THOMAS JEFFERSON'S FLOWERS

THOMAS JEFFERSON'S FLOWERS

HISTORIC GARDENS AT MONTICELLO

PEGGY CORNETT

G. S. WILSON
Contributing Editor

PUBLISHED FOR THE THOMAS JEFFERSON FOUNDATION
BY THE UNIVERSITY OF VIRGINIA PRESS
Charlottesville and London

The University of Virginia Press is situated on the traditional lands of the Monacan Nation, and the Commonwealth of Virginia was and is home to many other Indigenous people. We pay our respect to all of them, past and present. We also honor the enslaved African and African American people who built the University of Virginia, and we recognize their descendants. We commit to fostering voices from these communities through our publications and to deepening our collective understanding of their histories and contributions.

University of Virginia Press

Printed in Canada on acid-free paper

First published 2026
1 3 5 7 9 8 6 4 2

LIBRARY OF CONGRESS CATALOGING-IN-PUBLICATION DATA

Names: Cornett, Peggy, author | Wilson, G. S. (Gaye), editor
Title: Thomas Jefferson's flowers : historic gardens at Monticello / Peggy Cornett ; with G. S. Wilson, contributing editor.
Description: Charlottesville : published for the Thomas Jefferson Foundation by the University of Virginia Press, 2026. | Includes bibliographical references and index.
Identifiers: LCCN 2025045078 (print) | LCCN 2025045079 (ebook) | ISBN 9780813953502 hardback acid-free paper | ISBN 9780813953519 paperback acid-free paper | ISBN 9780813953526 ebook
Subjects: LCSH: Jefferson, Thomas, 1743–1826—Homes and haunts—Virginia—Monticello | Jefferson, Thomas, 1743–1826—Knowledge and learning | Historic gardens—Virginia—Monticello | Flowers—Catalogs and collections—Virginia | Monticello (Va.)—History | BISAC: NATURE / Regional | GARDENING / Ornamental Plants | LCGFT: Biographies
Classification: LCC E332.74 .C67 2026 (print) | LCC E332.74 (ebook) | DDC 973.4/6092—dc23/eng/20251118
LC record available at https://lccn.loc.gov/2025045078
LC ebook record available at https://lccn.loc.gov/2025045079

This publication was made possible in part by a gift from Teresa and Kenneth Wood of Chester Springs, Pennsylvania.

COVER ART: *Campanula medium* (Canterbury bells); FRONTISPIECE (page ii): *Iris pallida* (sweet flag iris); TABLE OF CONTENTS SPREAD (pages vi–vii): panoramic view of West Front and Gardens of Monticello, April 17, 2025; IMAGE PRECEDING SECOND HALF-TITLE (page xiv): *Consolida ajacis* (larkspur)
COVER DESIGN: Cecilia Sorochin

Nature intended me for the tranquil pursuits of science, by rendering them my supreme delight.

—THOMAS JEFFERSON TO
PIERRE SAMUEL DU PONT DE NEMOURS,
2 MARCH 1809

CONTENTS

PREFACE

In 1941, Edwin Morris Betts and Hazlehurst Bolton Perkins collaborated to publish a modest book, *Thomas Jefferson's Flower Garden at Monticello,* telling the story of what they understood to be a flower garden unlike any other in Virginia. The publication was written at the conclusion of a three-year project undertaken by the restoration committees of the Thomas Jefferson Memorial Foundation, chaired by Fiske Kimball, and the Albemarle and Rivanna regional members of the Garden Club of Virginia. Betts, a University of Virginia biology professor and student of Jefferson's interest in botany, gardening, and agriculture, and Perkins, former President of the Garden Club of Virginia and general chair of the club's restoration committee, were the leading forces in guiding the restoration of the flower garden according to Jefferson's plans.

A second edition was published in 1971. In 1986, a revised and enlarged edition by Peter Hatch, Monticello's Director of Gardens and Grounds, was published by the University of Virginia Press with color photographs and an annotated plant list.

This book, *Thomas Jefferson's Flowers,* tells a broader story. It begins with Jefferson's gardens at his boyhood home of Shadwell and then moves on to the gardens that he envisioned for Monticello as well as his retreat home, Poplar Forest. Additionally, it explores the gardens of many of his contemporaries, from George Washington at Mount Vernon and James and Dolley Madison at Montpelier, as well as the Philadelphia gardens of John and William Bartram and The Woodlands, William Hamilton's estate. Likewise, Jefferson's friendships abroad influenced and expanded his understanding and appreciation of the latest landscape gardening styles of the period. Today, his deep and often complicated relationships with his family, his friends, and the enslaved gardeners at Monticello continue to inform the ongoing restoration, preservation, and interpretation of the gardens themselves. This book illustrates the important role that flowers and flower gardening played in Jefferson's life from Monticello and in the broader and expanding world of eighteenth- and early nineteenth-century horticulture. In addition, it provides an updated, illustrated list of Jefferson's flowers and those that appear at Monticello today.

< *Papaver rhoeas* (corn poppy)

ACKNOWLEDGMENTS

I wish to recognize many who have encouraged the creation of this book over the years. This publication was made possible in part by a generous gift from Teresa and Kenneth Wood of Chester Springs, Pennsylvania. As longtime friends of the Thomas Jefferson Foundation, the Woods have supported numerous garden-related programs, including the production of botanically accurate paintings by local artist Tim O'Kane of 120 seed varieties offered through the Center for Historic Plants (CHP). Additional appreciation goes to the Richard D. and Carolyn W. Jacques Foundation, whose generous support has made possible Monticello's annual display of historic bulbs and the "In Bloom at Monticello" website page.

Monticello colleagues past and present have provided valued encouragement and guidance. Historian, scholar, and author Gaye Wilson of the International Center for Jefferson Studies was an essential partner, guiding the research and writing of this book from beginning to end. Peter Hatch, Monticello's Director Emeritus of Gardens and Grounds, continues to inspire through his decades of research and writing and his tenacious quest for horticultural accuracy. The leadership of Dr. Jane Kamensky, Monticello's President, is profoundly appreciated. Monticello's Senior Vice President for Preservation and Operations, Gardiner Hallock, and Senior Historian Emerita, Ann Lucas, as well as former CHP Curator Lily Fox-Bruguiere were early cheerleaders for this book. Under the leadership of Director Andrew Davenport, the International Center for Jefferson Studies provided significant support, from needed office space to staff expertise. Colleagues at the Jefferson Library, including Fiske and Marie Kimball Librarian Endrina Tay and the Jefferson Library's Public Services and Collections Development Manager Anna Berkes, and Megan Brett, Manager for Collections Processing and Digital Initiatives, never failed to find the most elusive documents and images. Likewise, the scholarship and ongoing research by members of the Papers of Thomas Jefferson: Retirement Series project, under Director Jeff Looney, and the Papers of Thomas Jefferson at

< *Viola tricolor*, painting by Tim O'Kane

Ipomoea quamoclit (cypress vine)

Princeton University project, including Associate Editor Merry Ellen (Melly) Scofield, were critically important and cannot be overestimated.

Other Monticello colleagues have helped with this research in many diverse ways, including Chad Wollerton and photographer Ian Atkins of Monticello's digital media team, Jefferson interpreter Bill Barker, guides Lou Hatch and Elizabeth Lukas, Senior Historian Emerita Cinder Stanton, and Monticello's Director of Horticulture, Roger Gettig, and Curator of Historic Gardens, Michael Tricomi. It goes without saying that the entire gardening team at Monticello and CHP deserve sincere appreciation. Special thanks go to Flower Gardener Debbie Donley and former Vegetable Gardener Pat Brodowski, both talented artists who contributed unique paintings to illustrate this book.

University of Virginia Press Editor Mark Mones shepherded the book through many drafts. Careful reading and generous suggestions from landscape architect and historian Will Rieley and from Poplar Forest's architectural historian Travis McDonald added depth and broadened the book's content.

Sister historic sites have supported this research in many ways, including Thomas Jefferson's Poplar Forest, George Washington's Mount Vernon, James Madison's

Montpelier, Adams National Historical Park, and Old Salem Museum and Gardens, with special thanks to Mount Vernon's Leslie Bird and researcher Hillarie Hicks of Montpelier. Invaluable material was gained through the Southern Garden History Society's "Southern Plant Lists," a joint project with the Colonial Williamsburg Foundation to publish a searchable database with an extensive array of period seed and nursery catalogues, diaries, and primary documentation.

The Garden Club of Virginia maintains strong ties with Monticello, and the close friendships with restoration committee members Candy Crosby and Lucy Huff are especially appreciated.

It is impossible to enumerate all the friendships and supportive counsel gained through the world of garden historians, native plant enthusiasts, and rosarians. But several individuals deserve mention: Denise Adams, Beate Ankjaer-Jensen, Bill Bergen, Fran Boninti, Carol Carter, Staci Catron, Cathy Clary, John Fitzpatrick, Wayne Goodall, Eleanor Gould, Greg Grant, Gail Griffin, Barbara Hall, Brent Heath, Connie Hilker, Jennifer Jewell, Scott Kunst, Ken McFarland, Keith Nevison, Reina Oostingh, Charlie Pepper, Barbara Wells Sarudy, Bill Welch, Dennis Whetzel, and Andrea Wulf. Special acknowledgment must also be offered for those no longer with us: Allan Brown, Flora Ann Bynum, Liz Druitt, Rudy Favretti, Joel Fry, Randy Harelson, Ruth Knopf, Patti McGee, Doug Seidel, Art Tucker, and Jane White.

Finally, without the loving support of my ever-patient husband, Chris Morash, I could not have completed this book. I dedicate it to the memory of my mother, a consummate vegetable gardener and seed saver who never had time to grow flowers, and to my sister Carole, who carried on the tradition of growing our family's heirloom pole beans for as long as she could.

THOMAS JEFFERSON'S FLOWERS

INTRODUCTION

G. S. WILSON

No occupation is so delightful to me as the culture of the earth and no culture comparable to that of the garden.

THOMAS JEFFERSON, 1811

THE LURE OF THE GARDEN was an all-encompassing passion for Thomas Jefferson throughout his lifetime. His interest never subsided. Innate curiosity led him to new ideas, new methods, and new and exotic plants. This was undergirded by his keen interest in the natural sciences as promoted in eighteenth-century Enlightenment thinking, which emphasized an empirical, hands-on approach. Horticulture and gardening formed a part of Jefferson's larger vision for the new American republic, as he believed agriculture would prove its economic backbone. But this was the larger role of horticulture in the socioeconomic and political realm. On a personal level, Jefferson demonstrated a genuine affinity for the flower garden. He could always delight in the "belles of the day," those ephemeral flowers that graced the gardens surrounding his homes at Monticello and Poplar Forest.

Flowers provided Jefferson with a more intimate encounter with gardening. At points of deepest grief, he turned to his flower gardens. Flowers helped connect him to his own family or to other friends and acquaintances, those who might be close at hand or an ocean away. An exchange of information—and an exchange of the plants themselves—formed these connections. Many family letters recount the lively interactions between Jefferson and his daughters and granddaughters, as his absences during his long political career necessitated their help and oversight of the flower gardens at Monticello. Additional memos and directives allow us some insight into how closely he worked with enslaved gardener Wormley Hughes and how much he depended on Hughes's expertise in the creation and maintenance of Monticello's flower gardens. Jefferson made the acquaintance of nurserymen and

< *Gomphrena globosa* (globe amaranth)

Tulips along walk, West Front

other gardeners who propagated flowering plants and could supply him with both familiar flowers as well as exotics that came from far parts of the world. Friendships established during his diplomatic tenure in Paris were sustained after his return to America through an exchange of plants that frequently included flowers.

This book offers a closer view of the private Jefferson through his affinity for flowers. It begins with his earliest entry in his Garden Book, a diary he began as a young man at his family's home on the Shadwell plantation, then moves to his early landscape plans for Monticello and, later, his retreat home at Poplar Forest. It follows him as he explores gardens in Europe during his diplomatic service abroad. As his public career continues, family letters allow us intimate glimpses of his reliance on daughters Martha and Mary and later, during his presidency, on granddaughters Anne Cary, Ellen, and Cornelia to implement and oversee his plans for his flower gardens. His granddaughters, along with Wormley Hughes, worked closely with Jefferson in creating the flower borders that defined the winding walk he designed to encircle the West Front of the Monticello house. The final chapters look at how these flower gardens were restored early in the twentieth century by the Garden Club of Virginia and how they continue to be maintained today by Monticello's gardening staff. This tour through Jefferson's long association with flowers and his gardens is led by a key member of the Department of Gardens and Grounds: Peggy Cornett, Curator of Plants at Monticello. She joined the Monticello crew in 1983 and is sharing her years of hands-on experience and knowledge of Jefferson's gardens and the flowers he introduced, which are on display at Monticello today.

1

JEFFERSON'S EARLIEST FLOWER GARDENS

1766, Mar. 30. Purple hyacinth begins to bloom.

ON MARCH 30, 1766, at the age of twenty-three, the young Thomas Jefferson (1743–1826) jotted a simple observation into a leather-bound book: "Purple hyacinth begins to bloom." Further records that spring charted the blooming periods of common ornamental and native flowers. This was the beginning of Jefferson's Garden Book,[1] ultimately a sixty-six-page personal diary that he would keep with regular entries until the autumn of 1824, just two years before his death.

Thomas Jefferson's first accounts of flowers and flower gardening came not from Monticello but from Shadwell, his boyhood home on the rolling terrain above the Rivanna River in the foothills of the Southwest Mountains of Virginia. Before early colonists settled in the region, this was the heartland of the Monacan nation and its people had trails that crossed the area. When he was born there in April 1743, in what is now Albemarle County, this portion of the Appalachian mountain chain formed the edge of colonial Virginia's frontier. Thomas was the eldest son of Peter Jefferson (1708–1757), a surveyor and tobacco planter, and Jane Randolph Jefferson (1720–1776) of Virginia's prominent Randolph family. The eight Jefferson children enjoyed an unpretentious yet comfortable gentry house situated at the center of the Shadwell tobacco farm. Shadwell was home as well to more than sixty enslaved people who worked on the land and served the Jefferson family.[2]

That his Garden Book begins with observations of flowers rather than more practical horticultural activities, or even fruit or vegetable gardening, is not extraordinary. Jefferson's early life experiences exposed him to a variety of gardening possibilities, which undoubtedly informed his understanding and appreciation of the

< *Hyacinthus orientalis albulus* (purple hyacinth)

more sophisticated ornamental landscapes and designs that were well established in Europe. He spent seven years of his childhood at the Randolph plantation, Tuckahoe, favorably placed on the bluffs of the James River near Richmond, Virginia. Later, as a young adult, he lived in Williamsburg, the colonial capital of Virginia, where he attended the College of William and Mary and then studied law under one of Virginia's leading jurists, George Wythe. During this period of study, Jefferson developed a lifelong friendship with schoolmate John Page, who, like Jefferson, would later enter politics and serve as a Virginia governor. Jefferson often visited him at his palatial family home, Rosewell, in Gloucester County, Virginia. John's grandfather Mann Page began building Rosewell in 1725 with the intent of having a house that could rival the luxury of the Governor's Palace in Williamsburg.[3] Although the documentary evidence of ornamental flowers in ambitious landscape gardens such as those at Rosewell, Tuckahoe, and other Virginia plantations has essentially vanished over time, certain elements of English landscaping styles, winding walks, terraces, and enclosures suggest the existence of ornamental gardens at one time that could have provided Jefferson his earliest experiences of the formal pleasure garden.

By the time Jefferson resided in Williamsburg in the 1760s, the gardening traditions that came to signify the town were in place. He could enjoy the ornamental garden layout at the College of William and Mary and the formal parterre gardens of the Governor's Palace. These gardens relied on the exchange of plants and ideas among gardeners earlier in the century. One who was quite influential was John Custis (1678–1749). Custis, a wealthy local resident, purchased eight lots in the heart of Williamsburg to establish gardens, where he hoped to display fine imported European plants alongside those native to Virginia. This led to his correspondence with Peter Collinson (1694–1768), a wealthy Quaker woolen merchant from London who was also extremely interested in plant exchanges. He wrote Custis in December 1735, "Wee brothers of the Spade find it very necessary to share among us." Custis was pleased to receive shipments from Collinson, though he complained that "the seeds in generall wee have from England very often never come up."[4] Still, they persisted. Collinson provided the link between Custis and the Philadelphia farmer and nurseryman John Bartram (1699–1777). Following an introductory letter from Collinson, Bartram called upon Custis during his tour through Virginia seeking new plants for his nursery. Custis also became acquainted with the British naturalist and artist Mark Catesby (1683–1749), who contributed to the gardening world by exploring the southern colonies and then publishing sketches of his findings in one of the earliest illustrated folios of native plants and birds.[5] The results of these efforts by early gardeners and their plant exchanges shaped Williamsburg's gardens and afforded Jefferson some of his earliest observations of formal pleasure gardens.

During the spring of 1766, when the Garden Book entries began, Jefferson was at Shadwell with his then widowed mother (Peter Jefferson had died in 1757) and his unmarried siblings. Throughout his life, spring was Jefferson's favorite season, especially in the land of his birth. During a trip through New England in May 1791, he longed for springtime in Virginia, which made "a paradise of our country," adding, "When we consider how much climate contributes to the happiness of our condition . . . we have reason to value highly the accident of birth in such an one as that of Virginia."[6] A few years later, in April 1797, Jefferson repeated this sentiment to French philosopher Constantin François de Chasseboeuf, comte de Volney, who had visited Monticello for two weeks in June 1796: "As far as my indisposition and solitude would permit I have been in the enjo[y]ment of our delicious spring. The soft genial temperature of the season, just above the want of fire, enlivened by the reanimation of birds, flowers, the fields, forests and gardens, has been truly delightful and continues to be so."[7] Yet the enjoyment of the spring of 1766 was marred by the particularly painful absence of his eldest sister, Jane, who had died the previous autumn at the age of twenty-five from an unknown illness.[8] According to family lore, Jane was her brother's constant companion and confidant. They shared a passion for music and often roamed the banks of the Rivanna River together. The epitaph he composed for her reflects their mutual love of nature.[9]

> Ah, Joanna, puellarum optima,
> Ah, ævi virentis flore prærepta,
> Sit tibi terra lævis;
> Longe, longueur valeto![10]

Together, as winter turned to spring, they would have encountered enchanting displays of ephemeral wildflowers gracing the riparian woodland slopes.

At that time, Jefferson's mastery of botanical nomenclature was rudimentary, and he often referred to plants, especially native species, with common names and regionally colloquial terms. On April 6, 1766, he wrote, "Puckoon open," calling bloodroot (*Sanguinaria canadensis*) by a name with an Indigenous American derivation.[11] On his birthday—April 13, just a week later—his observation "Puckoon flowers fallen" described the fleetingly fragile character of this diminutive woodland species with pure white, eight-petaled blossoms.

As April advances, the forest floor of Piedmont Virginia's winter landscape is transformed by expansive drifts of lush, gray-green foliage emerging along moist ravines and streambeds. Out of the warming, humus-rich riparian soil, arching stems with purplish-pink buds unfurl into sky-blue, sweetly fragrant bell-shaped blossoms.

Without knowing its botanical or even common name, Jefferson could only describe this glorious display with pure and innocent wonder, writing, "Apr. 16. a bluish colored, funnel-formed flower in low grounds in bloom." A month later, on May 7, he shared his understanding of its ephemeral nature: "blue flower in low grounds vanished." Interestingly, the Virginia bluebell (*Mertensia virginica*) was well known by early naturalists, having been introduced to British gardeners in the late 1600s by the Reverend John Banister (1650–1692).[12] In 1734 Williamsburg's John Custis sent roots to his London patron, Peter Collinson, calling it "Mountain Cowslip."

Jefferson's account of Virginia's wildflowers continued through that spring season. The deciduous pinxter azalea, which he called "wild honeysuckle" (*Rhododendron periclymenoides*), "dwarf flags" or dwarf crested iris (*Iris cristata*), and native violets were in bloom until his last entry on May 11, when he left on his first trip north through the colonies of Maryland, Pennsylvania, and New York. As he wrote in his gardening journal, "so observations cease."

Although never confirmed archaeologically with physical evidence, this first page of the Garden Book also indicates the existence of an ornamental flower garden near the Shadwell homesite. Purple hyacinths, narcissus, and purple flag iris suggest beds of well-established perennial flowering bulbs or "roots." Were Jefferson's observations of these cultivated plants part of an effort to document the family

Virginia bluebells along Monticello's north slope

flower garden and, in so doing, to preserve a comforting memory of the garden once shared with his most intimate relations, including his much-lamented sister Jane?

Shadwell—Gardening Begins

EARLY THE following year, on the second and third pages of his Garden Book, Jefferson's eagerness to continue recording garden activities was unmistakable. By February, pea planting was foremost on his agenda, with beds of "forwardest" and "midling" peas sowed on February 20, and he noted on March 9, "Both beds of peas up." But along with the asparagus, celery, onions, lettuce, and the first strawberries coming to table,[13] Jefferson also resumed his observation on March 23 of "Purple Hyacinth & Narcissus bloom," which was seven days earlier than the previous year. His propensity for charting the occurrence and duration of natural phenomena was a phenological bent that continued throughout his lifetime. These discrete observations were later summarized to accurately tabulate vegetables, fruits, and flowers at Shadwell and Monticello.

Despite his burgeoning law practice, which often required extended travel away from Shadwell, Jefferson was charting a remarkable variety of ornamental flowering plants throughout the spring of 1767 and into midsummer. He recorded lily bulbs, flowering shrubs—including suckering roses,[14] lilacs, laurel, Spanish broom, and wild honeysuckle azaleas—and even a native tree like the umbrella magnolia. He noted the first blossoming of many bulbous-rooted species, such as feathered hyacinths (a type of *Muscari*) flowering on April 25; a month later, he wrote that the yellow "Flower-de luces opened" (or fleur-de-lis iris [*Iris pseudacorus*]). Both were European species that sometimes naturalize in North America. The "Snap-dragon" (*Antirrhinum majus*), which came into bloom on May 28, is especially significant, as it is considered the earliest reference to this European wildflower in a colonial American garden.[15]

Beginning on the second day of April, Jefferson recorded the sowing of an extraordinary selection of flower seeds, listing "carnations, Indian pink, marigold, tricolor, Dutch violet, sensitive plant, Cockscomb (a flower like the prince's feather), lathyrus." He did not record the source of these primarily hardy and tender annual flower varieties, but they could have come from neighbors or been acquired on local trips from Williamsburg through the Blue Ridge associated with his law practice—or possibly from his trip to Annapolis, Philadelphia, and New York the previous year.[16] Jefferson's fourth sister, Martha Jefferson Carr (1746–1811), may have provided certain flowers, as his notations for "June 4–18 by information of Mrs. Carr" imply her connection with the Shadwell flower garden. Martha had married Thomas Jefferson's close friend Dabney Carr on July 20, 1765, and at the time of Jefferson's 1767 entries, she was living about forty miles away at Spring Forest in Goochland County, Virginia. The succession of flowers Jefferson associated with his sister included the following:

June 4: Larkspur & Lychnis bloom & Poppies
June 10: Pinks & Hollyhocks bloom
June 12: Carnations bloom
June 18: Argemone put out one flower.

On July 5, Jefferson added, "larger Poppy has vanished—Dwarf poppy still in bloom but on the decline." The two poppies (*Papaver somniferum* and *Papaver rhoeas*) are showy, hardy annuals that can persist and reseed in gardens for generations.

Significantly, Garden Book entries for 1767 verified the existence of organized flower beds, identified with Roman numerals designating "Rows V.c." and "VI.c." Four decades later, Jefferson would organize the twenty-four squares of his vegetable garden at Monticello in a similar way. Cultivating flowers in designated beds, rather than interspersing them more generally in an ornamental pleasure garden, appears to follow the directives in John Hill's *The Gardener's New Kalendar* (1758), a book that Jefferson owned. Hill wrote, "Flowers should be planted in distinct beds, and in a piece of ground devoted solely for that purpose, where flowers are to be the only object, and we seek nothing farther; this is the best disposition."[17] Jefferson's 1767 Garden Book entries carefully followed the appearance and flowering duration of his pinks and carnations in numbered rows in beds:

April 25. A pink in bed VI.c. blooming
July 5 pinks V.c. just disappear.—pinks in VI.c. still shew a few.
Carnations in full life.
July 18: Lesser poppy still blooming—pinks V.c. a few—pinks VI.c. a few.—a few Carnations—

The evolution of the name "pink" is explained in Raymond Taylor's *Plants of Colonial Days.* Taylor observes that the term "pinks" was derived from *pinksten* or *pfingsten,* the German name for flowers that bloomed at Pentecost (or Whitsuntide). Other sources say that "pink" comes from the "pinked" or jagged edge of the petals, as though cut by pinking shears. In either case, it appears that the idea of "pink" as a color occurred much later, for the color was named for the flowers rather than the other way around. In the eighteenth century, flowers were described as blush, pale red, rose, light red, flesh-colored, or carnation.[18]

Jefferson's interest in carnations, pinks, and other members of the dianthus family suggest his sophisticated knowledge of English cottage garden flowers. Dianthuses are among the oldest garden flowers in Europe and England, and their history is rich and complex. Many varieties had been cultivated long enough to have lost contact with a known wild species.[19] However, by the eighteenth century in America, pinks were not available to the degree—or with the diversity—they were in England. In 1795, John Lithen, a nurseryman and seedsman from Philadelphia, carried a simple offering of carnations, pheasant's eye pinks, and sweet William. The pheasant's eye pinks were a class often found in early nineteenth-century American seed catalogues. This name was used for a vast group of pinks that had evolved in Britain by the late seventeenth century and were characterized by flowers marked with a dark central blotch and a soft irregular band of color along the jagged margin of each petal. They were usually single, but, if double, the flowers had a ragged cluster of small petals near the center. Interestingly, this type of pink was considered passé in Britain by the late eighteenth century, a time when they were among the few forms available in America.

Pinks and carnations appear throughout Jefferson's lifetime in his Garden Book and correspondence. Jefferson's 1807 plan for his retirement garden prominently featured "Dianthus caryophyllus (single carnation)" and other annual and biennial dianthus in Monticello's East Front oval flower beds. An 1808 letter from his granddaughter Anne Cary Randolph Bankhead (1791–1826) referenced "a beautiful pink" that she hoped to obtain; in an 1811 planting memorandum for Poplar Forest, Jefferson directed the planting of "pinks. in locks of fence N. & W."[20]

Jefferson's Garden Book record of a family flower garden at Shadwell ceased after his midsummer observations of lesser poppies, pinks, carnations, larkspur, eastern mallow, and lychnis. His final note, from July 18, ended with his apparent delight in marvel of Peru, or four o'clock (*Mirabilis jalapa*); he found the "just opened" flower "very clever." There likewise was amusement in the much-anticipated "one flower" out of his yellow prickly poppy (*Argemone mexicana*).[21]

The following month, Jefferson was focusing on cherries and walnuts, and on August 3 he noted, "inoculated common cherry buds into stocks of large kind at Monticello." This is the earliest mention of his using this Italian word, "Monticello," for the farmland he had inherited from his father located on the southern side of the Rivanna River. Jefferson's final choice of a name for his "little mountain" was not evident in his Garden Book until "1769. MONTICELLO."

For the next two years, much transpired to draw his attention away from Shadwell and Monticello. His law practice and subsequent travels across the colony increased. He was elected to the House of Burgesses in 1769, which required his presence in Williamsburg. When not occupied by his law practice and political duties, Jefferson's mind was constantly directed toward construction of a new house. In May 1768, at the age of twenty-five, he had contracted with John Moore for the leveling of the top of the mountain to begin construction.[22] A cellar was dug by enslaved laborers for what would become the basement of the South Pavilion, the first building completed on the site.

Jefferson's Garden Book for 1769 recorded rows of fruits and nuts on the southeast side of Monticello and hills of cucumbers and watermelons. He was consulting Philip Miller's *The Gardeners Dictionary* (London, 1731) and *The Gardeners Kalendar* (London, 1732). Miller (1691–1771) served as head gardener at Chelsea Physic Garden for almost fifty years, beginning in 1722, and was considered an authority. At least three of his works were in Jefferson's library: *Dictionnaire des Jardiniers* (Paris, 1785), *The Gardeners Dictionary* in folio (London, 1768), and *The Gardeners Kalendar* (London, 1765).

In 1770 no entries were made in either the Garden Book or his Memorandum Books of accounts and legal records. For much of the year Jefferson was in Williamsburg, attending sessions of the House of Burgesses. Tragically, Shadwell burned during his absence, and most of the family's possessions, including Jefferson's cherished books, were lost. Fortunately, the Garden Book and memorandum book were likely at the unfinished house at Monticello and thus spared. Jefferson's gardening activities would resume the following year, as he began planning the Monticello landscape.

"The Open Ground on the West. A Shrubbery"

IN 1771, at age twenty-eight, Jefferson was developing elaborate conceptual plans for the broader Monticello landscape. As construction continued for a dwelling atop Monticello Mountain, Jefferson began clearing for a park on the north side, one that would be 1,850 yards in circumference. He was preparing for the future development of a shrubbery, or naturalized planting, on the mountain's steep, uncultivated slopes. Some of his ideas were quite fanciful but certainly inspired by the sublime elements of the eighteenth-century naturalistic English landscape movement. An initial concept suggested his intention to create a burial place in "some unfrequented vale in the park where is 'No sound to break the stillness but a brook. . . .' Let it be among antient and venerable oaks, intersperse some gloomy evergreens." In the center a "Gothic temple of antique appearance" was to be erected as a burial ground for members of his own family, as well as certain unnamed enslaved individuals. But this fantastical idea was quickly abandoned for another—a grotto at the North Spring paved with pebbles and spangled with translucent stones and shells and covered with moss. The figure of a reclining nymph on a couch of moss within the carved grotto would bear an inscription from Alexander Pope: "Nymph of the grot, these sacred springs I keep. / And to the murmur of these waters sleep: / Ah! spare my slumbers! gently tread the cave! / And drink in silence, or in silence lave!"[23]

Ultimately Jefferson came upon other, somewhat more pragmatic ideas for the grounds in general, which were gradually incorporated into practical designs. They included his earliest thoughts on the development of a grove, specifically described as "Open Ground on the West," which anticipated his ideals for an American grove. He would revisit these ideas more than thirty years later when he wrote, "Thin the trees. Cut out stumps and undergrowth. Remove old trees and other rubbish except where they may look well. Cover the whole with grass. Intersperse Jesamine, honeysuckle, sweetbriar, and even hardy flowers which may not require attention."[24]

Jefferson's specifications for the "shrubbery" contained a rich diversity of both native and ornamental shrubs, trees, climbing shrubby plants (or vines), evergreens, and hardy perennial flowers. Among the shrubs that, as he noted, would not exceed a growth of ten feet was the sweetbriar, specifically the pale pink, single-flowered *Rosa rubiginosa.* This is a native European species of rose with once-blooming spring flowers. Its foliage, light green when new, has a strong green apple fragrance. One of the most famous references to this rose occurs in Shakespeare's *A Midsummer Night's Dream,* when Oberon describes Titania's bower: "I know a bank where the wild thyme blows / Where oxlips and the nodding violet grows / Quite over-canopied with luscious woodbine, / With sweet musk-roses and with eglantine."[25] The visual combination of flowers through the spring and summer season, as planned by Jefferson, would range from deep bluish-purple false indigo bush (*Amorpha fruticosa*) to pale gray New Jersey tea (*Ceanothus americanus*) and from the pure white blossoms of wild cherry, magnolia, and dogwood to the purple of redbud.

Jefferson's selection of climbing shrubby plants focused primarily on showy native species: red wild honeysuckle (*Lonicera sempervirens*), orange trumpet flower (*Bignonia capreolata*), and yellow jessamine (*Gelsemium sempervirens*). Additionally, he included the perennial or everlasting pea (*Lathyrus latifolius*), a southern European species that bears attractive, bright purple, pea-like flowers. This selection of vines, some of which can grow fifty feet or more, suggests that he considered them in the same category as the trees upon which they could climb. Hence, Jefferson's vision echoed that of Philip Miller in *The Gardeners Dictionary.* Miller wrote that such trailing plants "should be planted in Large Wilderness-quarters, near the Stems of great Trees, to which they should be trained up, where, by their wild Appearance, they will be agreeable enough."[26] This idea of allowing ramblers to creep through the shrubbery and encircle the bases of trees was, in fact, pioneered a generation earlier by the influential English landscape writer Batty Langley (1696–1751) in *New Principles of Gardening* (1727).[27] The high-reaching vines Jefferson listed all have very desirable ornamental features, such as fragrance, showy flowers—of vivid yellow, light lavender, warm cantaloupe orange, or bright red—and, as in the case of poison ivy, brilliant fall color.

Jefferson would revisit this treatment of climbing plants on April 27, 1807, when he specified in his Garden Book that seeds of the North American clematis, or virgin's bower (*Clematis virginiana*), were to be planted "about the 3. springs on & near the road from the river up to the house & at the Stone spring." Here again, Jefferson's intention to create a scene where the vine tumbles and cascades over the woodland springs with a shower of fragrant, creamy-white flowers resonates with Philip Miller's dictionary entry for clematis: "These may also be planted to cover Seats in Wilderness-quarters, that are designed for shade; to which Purpose these Plants are very well adapted."[28]

The list of "hardy perennial flowers" contained an ambitious mixture of both exotic ornamentals and native species, and it included herbaceous and evergreen perennials and bulbs as well as annuals such as larkspur and poppies, which can easily reseed in open ground.[29] Several European species, such as gillyflower, pasque flower, and primrose, would have been more suited to a cultivated garden setting, while others, such as periwinkle, violets, flag iris, and sunflower, could thrive in open, uncultivated ground. The snapdragon and fleur-de-lis iris, first noted in the Shadwell flower garden in 1767, appear again in this plan for Monticello. That Jefferson included peonies as part of a designed and managed landscape is significant. Edwin Betts identifies Jefferson's peony as Chinese peony, *Paeonia albiflora* (a synonym for *Paeonia lactiflora*), yet it is more likely that Jefferson was referring to some form of the common or European peony, *Paeonia officinalis*. This long-lived, ancient species with cup-shaped, single, reddish-purple flowers in spring had been featured in the gardens of France and Britain since the sixteenth century, when it was grown in the medicinal gardens of monasteries. The genus name derives from the Greek name for Paeon, the physician of the gods and reputed discoverer of the medicinal properties of plants in this genus. Peonies were relatively new in eighteenth-century North American gardens; however, the first known citation for peony was recorded by John Brickell in *The Natural History of North Carolina* (1737). Jefferson could have obtained roots of herbaceous peonies from a few sources, including the gardens at Williamsburg or from his connections with Philadelphia nurseryman John Bartram, who reportedly sent roots of peonies to the botanical garden of Elizabeth Pitts Lamboll (1725–1770) and Thomas Lamboll (1694–1774) of Charleston, South Carolina, in 1761.[30]

As Jefferson built his house and planned the grounds for Monticello, he made another significant addition to his life. On January 1, 1772, he married a lovely young widow named Martha Wayles Skelton (1748–1782). According to family traditions, Martha was not only quite attractive but also well educated and very talented in music, a passion that she and Jefferson shared. Her father, John Wayles, hosted the wedding at his plantation, The Forest, located not far from Williamsburg. After the extended wedding festivities, the couple left for Monticello in a mild snowfall. The story told by their eldest daughter, Martha (named after her mother), described how the snow became so deep as they approached Monticello that the couple abandoned the carriage and traveled the last few miles on horseback. They arrived late in the evening at the only portion of Monticello completed at that time, now called the South Pavilion. It was dark and unattended. The story ends happily, however; according to their daughter, the newlyweds found a bottle of wine behind some books and ended the evening with laughter and song.[31] Over the next ten years, Mrs. Jefferson would see the house grow from the single South Pavilion, where she spent her first night, and the grounds around the mountain develop.

A Year of Loss and "A Calendar of the Bloom of Flowers"

IT WAS not until 1782 that many of the flowers first recorded at Shadwell and in the Monticello shrubbery landscape returned to another, more organized flower garden. Although no physical evidence of this garden has been found, it was possibly located in rectangular beds near the first version of the mansion (which was still under construction) and perhaps associated with the sweet shrubs that were collected from the Green Mountain area in 1778.[32] When Jefferson wrote from Paris to his gardener and vigneron Anthony Giannini in 1786, he confirmed the existence of this garden in a request for "Lilly of Canada. This is the lilly which George [Granger Sr.] found for me in the woods near the stone spring. I think that before I left home we took up some roots and planted them in the flower borders near the house."[33]

The nature of this garden is significant for several reasons. Horticulturally, the timing is curious. Jefferson notes that the flowers were "planted this spring and the season was very backward," meaning a cold spring, which would delay flowering. But the plants he documented were mostly perennial plants, including flowering bulbous roots (perennial hyacinths, feathered hyacinths, jonquils, lilies, ranunculus, iris, and even tulips), biennial hollyhocks and sweet William, herbaceous and evergreen perennials (peonies and dianthus or pinks), and flowering shrubs (dwarf crimson roses and the native *Calycanthus floridus,* or sweet shrub). Therefore, except for the tender annual nasturtium, all must have been transplanted as mature plants from another location (perhaps from a holding garden or even the shrubbery landscape) or newly acquired as mature plants, although there are no records of purchases or plant exchanges. Transplanting actively growing bulbs and long-lived perennials, such as peonies, is especially problematic, as the act of transplanting could easily delay or completely interrupt the flowering of some of the plants he was charting.

A second important aspect of this calendar is its diagrammatic format, which he created in his careful script beginning with March. Each subsequent month headed the columns below, with horizontal lines indicating the duration of flowering for each variety. Jefferson's penchant for recordkeeping was again reflected in this simple diagram comparing the blooming periods of flowers. This method of charting the garden would return years later for his vegetable garden, but in a more complex and comprehensive fashion. Beginning in 1809, the first season of his retirement to Monticello, Jefferson created a series of vegetable garden "Kalendars" in the pages of his Garden Book, which he continued annually through 1824.

But the most compelling aspect of Jefferson's 1782 gardening diary relates to what was happening within the Jefferson household during that spring and summer. His wife, Martha, in the final months of pregnancy, gave birth in May to their sixth child, Lucy Elizabeth, who was named after a daughter who had died the previous year. In a letter to James Monroe announcing the birth, Jefferson described Martha's deteriorating health as "dangerous."[34] Over the ensuing months, concern for her precarious condition weighed heavily on the entire Monticello household. Jefferson was never far from Martha's side and was joined in her care by her half sister Elizabeth Eppes and his widowed sister, Martha Jefferson Carr. An enslaved woman caring for her had a particular connection. This was Elizabeth Hemings (1735–1807), who had previously been enslaved by Martha's father, John Wayles, and was reputed to have been his long-term mistress. Six of her children are believed to have been fathered by Wayles and thus were Martha's half brothers and sisters. Elizabeth Hemings would have cared for Martha from the time she was a child and was at her bedside when she died.[35]

Despite Jefferson's grave depression over his wife's fragile condition, and perhaps as a distraction from it, he continued charting the duration of flowers over the months she lingered. Whether this task was shared with his dying wife or was a solitary contemplation, as he stood in the garden with a leather-bound book in hand, is unknown. Jefferson kept their relationship completely private and later burned their shared correspondence. But like his March 1766 observations of purple hyacinths

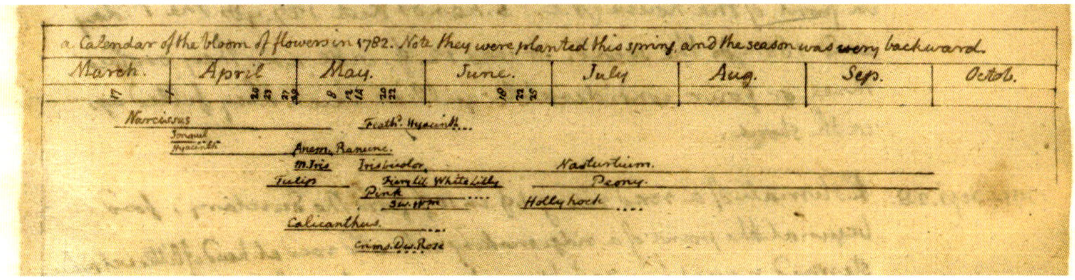
a Calendar of the bloom of flowers in 1782. Note they were planted this spring, and the season was very backward.
March. April May. June. July Aug. Sep. Octob.
Narcissus
Jonquil
Hyacinth
Feath. Hyacinth...
Anem. Ranunc.
M. Iris Iris bicolor
Nasturtium.
Tulips
White Lilly
Peony.
Pink
Sw. W'm
Holly hock
Calicanthus.
Crims. Dw. Rose

"Calendar of the bloom of flowers" (1782) from page 25 of Thomas Jefferson's Garden Book, 1766–1824

at Shadwell in the spring following his sister's death, Jefferson's careful attention to these common flowers may have provided some small comfort and consolation in a time of intense grief. It is not known whether this was the impetus and catalyst for the creation of this garden. Martha Wayles Skelton Jefferson died on September 6, and any written documentation of this flower garden ceased.

2

JEFFERSON'S EUROPEAN TOUR

ORNAMENTAL FARMS AND PLEASURE GROUNDS

MARTHA JEFFERSON'S DEATH was the greatest tragedy of Jefferson's life, one from which he never fully recovered. Now a forty-one-year-old widower, he found that life was about to change dramatically. The Congress, following a motion by James Madison, unanimously agreed to renew Jefferson's appointment to the commission in Paris, where the Americans and their allies were still negotiating a peace treaty with Britain. He had declined the first two appointments owing to his wife's failing health, but now he accepted, admitting that "the state of my mind concurred in recommending the change of scene proposed; and I accepted the appointment."[1] He traveled to Philadelphia, but before he could embark for Europe, notice arrived that a provisional peace treaty had been signed, and Jefferson's commission was consequently rescinded.

By mid-May he was back home at Monticello and spent the summer there with his three daughters and his sister Anna Scott Jefferson. This quiet domestic stay ended when Jefferson was summoned once more to public service, this time as a Virginia delegate to Congress. When he left Monticello in October 1783 for Philadelphia, he had no way of knowing that this would evolve into a significant absence from his Virginia home.

He took his eldest daughter, Martha, with him, as he felt that educational opportunities in Philadelphia were better. The younger daughter, Mary, and the baby, Lucy Elizabeth, stayed with their aunt Elizabeth Eppes in Virginia. Jefferson

< *Amaranthus tricolor* (Joseph's coat)

himself was in Philadelphia for only a short time, as the government was moving from its brief sojourn in Princeton on to Annapolis. He situated Martha with a trusted acquaintance, Mrs. Thomas Hopkinson, engaged a French teacher and a drawing master, and was off to Annapolis.[2]

In May 1784, things took a significant turn, as Jefferson received yet another appointment to Paris—now as a minister plenipotentiary to negotiate treaties of amity and commerce. There was no time to return to Monticello. His two youngest daughters would remain with their Aunt Eppes and her husband, Francis Eppes (1747–1808). A dependable friend, Nicholas Lewis, would join Francis Eppes in overseeing affairs at Monticello. Daughter Martha would accompany him; in addition, Jefferson sent for James Hemings (1765–1801), an enslaved eighteen-year-old at Monticello, and his older brother Robert. Robert Hemmings (1762–1819) traveled only as far as Boston, returning to Virginia with Jefferson's horses. The younger Hemings was off to Paris, where Jefferson planned to have him trained "in the art of French cookery."[3]

They sailed from Boston on July 5 aboard the *Ceres.* By August 6, 1784, Jefferson was in Paris, ready to join fellow ministers John Adams and Benjamin Franklin, who had remained in France following ratification of the peace treaty. Jefferson knew there was much to be done on behalf of the new United States—and much to personally learn and to experience. With this new European venture before him, Garden Book entries for Monticello were replaced with visual and written notes on the gardens of Europe.

On September 15, Jefferson made his first visit to Versailles. The American ministers met with the comte de Vergennes, French minister of foreign affairs, and presented their commission from the US Congress authorizing them to negotiate commercial treaties. On this first official visit, Jefferson made no comment on the grandeur of Versailles or its art or architecture, but he did note that he paid to see the gardens.[4]

Although Jefferson left few observations of his strolls in the gardens of Paris, we can surmise that numerous floral displays inspired him. At that time, formal French gardens were designed with elaborate "embroidery" parterres. The parterre was first developed in France by garden designer Claude Mollet around 1595 and evolved from earlier knot gardens with simple interlacing herbs. The more intricate embroidery parterre found in English gardens dates to the early seventeenth century. It contained dwarf boxwood hedges filled with colorful flowers and gravel and was meant to be viewed from above.

This was the predominant style, but elements of Anglo-Asian gardening influences were beginning to take hold, in keeping with the fashion of the day. At

Versailles, the South Garden, known as the Flower Parterre, was situated above the orangery. During the reign of Louis XVI (1754–93), brightly colored flowers were continually planted and replanted: wallflowers, hyacinths, jasmine, tulips, and daffodils. Early accounts of the gardens on the north side of the palace describe colorful and highly fragrant displays of jasmines, jonquils, hyacinths, veronicas, carnations, pasque flowers, tuberoses, violets, white lilies, sweet Williams, bellflowers, and more. Flowering plants were brought from all parts of Europe. The element of floral fragrance cannot be overemphasized.

Jefferson joined excursions with Parisian elites to various public gardens and sites including Versailles, the Louvre, the Palais Royal, Saint-Germain, the gardens of Bagatelle (built by Louis XVI's brother), and the chateau and park of Marly, Louis XIV's retreat in the hills above the Seine and near Versailles. He explored Le Désert de Retz, adjacent to Marly, late in the summer of 1786 with a lovely London visitor introduced to him by his friend John Trumbull, an American artist. The visitor was Maria Cosway; she was the wife of the artist Richard Cosway and a talented artist and musician herself. Their stay in Paris was prompted by Richard's commission to paint the children of the duc d'Orléans. Jefferson became quite infatuated with Richard's beautiful Anglo-Italian wife. Their initial infatuation, however, soon evolved into a long-distance correspondence that would continue over many years. This correspondence preserves glimpses of Jefferson's impressions of the sites they visited around Paris. In an early letter from Paris, he wrote to Maria in London and reminisced about their picnic "under the bowers of Marly."[5]

A more endearing and enduring friendship grew between Jefferson and Madame de Tessé (Adrienne Catherine de Noailles [1741–1814]), the aunt of the marquis de Lafayette. Their shared enthusiasm for horticulture began in 1784 and continued until her death. The comtesse was a connoisseur of gardening and the fine arts, and their mutual love of plants is well chronicled through their correspondence. She was quite interested in the plants of Virginia and the Carolinas and requested long lists of desirable North American trees and shrubs for the gardens at her Château de Chaville, a beautiful country estate near Versailles. Jefferson implored American naturalists and nurserymen to send collections of carefully packed young plants, including umbrella magnolias, tulip poplars, mountain laurels, red cedars, sassafras, persimmons, dogwoods, oaks, sweet shrub, and American beautyberry.

Jefferson continued sending plants to her estate after his return to America, but because Chaville was a Crown property, many specimens were eventually "nationalized." After the proclamation of the French Republic, garden plants were salvaged from émigrés' estates to enrich the Jardin du Roi in Paris, then renamed the Jardin des Plantes to better reflect the new political state. André Thoüin (1747–1824), the

French botanist and gardener-in-chief of the Jardin du Roi from 1764 to 1793, continued as the superintendent of the national garden and was commissioned to select rare exotics from former Crown properties that might prove useful to the nation. In the presence of Chaville's gardener, Cyrus Bowie, he chose 148 species from the estate, including many North American specimens.

Throughout his time in Paris, Jefferson sought not only to import North American species for his European acquaintances but also to send ornamental European garden flora back to Virginia. In a letter to his friend and kinsman Richard Cary, Jefferson requested numerous species of trees, shrubs, and vines as well as campanulas and native geraniums. In return, Jefferson attempted to ship seeds of ranunculus, carnations, and auriculas along with roots of tulips, tuberoses, hyacinths, and fritillaries to Cary.[6]

Thoüin also exchanged plants with Jefferson personally throughout the ensuing years. Jefferson often shared Thoüin's shipments with like-minded American plantsmen, such as Philadelphia nurseryman Bernard McMahon (1775–1816) and Dr. David Hosack (1769–1835) of the Elgin Botanic Garden in New York. Thoüin's packages were carefully curated, documenting the time the seed was gathered and the time and methods for planting "according to the French calendar."[7] Evidently, Jefferson planted many seeds at Monticello as well. When a large package of seed arrived in 1808, Jefferson wrote to his daughter Martha from Washington asking her to tell his granddaughter Anne Cary Randolph that "my old friend Thouin of the National garden at Paris has sent me 700. species of seeds. I suppose they will contain all the fine flowers of France, and fill all the space we have for them."[8]

Jefferson's Garden Book contains few specific references to the hundreds of varieties from Thoüin, but diary entries indicate a wide range of plants, from Spanish broom to sprout kale to "Ximenesia Encelioides," which is most likely *Verbesina encilioides* (golden crownbeard), an annual aster from the American Southwest and Mexico that had been introduced to European gardens by 1785. Perhaps a clue to the identity of some of the many species may come from a listing of plants, dated from about 1786, that Jefferson himself attempted to send from Paris to his brother-in-law Francis Eppes of Eppington plantation. This list included "roses of various kinds." There were as many as fifty varieties of roses available in France at that time, including various European shrub roses such as the gallica roses (apothecary's and Rosa Mundi), musk, centifolia, and damask. Also on Jefferson's list were carnations, pinks, an assortment of fine bulbs that could have included double hyacinths, tulips, narcissus, and fritillaries, among others, and several annual flowers such as "Velvet Amaranth" (possibly the crested cockscomb, *Celosia cristata*). It also contained Jefferson's only mention of the "delicious" flowering heliotrope (*Heliotropium*

Portrait of Anne Cary Randolph Bankhead by James Westhall Ford, oil on canvas, 1823

arborescens), a species native to the mountains of Peru and introduced to European gardens before 1757 by the French naturalist and explorer Joseph de Jussieu (1704–1779).[9] The shipment also contained the "three-coloured Amaranth," or Joseph's coat (*Amaranthus tricolor*), so popular in the Monticello gardens today.

In later years Jefferson's gardening interests would turn even more toward the culture of flowers, vegetables, and plants that repaid the labors of the year within the year. He wrote to Madame de Tessé, "death, which will be at my door, shall find me unembarrassed in long-lived undertakings."[10] In this regard, he found her resolve to plant long-lived trees even more admirable, acknowledging, "[T]here is more of the disinterested & magnanimous in your purpose." It is a testament to the bond developed from their shared interest in gardening. Even while serving his first term as President of the United States, Jefferson would write to his dear Parisian friend: "Altho' the times are big with political events, yet I shall say nothing on that or any subject but the innocent ones of botany & friendship."[11] On December 8, 1813, in his final letter to the comtesse and just a few weeks before her death, Jefferson discussed the botanical specimens collected during Meriwether Lewis and William Clark's western expedition in North America. He described some as curious, some ornamental, some useful, and some that "may by culture be made acceptable on our tables."[12] Jefferson had at Monticello one little shrub from the expedition—a snowberry bush (*Symphoricarpos albus*)—that was destined for her, but it is not known if it ever successfully made the transatlantic passage.

Tour of English Gardens—"Embellishing Landscape by Fancy"

IN MARCH 1786, Jefferson was summoned to London by John Adams, the American minister to Britain. Adams saw opportunities for commercial treaties that he felt could be better advanced through the efforts of both American ministers. But as negotiations moved very slowly, Jefferson had a chance to visit many of the English country gardens that he knew only through books. He launched his journey across the English countryside from London on April 1, visiting sixteen celebrated gardens, beginning with Chiswick. He returned by April 14 to Kew Gardens. John Adams joined him on April 4, and their tour took them through the English Midlands, from Birmingham in the north to Oxford on the western corner.

Jefferson planned to tour many of the gardens described by Thomas Whately in his book *Observations on Modern Gardening,* which Jefferson had in his library at Monticello. Before arriving in Europe, he was well acquainted with the picturesque English landscape gardening revolution that had swept the country. This revolution had begun with William Kent (ca. 1685–1748), who early in the century had introduced the Palladian style of architecture and is also credited with promoting the natural English landscape style with his design of Chiswick. This style was later popularized by the grandiose landscape designs of Lancelot "Capability" Brown (1716–1783), who has been described as the greatest landscape gardener of all time. His numerous landscapes for grand English estates and parks included pleasure grounds with flower gardens, serpentine lines, clumps of trees, and shrubberies placed where they would not obstruct the views through the use of the "ha-ha," a moat-like barrier that blended with nature. Jefferson later used a modified version of the ha-ha at Monticello. Nine of the sixteen gardens Jefferson and Adams visited were designed by Brown. Many of Jefferson's ambitious proposals for the Monticello landscape in 1771—specifically the "Ground in General" and the shrubbery for the "Open Ground on the West"—were inspired by these English landscape concepts that he could now study firsthand.[13]

Jefferson purchased guidebooks during his travels as well, including Benton Seeley's on Stowe.[14] This estate was much visited and publicized for having enormous influence on the "natural" garden design that began in the 1730s and remained influential throughout the eighteenth century. But Jefferson never let go of his copy of Whately's *Observations.* He began his "Notes of a Tour of English Gardens" by crediting Whately's work: "I always walked over the gardens with his book in my hand, examined with attention the particular spots he described, found them so justly characterised by him as to be easily recognised, and saw with wonder, that his fine imagination had never been able to seduce him from the truth." Jefferson was clear in his objectives: "My enquiries were directed chiefly to such practical things as might enable me to estimate the expence of making and maintaining a garden in that style." His gardens at Monticello never totally left his mind.[15]

Whately begins his *Observations* by acknowledging the state of gardening in his country: "Gardening, in the perfection to which it has been lately brought in England, is entitled to a place of considerable rank among the liberal arts. It is as superior to landskip painting, as a reality to a representation: it is an exertion of fancy; a subject for taste; and being released now from the restraints of regularity, and enlarged beyond the purposes of domestic convenience, the most beautiful, the most simple, the most noble scenes of nature are all within its province."[16] Whately had a direct and abiding influence on Jefferson's understanding of designing landscapes, which he echoed in 1805 when discussing the fine arts with his granddaughter Ellen Randolph. He wrote that gardening was a seventh fine art, adding, "not horticulture, but the art of embellishing grounds by fancy. . . . It is nearly allied to landscape painting, & accordingly we generally find the landscape painter the best designer of a garden."[17]

In his *Observations on Modern Gardening,* Whately seeks to convey the basic composition of nature: ground, wood, water, rocks, and buildings. Each of the book's sections begins with simple headings: of a farm, of a park, of a garden, of the seasons, and so on. Hence the gardens are described within the sections defined by these elements.

Jefferson's review of Painshill, Charles Hamilton's seat near Cobham in Surrey, was brief and not completely complimentary, remarking that "there is too much evergreen." But Whately's appraisal gives a fuller picture of this site, which incorporated many North American species as part of the overall landscape. Describing the parterre separating the park as being filled with exotic plants that, during the summer, were intermixed with common shrubs and a "constant succession of flowers," he added that "the space before the house is full of ornament; the ground is prettily varied; and several sorts of beautiful trees are disposed on the sides in little open plantations."[18]

Jefferson's notes on the gardens he and Adams visited often referenced their encounters with "pleasure gardens."[19] The ideal of a pleasure garden encompassed flower gardens along with clumps of trees and winding paths as part of an overall design concept referred to as a *ferme ornée,* or decorative farm. Jefferson viewed the gardens they visited with this concept in mind, even criticizing gardens when he deemed the design poorly executed, such as at Leasowes in Shropshire: "This is not an ornamental farm—it is only a grazing farm with a path round it."

Whately felt the ideal of a *ferme ornée* was best executed at Woburn Farm in Surrey, describing it as a farm whose objective was to "bring every rural circumstance within the verge of a garden."[20] Jefferson visited Woburn twice, once alone and later with John Adams. As Whately's *Observations* informed Jefferson:

> The buildings are not . . . the only ornaments of the walk; it is shut out from the country, for a considerable length of the way, by a thick and lofty hedgerow, which is enriched with woodbine, jessamine, and every odoriferous plant, whose tendrils will entwine with the thicket. A path, generally of sand or gravel, is conducted in a wavy line, sometimes close under the hedge, sometimes at a little distance from it; and the turf on either hand is diversified with little groups of shrubs, of firs, or the smallest trees, often with beds of flowers; these are rather too profusely strewed, and hurt the eye by their littlenesses; but then they replenish the air with their perfumes, and every gale is full of fragrancy. In some parts, however, the decoration is more chaste; and the walk is carried between larger clumps of evergreens, thickets of deciduous shrubs, or still more considerable open plantations. . . . [The] country has on the other hand been searched for plants new in a garden; and the shrubs and flowers which used to be deemed peculiar to one, have been liberally transferred to the other; while their number seems multiplied by their arrangement in so many and such different dispositions.[21]

Jefferson's comments on Woburn were brief. He observed, "All are intermixed, the pleasure garden being merely a highly ornamented walk through and round the division of the farm and kitchen garden." But his notes also revealed his attention to how such a garden could be managed: "Four people to the farm, four to the pleasure garden, four to the kitchen garden."[22] His awareness of the workforce required to maintain these pleasure gardens and grounds appeared throughout his tour of English gardens. At Wotton he wrote of "two hands to keep the pleasure grounds in order; much neglected." At Stowe: "Fifteen men and eighteen boys employed in keeping pleasure grounds." At Blenheim, Jefferson recorded the vast numbers of people needed to care for the 2,500-acre estate: two hundred cared for the grounds and fifty kept the pleasure grounds in order. He wrote about the "small thickets of shrubs, in oval raised beds, cultivated, and flowers among the shrubs." But he felt the graveled walks were too broad and there were not enough seats in the gardens.

In the month following Jefferson's tour, he wrote from Paris to his friend John Page: "I returned but three or four days ago from a two-month trip to England. . . . The gardening in that country is the article in which it surpasses all the earth. I mean their pleasure gardening. This indeed went far beyond my ideas."[23] Jefferson's observations, when taken as a whole, revealed the many ways in which these gardens informed and directed his thinking when, twenty years later, he contemplated the laying out of oval flower beds and a winding flower walk amid his personal "pleasure garden" on the West Lawn of Monticello.

Jefferson's Tour Through Southern France and Northern Italy

In the spring of 1787 Jefferson's travels continued, as he left Paris on a tour that would take him through southern France and into regions of northern Italy. He had made a list of the people he wished to call on and collected an impressive number of letters of introduction. These contacts afforded him entry into many of the châteaux along his route, with the opportunity of observing the gardens with their spring-blooming flowers. Notably, however, instead of recording details of the pleasure gardens, Jefferson's focus lay in a different direction. His travel notes indicated his intent to learn more about the viticulture of southern France and neighboring Italy as well as the agricultural products of the region, especially the olive trees and the fine oil produced by their fruit.

He made many notes on the various methods of planting and propagating grapevines, accompanied by an assessment of the quality of the red and white wines of each locality. Then his attention turned to the olive groves. He wrote in his journal, "Mar. 18. Principality of Orange. . . . Here begins the country of olives. . . . They are the only tree which I see planted among vines."[24] As to blooming things, he did add, "Thyme growing wild here on the hills."

As his travels took him into northern Italy, Jefferson visited the gardens of Count Giacomo Durazzo in Nervi, Italy, which exhibited "a very rare mixture of the *Utile dulci.*" He went on to compare Durazzo's gardens to those he had visited in England and decided that "Woburn farm in England is the only thing I ever saw superior."[25] During Jefferson's visits these gardens were known to exhibit the widespread use of buttercups, hyacinths, jonquils, and carnations as well as multicolored ranunculus.

The regions Jefferson toured were rich in wine and food. When on the coast of Italy near Albenga, he wrote, "The earth furnishes wine, oil, figs, oranges, and every production of the garden in every season."[26] His notes applauded the wine and food, while his principal comments upon things in bloom were directed to the almond, orange, and apple trees, with only a passing mention of the thyme, lavender, and broom covering many of the hills. The only specific flower described was outside Marseilles, where he saw the guelder rose, *Viburnum opulus* 'Roseum'.[27] Jefferson's travel notes do not specify ideas he may have gained from the elegant gardens of the châteaux he visited; however, years later in April 1807, he included guelder rose in his plantings around Monticello.

Jefferson's Tour Through Germany

ON MARCH 4, 1788, Jefferson left Paris to join John Adams in the Netherlands. Their goal was to negotiate a sizable loan for the struggling United States. With business successfully concluded with Dutch bankers, Adams was looking to his return to America, while Jefferson planned a tour down the Rhône River as far as Strasburg, Germany, at which point he would return to Paris. He made extensive notes on this journey in a "Memorandum on a Tour from Paris to Amsterdam, Strasburg, and back to Paris."[28] His excursion acquainted him with numerous châteaux, taverns, and hotels and introduced him to notable agricultural and wine-producing regions. His observations included a plantation of rhubarb in Kaeferthall and more fine European wine varieties.

He was most interested in visiting the gardens at Schwetzingen Palace, which, he wrote, were "not to be compared to the English gardens, but they are among the best of Germany."[29] The baroque-style gardens designed under Prince Elector Karl Theodor (1724–1799) were renowned for their rich variety, including lime tree–lined avenues and geometrically laid out circular parterres. Around the parterres were eight pairs of flower beds. In the late 1700s, the formal French-inspired garden was gradually being supplanted by an English-style landscape park, known as the Arborium Theodoricum, with native and exotic trees, ending at the Temple of Woodland Botany. At Schwetzingen, unlike at other baroque gardens that were demolished throughout Germany, both formal French and English landscape styles coexisted.

Following his tours through various parts of Europe and England, Jefferson volunteered to supply notes from his experiences for two young Americans on their Grand Tour, Thomas Shippen and John Rutledge. Among the many cultural objects and governing bodies that he noted as worth observation and study, he did not overlook gardens: "Gardens. Peculiarly worth the attention of an American, because it [the United States] is the country of all others where the noblest gardens may be made without expence. We have only to cut out the superabundant plants."[30] This advice would indicate that Jefferson had absorbed the outstanding features of the many gardens he had observed through England, Germany, France, and northern Italy and contemplated how these could be economically incorporated into the American scene.

In the following year, Jefferson made no plans for further travel in Europe, focusing instead on a brief trip to Virginia to attend to personal business and reposition his daughters among their Virginia relations. He petitioned Congress for a leave of absence with every intention of returning to complete the two years remaining in his diplomatic assignment—besides, there were stirrings of revolution in France that interested Jefferson greatly. He left Paris on September 26, 1789, and noted in his records that on November 23, he "landed at Norfolk a quarter before one P.M."[31] With all the business at hand, he was most likely not reviewing his plans for "noble gardens" on the European model. In fact, several years would pass before he could fully concentrate on his Monticello landscape and call upon the horticultural knowledge and personal observation that had enriched his European tour.

3

A BOTANIZING NORTHERN TOUR AND VISIT TO THE WILLIAM PRINCE NURSERY

SHORTLY FOLLOWING HIS LANDING in Norfolk, Virginia, on November 23, 1789, Jefferson learned that his plans of returning to Paris with the "spring winds" were apt to change. He had been appointed Secretary of State in President Washington's newly formed cabinet. Initially he argued with Washington that his diplomatic assignment in Paris was a much better fit for his abilities, but Washington was of a different opinion. Ultimately Jefferson felt he must accept the new appointment. Even though he would remain in the United States, never to return to Europe, he would again be away from Monticello for extended periods and would keep very few personal records of his own gardens at home. He described to James Madison "the reluctance I have to that office which has increased so as to oppress me extremely."[1] His forebodings proved prophetic, as he encountered differing political views and challenges that made his new position especially difficult. During his second year in office, he managed to escape the stresses for a brief period when he joined Madison on an excursion to the "Northern Lakes" of upstate New York and New England. This trip brought new horticultural experiences and culminated with a visit to the Prince Nursery of New York, which offered an abundance of roses.

< *Rosa x damascena bifera* (Autumn damask rose)

Jefferson delayed joining the federal government in New York until after the marriage of his eldest daughter, Martha, to her third cousin Thomas Mann Randolph Jr. (1768–1828) of Tuckahoe plantation. The ceremony took place on February 23, and shortly after, Jefferson was traveling north accompanied by two enslaved attendants, James Hemings and James's older brother Robert, whom Jefferson more often referred to as "Bob." The three arrived in New York on March 21. Once Jefferson was settled, Bob Hemmings returned to Virginia, while James Hemings remained with Jefferson to serve as chef and put into practice the culinary skills he had learned in Paris.[2]

Their stay in New York lasted only through the summer, as Congress voted to move the seat of government to Philadelphia. Jefferson made a quick visit to Monticello in the fall of that year, but he was in Philadelphia before Christmas and ready to set up housekeeping there. For the next few years, he would depend on his daughters or other relatives at Monticello to keep him informed of what might be blooming at his Virginia home. His letters were always full of questions.

During his first spring in Philadelphia, he wrote his daughter Martha and speculated, "I suppose you are busily engaged in your garden. I expect full details on that subject as well as from Poll [or Polly, the family's nickname for Maria] that I may judge what sort of a gardener you make." Martha's letter (which would have crossed her father's in the mail) informed him, "Polly and myself have planted the cypress vine in boxes in the window and also date seeds and some other flowers. I hope you have not forgotten the collection of garden seed you promised me."[3]

Thomas Mann Randolph Jr., Jefferson's son-in-law, was proving to be a keen observer of flora and fauna and natural phenomena in general. In a letter to Jefferson from Monticello on April 30, 1791, he gave a detailed account of the blooming times for both native and cultivated plants, including violas, dandelion, *Silene* (catchfly), fringe tree, yellow lady slipper orchid, tassel hyacinth, and native columbine.[4]

On May 8, Jefferson addressed a letter to Maria with a report of things blooming in Philadelphia. Though they still had "pretty constant fires here," the lilacs had blossomed and the guelder rose, dogwood, redbud, and azalea were coming into bloom. He used this letter to advise the family that they might not hear from him for some weeks, as he was off to meet Madison in New York and would be traveling with him up the Hudson to various points north. He did not anticipate their return to New York and Philadelphia until mid-June. This tour would introduce Jefferson to the "botanical objects," geography, and people of upstate New York and parts of New England and would give him the opportunity, on his return, to explore the William Prince nursery.[5]

A Botanical Tour of the Northern Lakes

ANY NEWS from Monticello of his family and gardens was certainly a welcome distraction for Jefferson during a period of political turmoil. Jefferson's ideological vision for America conflicted with the governmental system espoused by Alexander Hamilton, and it was causing political relationships to crumble and his already strained friendship with John Adams to deteriorate further. Consequently, Jefferson's monthlong "botanizing excursion" through New England with Madison in May and June 1791 was the subject of much speculation.[6] Hamilton and other political adversaries were convinced that this lengthy vacation of two republican Virginians through Federalist strongholds in the north had secret, ulterior motives. Yet apparently the trip was innocent of intrigue and intended primarily for, in Madison's words, "health recreation and curiosity."[7] This goal was successfully achieved, for both Jefferson's "periodical" migraines and Madison's "bilious attacks" vanished in the nearly four weeks they spent walking over historic battlefields; studying botanical curiosities, wildlife, and insects (including "musketoes" and the Hessian fly); recording observations on climate, the seasons, and the appearance of birds; and even boating and fishing on Lake George and Lake Champlain.[8]

Their journey did, nevertheless, incorporate elements of a working vacation, for Jefferson was seeking ways to advance the new nation through alternative domestic industries. He had promoted his idea—formulated while in Europe—of the addition "to the products of the U. S. of three such articles as oil, sugar, and upland rice."[9] While on his northern tour, he took advantage of his time in Bennington, Vermont, to study the possibilities of the sugar maple industry. Jefferson was not alone in considering the benefits of this tree. At that time, Quaker activist and philanthropist Dr. Benjamin Rush of Philadelphia, a close acquaintance of Jefferson's and an ardent opponent of slavery, sought to convince political leaders and slave owners to create a sugar maple industry in America. He was convinced that it would "lessen or destroy the consumption of West Indian sugar, and thus indirectly to destroy negro slavery."[10] Jefferson had the opportunity to purchase sugar maples on the return portion of his tour, when he visited the Prince Nursery on Long Island.

The Prince Nursery on Long Island, New York

IN THEIR quest for the sugar maple, Jefferson and Madison made a noteworthy visit to the Prince family's nursery in Flushing on the north shore of Long Island, New

York. Established on eight acres of land in the 1730s by Robert Prince—within a community chiefly of French Huguenot settlers—it became America's first commercial nursery and remained a thriving family business through four generations, until just after the American Civil War. Initially called the Old American Nursery, it soon became the largest supplier of fruit trees and grapes in the New World, producing most of the grafted apple, pear, and cherry trees that could be found in early northeastern orchards.

Robert's son William Prince, the nursery's second proprietor and the one who was in charge at the time of Jefferson's visit, was the first to propagate the native pecan commercially. In 1771, the nursery's first broadside advertised thirty-three different plum trees, forty-two pear trees, twenty-four apple trees, and twelve varieties of nectarines. Their offerings expanded and diversified by 1774, when they listed "Carolina Magnolia flower trees, the most beautiful trees that grow in America, and 50 large Catalpa flower trees," along with other flowering trees and shrubs, in the *New York Mercury.* The Prince Nursery was among the first to introduce Lombardy poplars and, in 1798, they advertised ten thousand trees. The nursery continued its focus on plum seedlings, among other fruits.

When William, in his advanced years, divided the operation between his two sons, Benjamin and William, the second William Prince purchased additional acreage nearby and, in 1793, began The Linnaean Botanic Garden and Nursery. It was named for Carolus Linnaeus (1707–1778), the renowned Swedish botanist and naturalist who, a mere half century earlier, had devised the system of plant classification called the binomial system, which revolutionized our way of identifying living things based on shared physical characteristics. William Prince's Linnaean Botanic Garden served to educate the public as well as encourage potential customers by displaying the richness and diversity of the world's botanical treasures.

As the Prince Nursery passed from father to son, each generation shared a common, underlying goal: to propagate and make available every known plant of merit, including North American species, not so much for profit as from a deep-rooted love of botany and the discipline of horticulture itself. This scientific approach toward the natural world was an attitude in keeping with the essential Enlightenment philosophical tenets also embraced by Jefferson and many of his contemporaries.

William Prince became an active member of the newly created New York Horticultural Society. Through this prestigious organization he was in fellowship with Dr. David Hosack,[11] who established the city's original botanical garden, the Elgin Botanic Garden, in 1801. (The garden now lies directly beneath Rockefeller Center.) Prince nurseries supplied Dr. Hosack with many of the trees for his seven-hundred-acre estate, Hyde Park, on the Hudson River.

Jefferson noted in his Memorandum Book: "June 15, 1791. Hamstead. Breakfd.– went to Prince's at Flushing." While at the home of William Prince, Jefferson left a note requesting "all you have" of sugar maples and bush cranberries (*Viburnum trilobum*) as well as three balsam poplars, six Venetian "sumachs" (American smoke-bush, *Cotinus obovatus*), and twelve "Bursé" (i.e., Beurré Gris) pears. Jefferson would later expand this order significantly, adding fruits for his south orchard—plums, apricots, nectarines, peaches, and Spitzenburg apples—as well as Madeira walnuts for his grove on the southwest slope of Monticello and filberts for the "room of the square of figs." He enhanced his selection of native and ornamental trees and shrubs with an eclectic collection of hemlocks, spruce, balsam fir, and poplar, native wisteria (which he called a "Carolina kidney bean tree with purple flowers"), and golden willows. He wanted the "monthly honeysuckle" (possibly the native *Lonicera sempervirens*) for planting at the base of weeping willows. The quantity and diversity of tree and shrub species Jefferson purchased from Prince in 1791 demonstrates the complexity of his long-ranging aspirations for Monticello.

Roses from Prince

IN ADDITION to this broad selection of trees and shrubs for the Monticello landscape, Jefferson went through Prince's entire inventory of roses and chose three each from all ten varieties the nursery had to offer that year.[12] In fact, this extensive assortment of rose varieties has proved to be the richest and most comprehensive documentation of Jefferson roses presently known. Until this time, the roses Jefferson documented at Shadwell and Monticello were not specific. The "suckers of roses" planted at Shadwell in 1767 could have been one of several suckering rose varieties, including the apothecary's rose (*Rosa gallica officinalis*), scotch briar rose (*R. pimpinellifolia*), or the cinnamon rose (*R. cinnamomea*), all of which were common in America at that time. Jefferson was more specific for his 1771 list of shrubs "not exceeding a growth of 10.f." when he noted "Rose . . . Sweet-briar."[13] The "crimson dwarf rose" Jefferson noted in the 1782 calendar of the bloom of flowers could have been another type of apothecary's rose or a miniature rose such as 'Pompon de Bourgogne', a *R. centifolia* variety, which was introduced before 1664 and later listed by Bernard McMahon as the Burgundy Rose in *The American Gardener's Calendar* (1806).[14]

On November 8, 1791, William Prince sent an invoice with the order; it included two rather than three of each of the ten roses, but the entire selection was filled.[15] Their success or failure is not recorded, although instructions on the reverse of the invoice from the Prince Nursery noted that the roses should be planted around the clumps of lilacs already established at the East Front of the house, a task that was overseen by Thomas Mann Randolph Jr.

At the time of Jefferson's rose order, America's love affair with the rose had barely begun, and the Prince Nursery list was typical of what was obtainable in the United States. Although British and European gardens were acquainted with upwards of two hundred roses by the 1780s, in America, the selection was more limited, especially of home-produced roses. Nurseries relied on imported roses from England through the turn of the nineteenth century. It is important to keep in mind that while Bernard McMahon's appendix to his 1806 edition of *The American Gardener's Calendar* contained eighty-three rose varieties, this is misleading. Benjamin Prince's catalogue of 1820 included a meager twenty-four rose varieties propagated at the nursery in Flushing, New York, and issued the following caveat regarding the imported offerings: "many of them, from the droughts of our summers, are difficult to propagate in America, the earth below the layers being too dry to admit of their striking roots; from which circumstance it is almost impossible to keep an assortment of them, unless newly imported, to supply the demand, which cannot be done at a price that would be satisfactory."

The ten roses from Prince Nursery were the traditional, spring-blooming varieties that were well known in European and American gardens at the time. Prince primarily used the common names of the day for the rose offerings. The "Moss Provence" was a variety of *Rosa centifolia muscosa,* or "hundred-leaved rose" (referring to the roses' multitude of petals, which are so thickly produced that sometimes the petals turn inward, producing a quartering effect to the blossoms). Another popular term for this variety is the cabbage rose, while the name "Provence" loosely referred to roses from regions of France. The moss form is a mutation of the cabbage or large Provence rose, having soft, pine-scented, resinous hairs on the buds before the blossoms open. In 1805, while president, Jefferson received from Washington nurseryman Thomas Main a "Provence Moss Rose," which was planted at Monticello in "the angles of the house." In addition to the moss rose, he also ordered "Large Provence Rose" or *R. centifolia* 'Major', which is a fully double cabbage rose with deep pink petals that are so quartered they form a distinct button eye in the center. This large shrub rose was popular by the late 1700s.

Jefferson ordered a particularly showy, variegated type of the apothecary's rose (*Rosa gallica officinalis*) known as Rosa Mundi (*R. gallica versicolor*). This variety is considered the oldest and best-known sport of the apothecary's rose, with a mixture of white and light crimson striping of the petals. The name Rosa Mundi has been used since the mid-sixteenth century. Many rose enthusiasts maintain that the name is associated with the romantic legend of the beautiful Fair Rosamund, the mistress

Moss rose

of Henry II, whereas others believe it simply refers to its popularity as the "rose of the world."

The "White Rose" in the order is a variety of the ancient European *Rosa alba,* whose antiquity may go back further than the Roman Empire. Pliny the Elder (23–79 CE) mentioned white roses in his *Natural History.* This rose produces tall, arching stems, handsome grayish or bluish-green foliage, and semidouble to fully double pure white blossoms. Jefferson's white rose could have been one of two albas. One was *R. alba semi-plena* 'White Rose of York' (also known as the "Yorkist" rose),[16] a semidouble variety cultivated in Europe since the sixteenth century, that was used in distilling attar of roses, an essential rose oil. The other was the fully double white rose, *R. alba maxima.*

A second white rose in the order, the musk rose (*Rosa moschata*), was another ancient species from southern Europe and the Middle East that was thought to be extinct before twentieth-century rose hunters rediscovered surviving shrubs in cemeteries and old home sites in both America and Britain. The fragrant, alabaster-white blossoms are produced in large clusters, and the tips of the gray-green leaflets are distinctly tapered. This rose species often sports, with semidouble and fully double flowers on the same plant. The musk rose is the parent of many important rose varieties developed in the nineteenth century, including the fragrant noisette class of roses. In England it is also known as the autumn rose because of its late-blooming habit, and it was mentioned in medieval herbals, was depicted in Renaissance paintings of the Virgin Mary, featured in the rose portraits by celebrated painter Pierre-Joseph Redouté (1759–1840)[17] for the Empress Josephine, and appeared in the writings of Shakespeare.

The cinnamon rose (*Rosa cinnamomea*) was named for the stems, which turn a reddish-brown cinnamon color. This rose originated in China and was being cultivated in Europe before the seventeenth century. Jefferson also called it the "May Rose." The "Yellow Rose" would be *R. lutea,* an Asian species native to southwestern and west central China, where it was cultivated by the sixteenth century. It has single, golden yellow flowers, chestnut-brown stems, and an erect habit, and it bears showy, round, bright red rose hips.

The identities of the remaining roses are not as straightforward. The "Monthly Rose" may describe a form of damask rose, *Rosa damascena bifera,* another ancient hybrid thought to be a cross between a gallica and a musk rose with highly fragrant, loosely semidouble, silk pink to white blossoms. The shrub's tendency to rebloom sporadically after the initial spring period gives it the name 'Royal Four Seasons' or 'Quatre Saisons' (and suggests the name "Monthly Rose" used by Prince).

Rosa gallica versicolor (rosa mundi)

The "Prim Rose" was most likely a variety of scotch briar rose, with striped petals (suggested by "prim," a term for "marbled"). In 1799 William Prince offered the same rose under the name "Prim, or Marbled Rose." In 1806 Bernard McMahon also used the term "Marble Rose" for another type of apothecary's rose and for a form of eglantine rose.

There are also several possibilities for the "Thornless Rose," including the alpine rose (*Rosa pendulina*), which is a European species dating to the early eighteenth century. It bears single, deep pink flowers followed by showy, orange-red hips. Another possible candidate for a "thornless" rose could be the North American swamp rose (*R. palustris*), a large shrub with gracefully arching stems and bearing fragrant, five-petaled, light pink flowers in early spring.

Jefferson's years away from his family and his little mountain meant that letters and memoranda were often his only source of news and updates. When at last he retired from the position of Secretary of State on December 31, 1793, and left Philadelphia for Monticello, he returned to find his plantation in deplorable condition under the supervision of overseers. He set about developing plans for regular crop rotations to improve the arable fields and to have fences repaired and peach trees planted to line the fields. Jefferson had little time to focus attention on ornamental gardens. His Garden Book entry for 1794 included a detailed chart of herbs and flowering trees and shrubs under "Objects for the garden this year." At the bottom of the second column, Jefferson simply wrote "roses."

Roses and Friendships

IT WAS not until 1802–3 that Jefferson resumed sending shipments of American plants to his Parisian friend Madame de Tessé. Jefferson was then serving his first term as President of the United States and living in Washington. Entries in his Garden Book and Farm Book had been scant to nonexistent since 1796, but correspondence indicated that planting in the Monticello fruit garden and nursery was especially active, including grapes in the southwest vineyard and fruit and nut trees in the nursery.

On December 9, Jefferson wrote to his Scottish-born professional gardener Robert Bailey with very detailed instructions.

> A friend of mine in France [Madame de Tessé] has asked me to procure the seeds and plants below mentioned, as this may not be out of your line, and the plants abound in this neighborhood, I will ask the favor of you to make

> the collection, and pack them well and properly for the sea, labelling each article so substantially as not to be erased. The sooner they are ready the better, should you not have the convenience of having the boxes made, and will send me a note of the sizes, they shall be made here.[18]

Jefferson once again asked for enormous amounts of seed and plants to be collected and prepared for shipment to Paris. Jefferson's request included pounds of red cedar berries, sassafras, dogwood, white ash, catalpa, and swamp laurel. He also asked for seed, by the half bushel, of black walnuts, poplar trees, oak acorns, and "wild roses of every kind." The most likely native species would be the Carolina or Virginia rose. *Rosa carolina* and *R. virginiana* are two common North American rose species. The Carolina rose, also called pasture rose, is more exclusive to dry, barren, sunny areas, whereas the Virginia rose inhabits moister regions along woodland edges. Both bear five-petaled, deep rose-pink flowers in spring, followed by deep red rose hips.

Jefferson received roses from various sources during his presidency, including from John Milledge, a Revolutionary patriot and Governor of Georgia who sent Jefferson seeds of the Cherokee rose.[19] *Rosa laevigata,* an Asian species, was believed to have been brought to America by the mid-eighteenth century and naturalized so extensively that it was thought to be native. Some feel, however, that it perhaps moved across the Asian landmass when the continents were connected. The French botanist André Michaux (1746–1802) saw it in great abundance during his botanical tour of the American south in 1803. On April 29, 1804, Jefferson noted, "[P]lanted seeds of the Cherokee rose from Govr. Milledge in a row of about 6.f. near the N.E. corner of the Nursery. Goliah stuck sticks to mark the place."[20] Goliah (1731–1810) was an enslaved worker at Monticello; at age seventy-three, he had been assigned the lighter work in the mountaintop gardens. In a letter to his daughter Maria, Jefferson wrote, "Goliah is our gardener, and with his veteran aids will be directed to make what preparations he can for you."[21] This message suggested that Goliah was an enslaved gardener with assistants.

Throughout his presidency and beyond, Jefferson maintained a relationship with another horticulturally minded friend, Mrs. Samuel Harrison (Margaret Bayard) Smith (1778–1844). Her husband was the founder and editor of the *National Intelligencer* and a strong supporter of Jefferson's. Margaret Smith became a close friend in her own right and has proved a resourceful observer of Jefferson and his family as well as other figures in early Washington society at the time. Following Jefferson's retirement, she visited Monticello. Her account of Jefferson's apartment in the President's House reveals his fondness for all living things and provides insight into plants being cultivated in flowerpots.

> In the window recesses, were stands for the flowers and plants which it was his delight to attend and among his roses and geraniums [*Pelargonium inquinans*] was suspended the cage of his favorite mockingbird, which he cherished with peculiar fondness, not only for its melodious powers, but for its uncommon intelligence and affectionate disposition, of which qualities he gave surprising instances. It was the constant companion of his solitary and studious hours. . . . How he loved this bird! How he loved his flowers! He could not live without something to love, and in the absence of his darling grandchildren, his birds and his flowers became objects of tender care.[22]

Although the identity of the rose in the window recesses of his cabinet was not specified, it could possibly be the repeat-blooming 'Old Blush' China rose (*Rosa chinensis* cv.), which created a sea change in rose breeding when it was introduced to the West by the 1790s.[23]

Rosa alba semi-plena (White Rose of York)

Margaret Smith sent another unidentified rose to President Jefferson in 1808 with a package she received from James Hugh McCulloch (1756–1836):[24]

> Mrs. H Smith presents her compliments to Mr Jefferson & sends him some plants of the Antwerp-raspberry which she has just received from Baltimore, with a number of other shrubs. The label was only round one stock, & she is not absolutely certain that the others are the same plant. The black-rose Mr McCulloch mentions on the label, she cannot distinguish among the other shrubs. If the President's grounds afford no safe spot for these plants, Mrs. S. will take great pleasure in attending to them until next winter, if Mr Jefferson will trust them to her care.—[25]

Jefferson responded, confirming that the plants would be sent to the Georgetown nurseryman who was caring for other plants intended for Monticello: "Th: Jefferson returns mrs Smith many thanks for the plants she was so kind as to send him yesterday, and which are very acceptable. he will not give mrs Smith the additional trouble of taking care of them through the season, but sends them up to mr Maine who has some others in charge for him."[26]

Roses at Poplar Forest

SOME OF the predominantly spring-flowering roses undoubtedly found their way to Jefferson's retreat home, Poplar Forest. The apothecary's rose, common in early American kitchen gardens for its medicinal and culinary uses, could be the "rose bushes" noted in Jefferson's planting memorandum dated February 21, 1811, for the "N. side of [the patch], at W. end." Jefferson was likely referencing these same bushes in his instructions to "weed roses" growing with the gooseberries and strawberries.

Jefferson's December 1812 planting memorandum to his Poplar Forest overseer, Jeremiah A. Goodman (ca. 1780–1857),[27] suggested that roses were also used in the mixed landscape plantings on the right and left banks flanking the sunken lawn on the south side of the house, where the following were planted: "a row of lilacs, Althaeas, Gelder roses [*Viburnum opulus* 'Roseum'], Roses, Calycanthus [sweet shrub]." Large, vigorous roses that would appropriately complement the surrounding shrubbery in this location could include the European musk rose (*Rosa moschata* and *R. moschata plena*), which, unlike the spring-flowering roses, bears fragrant, single to double, pure white flowers from June through frost.

Jefferson's November 1, 1816, planting memorandum offered more clues for roses in the ornamental oval flower beds on the north front of the house: "Planted large roses of difft. kinds in the oval bed in the N. front" and "dwarf roses in the N. E. oval." This reference to different large roses suggests his desire to add a variety of rose types, which could include the musk rose as well as the white rose (*Rosa alba maxima*) and the "large Provence" or cabbage rose (*R. centifolia* 'Major'). Because of the lack of any contemporaneous correspondence with friends or nursery orders confirming receipt of these roses, it is quite possible that the white rose varieties as well as the suckering gallica roses and the dwarf Burgundian rose could have been propagated from root divisions, cuttings, and other vegetative means from the roses that were well established at Monticello since at least the 1790s. This also would suggest a high degree of horticultural skill from the enslaved gardeners and overseers, a fact that was never documented.

During the early 1800s, Jefferson was on the cusp of a major transformation in rose culture and enthusiasm in the West, especially with the newly introduced everblooming roses from China. His desire to create a garden of roses at Poplar Forest reflected an emerging trend as the popularity of roses gained momentum in North America.

4

THE NATIVE FLORA OF VIRGINIA AND JEFFERSON'S CURIOUS MIND

. . . every bud that opens . . .

THE BOTANICAL KNOWLEDGE JEFFERSON GAINED from the days of his youth to old age was informed and enhanced by his intensely curious mind and keen, almost microscopic observation of the natural world. While his devotion to science and Enlightenment ideals is often described as dispassionate and aloof, his sense of innocent, almost spiritual wonder derived from the minutest details of nature was often disarming. His most intimate reflections filled those letters he wrote from Philadelphia to his daughters at Monticello, imploring them for news from home and the smallest of family particulars. He reminded Martha, "There is not a sprig of grass that shoots uninteresting to me."[1] Writing from Monticello to James Madison in June 1793, after retiring from the position as Secretary of State and what he described as the "tumult of the world," Jefferson began with a prosaic longing for domestic tranquility but then transitioned to a desire for a quiet peace in which he had "an interest or affection in every bud that opens, in every breath that blows around me, in an entire freedom of rest, of motion, of thought—owing account to myself alone of my hours and actions."[2] Jefferson's continual return to nature became a means of self-discovery and rejuvenation.

By the time he was governor of Virginia (1779–81), Jefferson's knowledge of the natural sciences was well known and publicly acknowledged by his peers. He was elected to membership in the American Philosophical Society (APS) in January 1780 and became president of the society on March 3, 1797, the day before he was

< *Asclepias tuberosa* (butterfly weed)

inaugurated Vice President of the United States.[3] He continued in this role at APS while serving two terms as President of the United States. Following his retirement to Monticello, he offered his resignation owing to the logistical difficulties of attending the meetings held in Philadelphia; his resignation was declined, however, until 1814. Following his long tenure as president, he continued his correspondence and involvement as an elected councilor until his death in 1826. During his association with the APS, Jefferson published his only book, *Notes on the State of Virginia,* secured funding for the purchase of the Louisiana Territory, and commissioned the Lewis and Clark Expedition to explore this newly acquired western region of the United States. At Monticello he oversaw the construction of a massive, one-thousand-foot vegetable garden terrace as well as ornamental flower gardens, filled with native and exotic species, near the house. At the same time, he planned the construction of Poplar Forest, his retreat home in Bedford County, Virginia.

Jefferson's Botanical Catalogue in Notes on the State of Virginia

THOMAS JEFFERSON'S record of North American plants in *Notes on the State of Virginia* not only offers insights into the native species he deemed valuable to early Americans but also serves as an important reference and primary resource document. He began writing in 1781–82, while serving as wartime Governor of Virginia, in response to a list of queries made by François Marbois, the secretary to the French legation in Philadelphia. He dutifully responded to Marbois's queries while pursuing a major goal of refuting European misconceptions about the natural history of North America. Ultimately his work developed into a comprehensive portrait of his native land. Jefferson included observations on race and slavery that have remained controversial. Nevertheless, James Madison concluded the work in its entirety was "too valuable not to be made known."[4]

Jefferson organized the chapters as queries. Under "Query VI: A notice of the mines and other subterraneous riches, its trees, plants, fruits, etc.," Jefferson designated plants into four major categories: "medicinal," "esculent," "ornamental," and "useful for fabrication." The North American species within these categories primarily included woody trees and shrubs, but the many native herbaceous species that Jefferson considered for his shrubbery and later for the ornamental gardens at Monticello are significant.

Jefferson consulted the floras and botanical treatises of the most learned scholars of his day, on which he would base his own scientific conclusions. In the introductory paragraph to his essay on Virginia's flora in Query VI of *Notes,* Jefferson clarified that he added "the Linnaean to the popular names, as the latter might not convey precise information to a foreigner." As noted above, the Swedish scientist Carolus Linnaeus, considered the "father of taxonomy," created the binomial system used internationally in the biological sciences. Among his many scientific tomes, Linnaeus's great work *Systema Natura* (1735) ran through twelve editions, and his *Species Plantarum* (1753) was published within Jefferson's lifetime. In addition to Linnaeus, Jefferson cited the English-born botanist John Clayton (ca. 1695–1773), who lived for many years at Windsor in Gloucester County, Virginia, and whose botanical investigations appear in *Flora Virginica* (1739), published by Jan Frederik Gronovius.[5] Jefferson's "of Millar" references indicate his third source, Philip Miller, the English botanist of Scottish descent and head gardener at Chelsea Physic Garden whose *The Gardeners Dictionary* (1731) and *The Gardeners Kalendar* (1732) informed Jefferson on many gardening-related topics throughout his lifetime. It was not until the seventh edition of the *Kalendar,* published in 1759, that Miller used the Linnaean scientific system of binomial nomenclature. Jefferson's library contained at least three of Miller's books, including the 1768 edition of the *Dictionary* and the 1765 edition of the *Kalendar.*

The third category, encompassing "ornamental" plants, contained the most extensive listing: forty-three primarily spring-flowering woody plants, including flowering dogwood, redbud, red maple, fringe tree, yellow jessamine, red buckeye, sweet shrub, Virginia sweetspire, hawthorn, catalpa, pawpaw, mountain laurel, spicebush, tulip poplar, trumpet honeysuckle, red bay, rosebay and pinxter flower rhododendrons, and cucumber, umbrella, and sweet bay magnolias. Additional broadleaf evergreens included wax myrtle and American holly. Jefferson's admiration of these native species harkened back to his earliest ideas for embellishing the landscape at Monticello when, in 1771, he developed elaborate plans for ornamental shrubberies on the western slopes of the mountain. Again and again throughout his lifetime, Jefferson's letters, memoranda, and Garden Book entries substantiate that he requested, recommended, shared, and planted these North American trees, shrubs, and vines both at home and abroad. Judging from the times Jefferson requested these species from his botanist friends John Bartram Jr., Richard Cary, and John Banister Jr. while he was minister to France in the 1780s, his *Notes on the State of Virginia* was obviously informing and inspiring many, including his Parisian friend Madame de Tessé.

Nearly all the choices for "medicinal" plants were herbaceous species used by Native American tribes for curative purposes as well as some that are considered poisonous when improperly used, including "Palma christi" (castor bean, *Ricinus communis*) and "James-town weed" (jimsonweed, *Datura stramonium*). The species most recognized now as ornamental included "Lobelia of several species," various mallows, gentians, angelica, and ginseng.

Many botanical names used by Jefferson have changed in some fashion during the intervening two centuries. Jefferson's "Pleurisy Root," *Asclepias decumbens,* is now *Asclepias tuberosa,* or butterfly weed. His "Indian Physic," *Spiraea trifoliata,* is now *Gillenia trifoliata* (Bowman's root). Other translations are more problematic. Was Jefferson's *Bignonia sempervirens* (yellow jasmine) actually *Bignonia capreolata* (trumpet or cross vine) or *Gelsemium sempervirens* (Carolina yellow jessamine)? Ann Leighton, in her classic book *American Gardens in the Eighteenth Century,* concludes the latter.[6] In another instance, Jefferson's "*Hedera quinquefolia*—Ivy" is most certainly not the European ivy (*Hedera helix*) but rather our native Virginia creeper, *Parthenocissus quinquefolia.* Conversely, the botanical name for Jefferson's "Black snake-root" (black cohosh) has recently changed from *Cimicifuga racemosa* back to *Actaea racemosa,* the name that appeared in *Notes on the State of Virginia.* This handsome North American perennial grows abundantly in the Monticello woodlands, where it produces towering spires of snow-white flowers in early summer above rich, broad mounds of astilbe-like dark green foliage. Black cohosh is a long-lived perennial that is grown today in Monticello's East Front oval flower beds.

A Botanical Namesake

In 1792, Jefferson received perhaps the highest honor in the realm of botany: the naming of a native plant after him. In a meeting in Philadelphia before the American Philosophical Society on May 18, the American botanist and naturalist Benjamin Smith Barton (1766–1815) read his paper describing a delicate, spring-blooming woodland wildflower. Although it resembled both bloodroot and mayapple in flower and habit, Barton determined it to be a unique genus, naming it *Jeffersonia* "in honour of Thomas Jefferson, esq. Secretary of State to the United-States." Barton went on to say that he "had no reference to [Jefferson's] political character [but rather] with his knowledge of natural history. In the various departments of this science, but especially in botany and zoology, the information of this gentleman is equalled by that of few persons in the United-States." The common name, twinleaf, refers to its large two-part leaves, which resemble butterfly wings.

Barton's description was based on plants collected in Virginia's Blue Ridge Mountains by another member of the APS, the French botanist André Michaux.[7]

Botanical watercolor of *Jeffersonia diphylla* by Pierre Jean Francois Turpin, undated

Twinleaf was blooming in Bartram's Garden in Philadelphia in 1791, although Barton did not observe twinleaf in the wild until he saw immense quantities near Harper's Ferry in 1802. Several years later, in April 1807, the seed was planted at Monticello in a northeast oval flower bed.

Horticultural Potential of Western Plants: "Peculiar to the Countries He Has Visited"

THE LURE of the West, with its promise of untold discoveries, was irresistible to most eighteenth-century Americans, and Jefferson was no exception. Monticello's position at the edge of the Virginia frontier, with commanding views of the Blue Ridge Mountains, inspired Jefferson to dream of explorations westward with feverish enthusiasm. By the time of the American Revolution, he was preparing directives for transcontinental scientific journeys that never materialized. Jefferson voiced this long-held desire in his 1801 inaugural address, when he dared to envision a "rising nation, spread over a wide and fruitful land, advancing rapidly to destinies beyond the reach of mortal eye." Two years later, he commissioned Meriwether Lewis, who recruited Captain William Clark to join him in leading the Corps of Discovery.

Lewis and Clark were true "pioneering naturalists," making collections and observations across the continent for the advancement of science.[8] Their three-year journey led them through the central prairies and the windswept high plains, the arid Rockies, and seasonally moist, temperate West Coast regions. These diverse climatic and geographic environments obviously resulted in growing conditions quite dissimilar from those of the woodlands, swamps, fields, and savannahs of eastern North America. Recognizing this, Jefferson wrote to Philadelphia nurseryman Bernard McMahon in 1807, at the conclusion of the mission, "Capt. Lewis has brought a considerable number of seeds of plants peculiar to the countries he has visited."[9] At the time, it was difficult to recognize or sort out the plants that might prove amenable to gardens from those requiring very specific (and difficult to reproduce) environmental conditions. Although Jefferson, McMahon, William Hamilton (1745–1813), and many others were enormously interested in cultivating these rare new introductions from the West, determining which would survive would require years of experimentation and trial and error.

Some plants with ornamental potential were quickly distributed and entered the nursery trade early on, such as Lewis's prairie flax (*Linum perenne lewisii*), which McMahon was offering by 1815. Other showy flowers, like the annual and perennial blanket flowers (*Gaillardia* sp.), were familiar asters that soon emerged as garden favorites. But widespread production and marketing of the Lewis and Clark plants occurred gradually over time, and, in some cases, it required the plants to be "rediscovered" by other intrepid explorers with more influential connections.

Often, these western North American species fared better in England than they did in the eastern United States. The elegant clarkia or "elkhorn flower," named for Captain William Clark by the German botanist Frederick Traugott Pursh

(1774–1820),[10] became widely popular in nineteenth-century British gardens. Accounts of London exhibitions in which clarkias received first-class certificates appeared in American magazines of the 1860s. After traveling to Britain, nurseryman and seed merchant James Vick of Rochester, New York, wrote enviously of "immense fields ablaze with bright colors, acres each of pink, red, white, purple, lilac," which he encountered in an Essex country village. Although (like most seedsmen) he offered a broad selection of both single and double cultivars, he readily admitted, "The Clarkia is the most effective annual in the hands of the English florist. It

Botanical drawing of *Clarkia pulchella* from *Flora Americae Septentrionalis* by Frederick Pursh, 1814

suffers with us in hot dry weather."[11] Clarkia has been found to perform best when planted in the fall, especially in southern states, so that it blooms as the season cools.

Snow-on-the-mountain (*Euphorbia marginata*), which was new to science when collected by Lewis and Clark in 1806, soon became a common annual flower in nineteenth-century seed catalogues. Although its natural distribution is along the west side of the Missouri River in North Dakota, it proved adaptable to a wide range of soil types and growing conditions and likely escaped from cultivation into farmlands from Minnesota to Texas and New Mexico. Still other adaptable western species, like the western Jacob's ladder (*Polemonium pulcherrimum*) and even Lewis's prairie flax, never managed to captivate American nurserymen, even though they grow with equal vigor and beauty. Catalogues generally offered only the traditional European counterparts, probably because it was easier to acquire these perennials from seed sources abroad.

Present-day ecological concerns must temper our rush to obtain certain species, especially those threatened by overzealous collectors. The prairie coneflower (*Echinacea angustifolia*), for example, has a long history of medicinal use by Indigenous Americans. Its common name, mad dog plant, refers to the belief that it cured the bite of rattlesnakes and rabid dogs, but our modern-day infatuation with herbal remedies for colds and respiratory problems has led to its near devastation by widespread digging of wild plants.

Now we can reflect upon the pristine landscape, stretching out beyond the horizon, that was viewed with awe and wonder by the men of the Corps of Discovery. While we know they endured near starvation and exhaustion, sickness, scorching heat, arduous winters, monumental hardships, and profound uncertainty about the road ahead, we can still envy their experiences and take pleasure in their discoveries just as Jefferson certainly did, though he never traveled west beyond the mountains of Virginia. Jefferson's destiny was to remain behind and wait with excited anticipation for the seeds, plants, and roots that returned with the corps. In the ensuing years he would pursue the study of new and sometimes peculiar flora from western regions, content in the belief that "Nature intended me for the tranquil pursuits of science, by rendering them my supreme delight."[12]

Jefferson's Horticultural Mentors: McMahon and Hamilton

IN 1806 Lewis and Clark returned with an astonishing collection of herbarium specimens as well as live plants and seeds, many of which were sent directly to President Jefferson. While in Washington, Jefferson attempted to grow some of these

Portrait of Bernard McMahon, artist unknown, undated

plants, but he relayed most of the collection of seeds to his close associates in Philadelphia: William Hamilton and Bernard McMahon.

Hamilton was born into a wealthy Philadelphia family and inherited over three hundred acres of land, which he named The Woodlands, on the west side of the Schuylkill River. Hamilton was an eminent botanist and plant collector and made his estate a New World model of contemporary English landscape gardening techniques. Jefferson described The Woodlands as the "only rival I have known in America to what may be seen in England."[13]

Perhaps of even greater influence than William Hamilton was another Philadelphian, Bernard McMahon. Born in Ireland, McMahon emigrated to the United States in 1796 and established a nursery and seed house in Philadelphia. He issued his first broadside catalogue in 1802–3 and authored and published *The American Gardener's Calendar* in 1806.

After receiving seeds from President Jefferson, McMahon met with success. He reported to Jefferson in 1808 that in addition to a variety of currants and gooseberries, he had fine specimens of about twenty new species, including five or six new genera. He would later send Jefferson seedlings of *Symphoricarpos albus,* a shrub found on the banks of the Columbia River, which became a garden favorite in England by 1815. He remarked, "I have given it the trivial english name of Snowberry-bush."[14]

McMahon played a key role in Jefferson's use of North American species in the garden that went beyond the specimens that returned with Lewis and Clark. In 1806 Jefferson received a copy of McMahon's newly published *Calendar,* which would become one of the most influential books on gardening in America for the remainder of the nineteenth century. The *Calendar* paid particular attention to North American natives and their desirability in the garden. A passage from McMahon's work gives a timeless argument for gardening with natives:

> Many flower-gardens . . . are almost destitute of bloom, during a great part of the season; which could be easily avoided, and a blaze of flowers kept up . . . in the borders of the pleasure-garden, from March to November, by introducing from our woods and fields, the various beautiful ornaments with which nature has so profusely decorated them . . . in Europe plants are not rejected because they are indigenous, on the contrary, they are cultivated with due care; and yet here, we cultivate many foreign trifles, and neglect the profusion of beauties so bountifully bestowed upon us by the hand of nature.[15]

Jefferson evidently took McMahon's recommendations to heart, for it is estimated that around a quarter of the flowers in his gardens were native species collected from the surrounding countryside. Jefferson's 1807 sketch for twenty oval flower beds situated in the angles of the house and terraces included native lobelias, lupines, and even his botanical namesake, the twinleaf, alongside beds of pinks, carnations, ranunculus, and tuberose.

One large shipment from McMahon's nursery included seed of "the Scarlet Cardinal's flower," which was sowed in an oval flower bed on the northwest side of Monticello. The cardinal flower (*Lobelia cardinalis*), which Jefferson included among the medicinal plants in *Notes on the State of Virginia,* is one of our most striking natives in the landscape. Its deep scarlet flowers on three-foot spikes are spectacular during July and August in central Virginia. Eighteenth-century Swedish naturalist Peter Kalm (1716–1779) listed it with bee balm and catchfly when he remarked that "the land [in America] is undoubtedly adorned with the finest red imaginable."[16] Judging by the request for seed made by the marquis de Lafayette to George Washington in 1784, it was a flower deemed suitable even for the king in his Royal Garden in Paris. Another unusual native likely from McMahon was the American larkspur (*Delphinium exaltatum*). Introduced into Britain in 1758, it became part of the parentage in early delphinium hybridization, creating the magnificent forms we know today. The spectacular Turk's-cap lily (*Lilium superbum*) could certainly have qualified as one of the "handsome lilies" sent to Jefferson by McMahon in 1812. Also known as martagon lily, it was introduced into Britain around 1727.

Preservation of Nature

WHILE PRESENT-DAY environmentalists can marvel at eighteenth-century gardening sensibilities that sought to include native plants in ornamental gardens, their admiration must be tempered by the realization that species extinction and the long-range consequences of habitat destruction were not fully understood at the time. Eighteenth-century intellectuals, scientists, and naturalists, such as the renowned geographer and explorer Alexander von Humboldt (1769–1859), were just beginning to articulate the dynamic interconnectedness of nature. Humboldt, a Prussian scientist, naturalist, and explorer, wrote more than thirty-six books based upon his travels on four continents, including the Spanish colonies of the Americas, in which he put forward a prescient concept of human-induced climate change. Humboldt met with President Jefferson several times during his 1804 visit to the United States, and they continued to correspond for twenty-one years.[17] Nevertheless, Jefferson and most of his contemporaries loved growing exotic plants and yearned for new introductions with little awareness of future problems associated with invasive species and indiscriminate plant introductions. This could be viewed as a drawback of Jefferson's inquiring mind. Yet within the broader context of his times, through his writing and participation, he made significant contributions toward the aim of the American Philosophical Society: "promoting useful knowledge."

5

THE ARDENT AMATEUR

When I return to live at Monticello . . .
I believe I shall become a florist.

OUR MODERN IMAGE of a florist likely does not conform to the occupation Thomas Jefferson envisioned for his retirement years. Floristry, as a major commercial industry, did not evolve until the turn of the twentieth century. In 1935 American horticulturist and author Liberty Hyde Bailey described floriculture as a kind of "intensive agriculture" for the purpose of growing ornamental plants, either under glass or outdoors, for their disposal in wholesale and retail markets.[1] The eighteenth-century florist was more often the ardent amateur, as presented in books like H. [Hermon] Bourne's *Flore Poetici: The Florist's Manual . . . for Cultivators of Flowers* and Joseph Breck's *The Young Florist; or Conversations on the Culture of Flowers, and on Natural History* (both published in 1833). The florist in Jefferson's time was a serious gardener who devoted his attention to carefully cultivating, observing, selecting, and even systematically improving flowers for their beauty, fragrance, color, and grace, but not as a commercial venture.

Historically, the kinds of flowers typically connected with the florist have remained remarkably similar. By the last two decades of the nineteenth century, the florist's attention began to focus on certain types of flowers: those that, as Peter Henderson described it in 1890, "displayed perfection in habit of plant, and in form of flower, with distinct coloring."[2] Both Henderson and George Nicholson, in *The Illustrated Dictionary of Gardening* (1885), cite the auricula, carnation, chrysanthemum, dahlia, fuchsia, gladiolus, hyacinth, show and zonal pelargonium, and tulip as some of the best-known examples, "each and all exhibiting evidence of the success attending the Florist's work."[3] But this litany of "florist flowers" echoes through

< *Dianthus barbatus* (Sweet William)

previous centuries in countless garden dictionaries and calendars. Philip Miller, the head gardener at Chelsea Physic Garden, repeated monthly directions on the care of "choice" and "fine" carnations, pinks, polyanthus, auriculas, hyacinths, and tulips in *The Gardeners Kalendar* (the 1765 edition of which Jefferson owned). Bernard McMahon repeated the very same flowers in *The American Gardener's Calendar* (1806). Moreover, many of these flowers recur in Jefferson's own journals and letters, whether he was searching the Parisian markets in 1786 for "Carnations, Auriculas, Tuberoses, Hyacinths, & Belladonna lilies," describing his extensive flower border of "tulips, hyacinths, tuberoses & Amaryllis," or ordering seeds and plants of auricula, double anemone, double carnation, crown imperial, and double ranunculus for his collection of "handsome or fragrant" flowers at Monticello. All were the classic subjects for the amusement of the eighteenth-century florist.

Jefferson's hopes and plans, however, were often more lavish than the results. His success as an ardent amateur florist, whether in growing fine garden flowers or choice indoor plants, was likely uneven. We know from his Garden Book that he recorded the sowing of carnations, pinks, sweet William, and auricula seed as early as 1767 at Shadwell. As spring progressed, he went on to record the pinks (*Dianthus plumarius*) and sweet William (*D. barbatus*) in bloom and carnations (*D. caryophyllus*) "in full life," but there were no further observations on the auriculas (*Primula auricula*). The Garden Book gives occasional verification that garden pinks and sweet William thrived at Monticello, as did the common primrose (*Primula vulgaris*). The success of the more difficult double carnations and auriculas seemed more elusive.

Seasoned gardeners will attest that the auricula demands a fair amount of gardening skill to bring the flower to perfection in Virginia. Native to the northern Alps and south into Italy, the wild, yellow-flowered primrose was described as early as 50 CE by Dioscorides. By the late 1400s it was called *Auricula ursi,* meaning "bear's little ear," in reference to the shape of its leaf. In the sixteenth century Dutch botanist Carolus Clusius (1526–1609) and English herbalist John Gerard (1545–1612) described various color forms and natural hybrids, which were known as "garden auriculas." These became one of the most fashionable spring-flowering plants for pots and parterres in seventeenth-century Britain and Europe, especially in the gardens of the wealthy. Ironically, it was in the hands of the British working class that the auriculas became true florists' flowers. During the nineteenth century, the development of show auriculas was taken to new heights in northern mill towns, where the social life of Lancashire communities revolved around auricula societies and shows.[4]

Jefferson's interest in auriculas was aroused again in 1807, when Bernard McMahon wrote that "of Auriculas we have none here worth a cent, but I expect some

Botanical drawing of *Primula auricula* after Pierre-Joseph Redouté (engraved by Victor), from *Choix des plus belle fleurs (Selection of the Most Beautiful Flowers)*, 1827–33

good ones from London this spring; if they come safe, you shall have a division next season."[5] When, in February 1812, McMahon forwarded a box of plants and roots to Jefferson, the box included "6 pots of Auriculas, different kinds," suggesting that the plants were likely some of the "choice" varieties, possibly from London, requiring special attention and care. McMahon understood that Jefferson had an unheated greenhouse, which could potentially provide a perfect environment for pots of auriculas and the pot of "a beautiful polyanthus."[6]

"Handsome or Fragrant"

THE DESIRABILITY of fragrant flowers during the eighteenth and nineteenth centuries cannot be overstated. In the language of flowers, it is said that fragrance speaks volumes. The sensory experience was central to the overall enrichment of a garden, whether in simple English cottage gardens or the grand formal palace gardens of Versailles and the Trianon, which highlighted frequently rotated plantings of fragrant hyacinths, tulips, primroses, and roses.[7] For Thomas Jefferson, the qualities of beauty and fragrance carried equal weight. Wallflowers (*Cheiranthus cheiri*) ranked highly among the favorite perfumed blossoms in early American gardens. *Cheiranthus* means "hand-flower," and in the Middle Ages it was carried in the hand at festivals. British herbalist John Parkinson (1567–1650) wrote that "the sweetnesse of the flowers causeth them to be generally used in Nosegayes and to deck up houses."[8] While serving as President of the United States, Jefferson sent his daughter Martha a "bundle of Wallflowers" on November 21, 1806. The flowers were transported by David "Davy" Hern Jr., an enslaved wagoner. Jefferson ordered wallflower seed from Bernard McMahon in 1807.

Mignonette (*Reseda odorata*), a native of Egypt, was first described in the sixth edition of Philip Miller's *Gardeners Dictionary* (1752) as a flower "of a dull colour, but hav[ing] a high ambrosial scent."[9] Napoleon is credited with collecting mignonette seeds during his Egyptian campaign and sending them to the Empress Josephine at Malmaison. Josephine set the fashion of growing mignonette in pots for its perfume. Its tiny pale green and white flowers are hardly showy, and yet, despite its humble appearance, the mignonette retained legendary esteem. In 1791 James Madison Sr., the father of America's fourth president, received mignonette seed from George Morris, a Philadelphia seedsman, for the gardens at Montpelier in Orange County, Virginia. In his *Calendar,* Bernard McMahon recommended mignonette for its "sweet and agreeable odour, for which purpose it is extremely worthy of cultivation."[10] In 1811 Jefferson situated this flower near the northwest cistern at Monticello.

Of the scented flowers, few can compete with poet's jasmine (*Jasminum officinale*). The mere word "jasmine" conjures fragrance and romance, and the delicious odor of this flower, which pours forth in the evening, is often the muse of amorous poetry. Jefferson included the "white jasmine" among his "Objects for the garden" in 1794, and in 1809 "star jasmine" was planted in a southwest oval flower bed.

Fragrance was likewise an important element in the gardens of James and Dolley Madison at their Virginia home, Montpelier.[11] Evidence suggests that the Madisons' formal garden was designed about 1810 by Charles Bizet, a gardener who fled France during the Revolution. Bizet would later become the gardener for the President's House in Washington, DC, under James Monroe. As described by Dolley Madison's niece Mary Cutts, the garden at Montpelier not only produced a variety of fruits but was also "a paradise of roses and other flowers." A remembrance of the flowers grown by James and Dolley Madison was recorded by Anne Mercer Slaughter, who visited Montpelier in 1825. Slaughter recalled the scent of jasmine and roses wafting through the drawing room, writing that "into this lovely apartment came the sweet odours of the jessamine and roses, which twined around the pillars of the rear porch, and gave an air of indescribable charm to the whole scene, like a bit of faery in this prosaic world."[12]

Scent and memory are known to share a primal bond. A similar remembrance was recorded years after Thomas Jefferson's death by Jane Cary Smith, niece of Jefferson's son-in-law Thomas Mann Randolph Jr., who often visited Monticello during Jefferson's later years. Smith described a flower bed "under each low French window" below the dining room with trellises "covered with yellow Jessamine & climbing roses, a nest of sweets." She went on to describe the scene "from the breakfast table [where she] looked down on the dew sprinkled blossoms in earliest spring, when the mountain air was too fresh to be admitted into the apartment, for frost and blight seemed to linger in this favored spot for a brief space only, just long enough for nature to rest in sleep and wake refreshed, for her perpetual youth."[13] The identity of the yellow jessamine was likely not the white star jasmine but rather the evergreen Carolina jessamine (*Gelsemium sempervirens*), a vine native to the southern United States, Mexico, and Guatemala, which bears highly scented yellow flowers in very early spring. The climbing rose, likewise, is not specified, but early spring flowering suggests the sweetbriar (*Rosa rubiginosa*), known as Shakespeare's eglantine rose, which bears sweetly fragrant, five-petaled, soft pink flowers and apple-scented foliage.

A Greenhouse for Delicious Flowering Shrubs and Cape Bulbs

IN HIS book, Bernard McMahon quite precisely distinguished the essential differences between greenhouses, hothouses or stoves, and conservatories. The greenhouse, he wrote, "is a garden-building fronted with glass, serving as a winter residence, for tender plants . . . which require no more artificial heat, than what is barely sufficient to keep off frost, and dispel such damps as may arise in the house." The hothouse, according to McMahon, required continual heat for the survival of its tropical flora. Furthermore, whereas the hothouse was designed to maintain humidity, the greenhouse was meant to dispel it.[14] The conservatory, on the other hand, was something entirely different. McMahon explained that "in the Green-house, the trees and plants are either in tubs or pots, and are placed on stands or stages during the winter. . . . In the Conservatory, the ground plan is laid out in beds and borders, made up of the best compositions of soils that can be procured, three or four feet deep."[15] Greenhouses and orangeries were features of several eighteenth-century country estates in Virginia and Maryland, including Green Spring Plantation near Williamsburg; Margaret Carroll's greenhouse at Mount Clare, outside Baltimore; and George Washington's orangery at Mount Vernon, overlooking the Potomac River. Jefferson also visited the greenhouses of The Woodlands, William Hamilton's estate on the banks of the Schuylkill River in Philadelphia.

As early as the 1770s, Jefferson displayed a fondness for certain plants that would require winter protection, including the flowering acacia (*Acacia farnesiana*), which he encountered on one of his many visits to Green Spring. Originally the family residence and estate of Sir William Berkeley (1605–1677), the Royal Governor, Green Spring then became home to successive generations of Ludwells and Lees from 1680 through the early nineteenth century.[16] On May 24, 1778, Thomas Jefferson noted in his memorandum book, "Pd. a gardener at Greenspring for two Acacias." Green Spring, located three miles from Jamestown, was a frequent side trip for Jefferson when he traveled to Williamsburg. There he could admire the estate's three extensive orchards, vegetable garden, field of indigo, and the substantial orangery (ca. 1730) or free-standing greenhouse, which was heated and most likely had glazed, triple-sashed windows. Philip Ludwell III likely had the structure built between 1725 and 1740.[17] The acacias Jefferson acquired had surely spent the previous winter in the Green Spring orangery; as he recorded later in his Garden Book, "They are from seeds planted March 1777."[18] Although this tender shrubby member of the bean family has a somewhat straggly habit, formidable thorns, and malodorous roots, its small, yellow pom-pom-like blossoms are extremely fragrant, and Jefferson would later describe the acacia as "the most delicious flowering shrub in the world."[19] Unfortunately, it is doubtful that Jefferson's young plants thrived far beyond September, when he measured their heights at eighteen and twenty-three inches. At the time, he lacked an appropriate structure to sustain them.

Jefferson would often return to the idea of growing tender plants in a glass enclosure, and he was well acquainted with the possibilities such structures could afford. In the 1790s, he visited William Hamilton at The Woodlands, where he encountered an enormous greenhouse measuring 140 feet in length and divided into a series of compartments.[20] Hamilton was an insatiable collector, and his carefully arranged collection, at its peak, was estimated to contain ten thousand plants from every explored corner of the globe, including the East Indies, Botany Bay, Japan, and the Cape of Good Hope. He went to great lengths to procure some of the most unusual and rare plants of his time, and he apparently had the reputation of being quite protective of them. Although Jefferson requested seeds of various greenhouse plants, including the sweet acacia and Venus flytrap, on several occasions, he was not always successful in securing them from Hamilton. Similarly, McMahon reported to Jefferson, "I have from time to time given Mr. Hamilton a great variety of plants, and altho' he is in every respect a particular friend of mine, he never offered me one in return . . . I well know his jealousy of an person's attempt to vie with him in a collection of plants."[21]

At Mount Vernon, George Washington's substantial, two-story orangery was, in turn, inspired by Margaret Carroll's greenhouse at Mount Clare.[22] The Mount Vernon orangery was heated by a furnace with a series of ceramic flues set in a separate room to the east of the main room. In 1789, upon the completion of Mount Vernon's structure, Mrs. Carroll sent President Washington pots and boxes of oranges, lemons, a "fine balm scented Shrub," aloes, and tufts of knotted marjoram.[23] Other references indicate what Washington called the "opopantax," or sweet acacia, among the plants cultivated in Mount Vernon's greenhouse. Jefferson's visits to Mount Vernon during the 1790s coincided with this active period in Washington's orangery.

Jefferson had twice envisioned a greenhouse for himself at Monticello. A freestanding, two-story structure on Mulberry Row was first designed during the late 1770s and again around 1805.[24] His second, more elaborate design included a terrace on the kitchen garden side and an entrance on two levels. Ultimately, however, Jefferson decided to incorporate his greenhouse within the body of Monticello as a small, glass-enclosed arched loggia, which he called the South Piazza. It was not until shortly before his final retirement to Monticello that his dream was realized. Construction began in October 1804, when he contracted James Oldham of Richmond to build five semicircular sashes and five pairs of square sashes "for the South Piazza as a Greenhouse," which were sent by boat to Monticello in April 1806.[25] The double-sashed windows functioned as doorways, opening onto the South Terrace and to the East and West Fronts of the house. Jefferson's simple yet elegant enclosure was balanced by an open gallery on the north end of Monticello.

While the completion date for the greenhouse is not known precisely, the event was anticipated by 1807 when Jefferson's granddaughter Anne Cary Randolph wrote from Edgehill, the Randolph family's plantation home, to Jefferson in Washington: "Ellen & myself have a fine parcel of little Orange trees for the green house against your return."[26] A year later, however—after the oranges had been ravaged by grazing sheep—Anne reported that "the green house is not done."[27] It was not until 1809 that Jefferson's South Piazza seemed complete, according to Jefferson's friend Margaret Bayard Smith. She was particularly fond of the plants Jefferson kept while in Washington, especially his pot of geraniums, which she entreated him to leave with her in 1808 upon his retirement to Monticello, writing, "I cannot tell you how inexpressibly precious it will be to my heart."[28] Jefferson obliged her with the geranium on March 6, 1809, apologizing for its neglected condition but assured of her nourishing hand, observing that "if plants have sensibility, as the analogy of their organisation with ours seems to indicate, it cannot but be proudly sensible of her fostering attentions."[29]

Rubens Peale with a Geranium by Rembrandt Peale, oil on canvas, 1801

Mrs. Smith gave a lengthy account of her visit to Monticello that summer in which she described Jefferson's "suite of apartments" consisting of the library, his cabinet, and "a green house divided from the other by glass compartments and doors; so that the view of the plants it contains, is unobstructed. He has not yet made his collection, having but just finished the room, which opens to one of the terraces." Mrs. Smith also described a storage closet in Jefferson's cabinet adjacent to the greenhouse, noting, "He opened a little closet which contains all his garden seeds. They are all in little phials, labeled and hung on little hooks. Seeds such as peas, beans, etc. were in tin cannisters, but everything labeled and in the neatest order."[30]

Jefferson was insistent that his greenhouse was not meant for an extensive collection of plants, writing on more than one occasion that the acacia "is the only plant besides the Orange that I would take the trouble of nursing in a green house. I rely on the garden & farm for a great portion of the enjoyment I promise myself in retirement." Yet we know that Jefferson used his South Piazza to start seeds of a variety of plants in wooden boxes, including those that were tender sorts. The "several sprigs of Geranium [stuck] in a pot" that he sent to his daughter Martha Jefferson Randolph in 1807, likely taken from the very plant given to Mrs. Smith, were surely intended for the greenhouse.[31] In November 1809 he tried again the delicious but temperamental acacias, along with an orange and a lime. That same year another noteworthy Garden Book reference regarded his planting of fourteen golden rain tree seeds (*Koelreuteria paniculata*) in boxes and pots.[32] The seeds of this small Asian tree, which bears lovely spikes of yellow blossoms in midsummer, were sent to him from France in June 1809 by his Parisian friend Madame de Tessé. The tree was introduced to Europe in 1753 but was not likely grown in America until Jefferson's successful planting. By year's end, he happily announced to Anne Cary Randolph Bankhead that "the plants in the green-house prosper."[33]

With the publication of *The American Gardener's Calendar* in 1806, Bernard McMahon became Jefferson's major source of seed, bulbs, and plants for his gardens. Jefferson studied McMahon's monthly instructions carefully and directed his family to follow them as well in their gardening endeavors at Monticello.

Cape Bulbs for the "Greenhouse Department"

AFTER THE Portuguese explorer Bartholomew Diaz (1450–1500) first rounded the Cape of Good Hope in 1488, unusual species from the Cape filtered into Europe by the 1500s. Some of the earliest species were grown by British herbalist John Gerard in his garden in London during the late sixteenth century. By the mid-seventeenth century, the Dutch had established a trading post on the Cape and plants began to reach Amsterdam. The eighteenth-century Swedish botanist Carl Linnaeus described this rich floristic region as "that paradise on earth, the Cape of Good Hope, which the Beneficent Creator has enriched with His choicest wonders."[34]

Exploration of this region accelerated during the 1770s, when a great wave of botanical discovery was issued by London's Royal Botanic Garden at Kew, shortly before Jefferson's tour of English gardens in 1786. Under the direction of Sir Joseph Banks (1740–1820), plant collectors sent from Kew imported beautiful and extraordinary specimens from South America, Mexico, and western North America, but the species from South Africa garnered particular interest. The most familiar plants from this region are our common garden and scented geraniums (*Pelargonium* sp.), but other species, such as heaths and a great multitude of bulbs, also intrigued garden enthusiasts. Scottish botanist Francis Masson (1741–1805), the first plant collector engaged by Banks in 1772, made his first voyage to the Cape of Good Hope aboard the *Resolution,* Captain James Cook's ship. Two Swedish plant collectors—Anders Sparrman and Carl Peter Thunberg—arrived at Cape Town at the same time. The three men discovered most of the Cape bulbs known today. Their introductions fostered a new fashion in British gardening and inspired plant devotees such as William Curtis (1746–1799) of London, who featured them in his highly influential *Botanical Magazine.*[35]

In America, South African species were still considered novelties from abroad. McMahon realized that Jefferson's greenhouse might provide an environment perfectly suited to the needs of this class of plants. Among the auriculas and polyanthus in McMahon's February 1812 shipment were "2 Roots Amaryllis Belladonna" from the Cape of Good Hope. These bulbs were most certainly intended for indoor culture. The *Amaryllis belladonna,* or Cape belladonna, was first introduced into England by way of Portugal in 1712 but was not likely available through American nurseries until after 1800. By the nineteenth century it was cultivated abundantly in Italy and exported to northern Europe. Linnaeus gave this lovely bulb the species name *belladonna,* or "beautiful lady," for the "exquisite blending of pink and white in that flower, as in the female complexion."[36] Because the foliage, following the rhythms of the southern hemisphere, grows throughout the winter months and dies to the ground by late summer when the leafless, bronzy green flower stalks emerge, the bulb is most known as naked-lady lily. Throughout the arid, mountainous regions of the southwestern Cape Province, these heavily scented blossoms burst suddenly from the heat-baked soil in just a few days during early spring, corresponding with early fall in North America. Thus, when McMahon sent a second parcel of three more "roots" of the "Belladonna Lily" in October, his directions noted that "if their strong succulent fibres or roots retain their *freshness* on receipt of them, do not have them cut off, but let them be planted with the bulbs in pots of good rich mellow earth; the flowers are beautiful and fragrant; their season of flowering is Septr. & Octr.," indicating that the fleshy roots were still actively growing and that they had likely just finished flowering.

McMahon's packages to Jefferson sent on October 24 contained other, even more unusual South African bulbs. "With this letter," he wrote, "I expect you will receive a small box containing, 6 Roots Watsonia Meriana . . . 6 [roots] Trittonia fenestrata [*Tritonia hyalina*] . . . 6 Morea flexuosa [*Hexaglottis longifolia*] All Cape of Good Hope bulbs and consequently, with you, belonging to the Green-House department."[37] The three somewhat obscure species are all members of the iris family. Of the three, the windowed- or open-flowered tritonia was the most recent introduction, having just arrived from the Cape in 1801. The flowers of this species are widely cup-shaped and a bright, fiery orange-red. What is most intriguing is the base of each petal, which is nearly translucent, like clouded glass.

In an earlier shipment that fall, McMahon also sent "3 Roots of Antholyza aethiopica [*Chasmanthe aethiopica*], a Green House bulb"—again, another South African iris species. This particularly stately plant forms a lush stand of sword-like leaves two to three feet tall. Its curved, hooded, scarlet and green flowers open like the mouth of an enraged animal, hence the derivation of its genus name from the Greek *chasme,* meaning "gaping." If Jefferson had any success with his South African bulbs, it would surely have been with this species, for it grows so easily and abundantly that it is today considered a weed in southern California.

McMahon's perseverance in enticing Jefferson to try his hand with plants intended for the "Green-House department" is admirable, considering Jefferson's repeated reluctance to provide a hospitable environment for them. In April 1811, a year before the Cape bulbs arrived, he wrote to McMahon, "You enquire whether I have a hot house, green-house, or to what extent I pay attention to these things. I have only a green house, and have used that only for a very few articles. My frequent and long absences at a distant possession render my efforts even for the few green-house plants I aim at, abortive. During my last absence in the winter, every plant I had in it perished."[38]

Jefferson's comments suggest that perhaps McMahon was encouraging Jefferson to try to provide some heat. In any case, by 1816 most references to plants for the "Green-House department" were in the distant past. Jefferson's South Piazza was serving more as a storage space and utilitarian room where he kept his large rectangular workbench and chest of tools that he had acquired in London. On November 16, Jefferson wrote to his daughter Martha from Poplar Forest, directing her to "tell Wormley [Hughes] also to send . . . about a bushel of Orchard grass seed out of the large box in the Green house."[39]

Stewardship of the tender plants at Monticello may ultimately have fallen to Jefferson's granddaughters, especially to Ellen Wayles Randolph (1796–1876) and Cornelia Jefferson Randolph (1799–1871), who inherited their "grandpapa's" devotion to gardening. Correspondence between the young women in later years indicated that plants were removed from the frigid greenhouse during winter months. Cornelia Randolph wrote to her sister Virginia on December 1, 1820, "I had all our plants moved into the dining room before I left home and yours along with them. I hope they may be able to bear this bitter cold weather." Again, on October 31, 1825, Cornelia would write, this time to her sister Ellen, "Mary and myself are established in mama's room with all her furniture and the sunny window in which I shall range my green house plants when the weather is cold enough to take them in."[40]

Writing to her mother from Poplar Forest in July 1819, Ellen Randolph specified a most unusual treasure: "I rely on Virginia's care of my pride of Barbadoes and multiflora rose if my mocking birds and other multiflora should arrive, I recommend them most particularly to the whole family."[41] Again, in September of that year, she wrote to Virginia Randolph, "Thank Aunt M for taking such good care of my pride of Barbadoes." In the appendix of *The American Gardener's Calendar* (1806), McMahon classified "pride of Barbadoes" as "Barbadoes Prickly Flower-fence . . . *Caesalpinia pulcherrima*" under his listing of "Hot-House Trees and Shrubs." This curious tropical American species, a relative of the brazilwood, was brought to Europe as early as 1691. A member of the bean family, this lanky shrub or small tree with formidable thorns resembles the acacia in foliage. Its highly ornamental blossoms, distinguished by long and gracefully curled red stamens, vary in color from scarlet red edged with yellow to rose-colored to pure yellow. William Curtis's *Botanical Magazine* described the plant in 1807 under its synonym *Poinciana pulcherrima,* noting, "Although common in the West Indies . . . it was probably imported into Barbadoes from the Cape de Verde Islands." The descriptive text also indicated that, even in England, the plant "cannot be preserved out of the stove."

By the end of his life, Jefferson's greenhouse appears to have functioned more as an enclosed porch. A few years after his death, Mary Jefferson Randolph wrote to Nicholas Trist that "the green house had been used so long as a common sitting room for the whole family that there were many of our things in it and in packing up some may have escaped our observation."[42] She also described the transformation of the greenhouse space in a letter to Ellen Randolph Coolidge: "[H]ow often I wish I could see your two sweet babies, added to the four that now run about the house or roll & tumble on the floor in the green house, which serves as a very pleasant little sitting room for us, during a part of the day (when the sun does not shine upon the windows) & is at all times a favourite play place for the children."[43]

Many years after Thomas Jefferson's death, Cornelia Randolph's gardening legacy would be further confirmed through the publication of a small book on indoor gardening, originally printed in France, which she translated and edited. *The Parlor Gardener: A Treatise on the House Culture of Ornamental Plants* (1861), complete with Victorian-style line drawings of parlor flower stands, étagères, and chandelier vases, includes instructions on propagating plants in portable greenhouses and creating gardens upon the balcony, terrace, window, and even mantelpiece—certainly well beyond the scope and breadth of her grandfather's interests. Cornelia studied a whole host of unusual as well as traditional floral subjects, becoming an ardent amateur florist in her own right.

6

JEFFERSON'S RETIREMENT FLOWER GARDENS

I have an extensive flower border . . .

DURING THE FINAL YEARS of his presidency, Jefferson was anxiously anticipating his retirement to Monticello and spending his remaining days with his family on his farms and in his gardens. His focus on gardening continued into the early years of his retirement, making 1806 through 1812 the most active and consequential period for the transformation of the Monticello landscape. Jefferson was planning not only an extensive ornamental flower garden but also the construction of a one-thousand-foot-long vegetable garden as well as the design, building, and landscaping of a retreat home at Poplar Forest, his nearly five-thousand-acre plantation located ninety miles away in Bedford County, Virginia. His plans for flower gardens at Monticello were detailed in numerous memoranda to his overseer of sixteen years, Edmund Bacon, and in letters to his family, especially his horticulturally minded granddaughters Anne Cary Randolph and Ellen Wayles Randolph.

Jefferson was corresponding, too, with his friend Bernard McMahon, the Philadelphia nurseryman who, in the early part of 1806, published *The American Gardener's Calendar.* McMahon sent a copy to Jefferson soon after publication, which Jefferson received with great appreciation. He responded to McMahon that even with his cursory read, he had no doubt that "it will be found an useful and to the friends of an art, too important to health & comfort & yet too much neglected in this country."[1] Jefferson realized the book's importance for its specific treatment of horticultural growing conditions in America. As Peter Hatch has observed, McMahon's *Calendar* was "the most comprehensive gardening book published in the

< Monticello flower garden by Pat Brodowski, oil on canvas

United States in the first half of the nineteenth century."[2] Prior to this time, Jefferson's library contained gardening books exclusively by European authors.

In July 1806 McMahon was already sending shipments of dormant tulip bulbs to Jefferson, writing:

> I take the liberty of requesting your acceptance of a few Tulip roots, the bloom of which I hope will give you satisfaction: they may remain in the state I send them till October, and be then planted as directed in page 528 of my book. . . . Prefixed to the names of the Tulips you will find the following marks, significant of the Florist's divisions of the family; Bz signifies the flower to belong to the Bizards, B. to the Bybloemens, I. to the Incomparable Verports, R. to Baguet Rigauts, r. to the Rose coloured or Cherry, & P. to the Primo Baguets.[3]

Jefferson received this remarkable collection of tulips on July 14 and responded that he planned to take the package with him when he returned to Monticello in a week and have them planted in the proper season. Tulips, which were mentioned more than any other flower in Jefferson's Garden Book, were an indisputable favorite. Jefferson was not unique in this, even in America. In the 1730s, Williamsburg's John Custis received "Double Tulips" and "early tulips" from his mentor Peter Collinson of London, and a portrait of Custis clearly shows him holding a well-worn book with the words "of the Tulip" legible on its spine and a streaked tulip blossom beside it.

"Tulipomania," a seventeenth-century European tulip "fever" where fortunes could be made or lost through the purchase of a single bulb, had long subsided from its peak in the 1630s. Yet tulips retained universal appeal and remained the intense focus of florists well into the nineteenth century. The tulips sent by the discriminating Bernard McMahon included such classics as Bizarre (mustard yellow flowers marked red or brownish black), Bybloemen (white ground marked with deep rich purple), and Rose (white feathered with red or rose markings). Also in the package were the Baguet Rigauts and Primo Baguets, which had rosy-purple or brownish-red markings on a white ground with pure white bases. The Baguets, a Flemish specialty, were among the most sought-after tulips of the late seventeenth and early eighteenth centuries. They were wide-cupped, round-petaled flowers, said to be capable of holding "a pint of wine" in their blossoms. While we can be impressed with Jefferson's florist tulips, their major limitation was that they were not really meant for the garden; rather, they were the aristocrats, meant to be cosseted and protected from harm.[4]

Double parrot tulip

In his response to McMahon, Jefferson admitted that he could not provide ideal conditions for this ambitious collection of tulips, as his situation at Monticello limited his wishes to only a few remarkable flowers "for beauty or fragrance." And yet in his next letter, written from Washington on January 6, 1807, Jefferson reported to McMahon that "the tulip roots you were so kind as to send me, I planted at Monticello last autumn." Jefferson's excitement at the prospect of a flower garden was palpable as he continued to request more plants and seeds for planting in early March. Jefferson trusted McMahon's judgment in determining the best manner of packing flower seeds and fibrous roots, "in moss or any thing else not too bulky." For safe transport, he recommended that McMahon delay the package until after February 25. His order for globe artichoke, Antwerp raspberry, and alpine strawberry also included "Lillies of a few of the best kinds" as well as tuberose, crown imperials, anemone, auricula, sweet William (*Dianthus*), ranunculus, hyacinths, "Wall flower," marigold, and saffron.[5]

Jefferson's spring visit to Monticello in 1807 was delayed until early April, but once home, he began implementing his gardening plans immediately. From April 11 to 13, he and enslaved gardener Wormley Hughes laid out oval and circular beds on the East and West Lawns around the house. Hughes, born at Monticello in March 1781, was the son of Betty Brown and the grandson of Elizabeth (Betty) Hemings, the Hemings family matriarch. He likely received training as a gardener from Robert Bailey, the Scottish-born gardener who worked at Monticello from 1794 through 1796. Jefferson's gardening directives often delegated skilled horticultural tasks to Hughes, including seed sowing in the nurseries, collecting and packaging seed and plants for Jefferson's gardening friends, planting exotic trees around the house, and planting bulbs in the flower borders that he had prepared.

By April 13, Jefferson's birthday, the beds had been planted with shrubs, trees, and flowers. In the circular beds at the four corners of the house, remarkably dense clumps of trees and shrubs were planted: thirteen paper mulberries, six horse chestnuts, a tacamahac poplar (*Populus balsamifera*), four purple beech trees (*Fagus sylvatica*), two moss or bristly locusts (*Robinia hispida*), two chokecherries, three European mountain ash (*Sorbus aucuparia*), two yellowroot (*Xanthorhiza simplicissima*), one redbud, one fraxinella (*Dictamnus albus*), and two guelder roses (*Viburnum opulus* 'Roseum'). A few days later, nine fragrant mock orange shrubs (*Philadelphus coronarius*) were added to the circular beds of shrubbery.

Most of the plants came from the Thomas Main nursery in Washington. The careful observations of Jefferson's close friend Margaret Bayard Smith provide an account of his pleasure in exchanges with local nurseries in the Washington area:

> There were two nursery-gardens he took peculiar delight in, partly on account of their romantic and picturesque location and the beautiful rides that led to them, but chiefly because he discovered in their proprietors, an

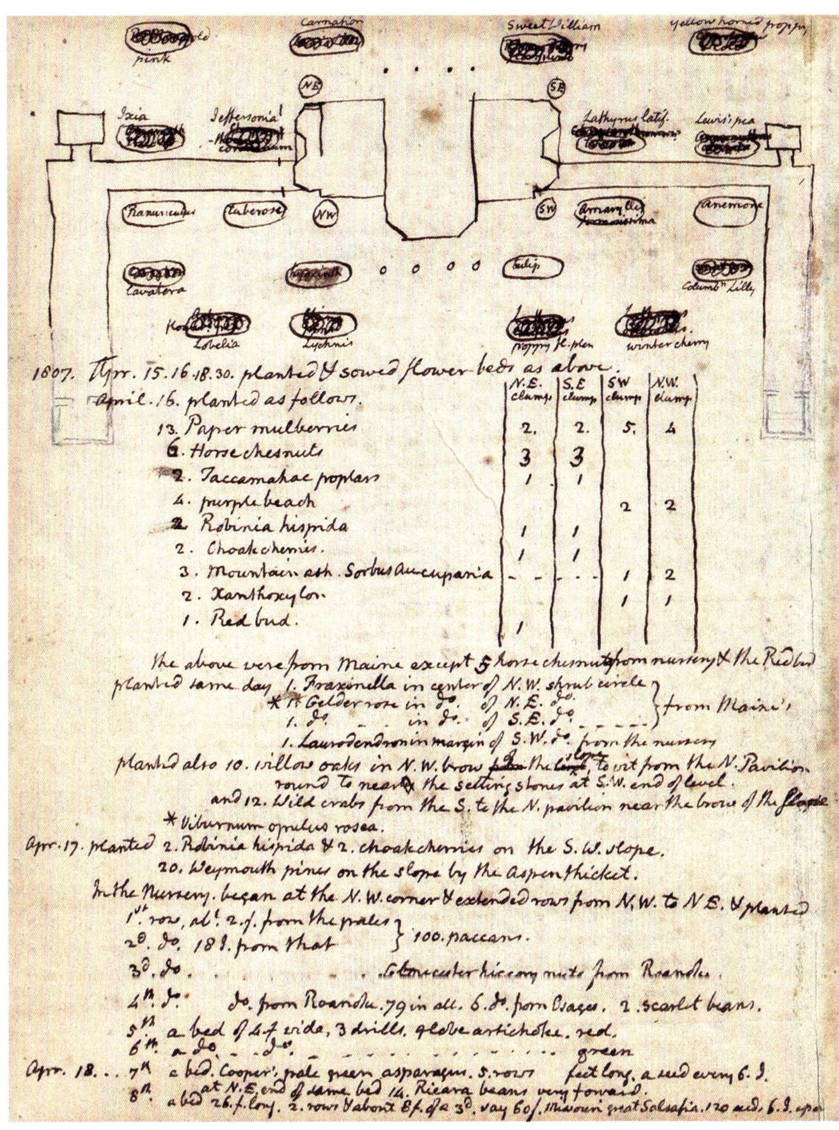

Draft of garden plan drawn by Thomas Jefferson, 1807

uncommon degree of scientific information, united with an enthusiastic love of their occupation. Mr. Mayne [Main], a shrewd, intelligent, warm hearted Scotch-man, rough as he was in his manners and appearance, could not be known, without being personally liked. . . . Rare fruits and flowers were his pride and delight: this similarity of tastes made Mr. Jefferson find peculiar

> pleasure, in furnishing him with foreign plants and seeds, and in visiting his plantations on the high banks of the Potomac.[6]

In Jefferson's directive to his overseer Edmund Bacon, he communicated precise planting locations, noting that Wormley Hughes would know especially where to plant the four purple beech (in clumps on the southwest and northwest angles of the house) and locusts (in the clumps on the northeast and southeast angles). While such dense plantings seem unreasonable by modern standards of landscape design, this intensive planting style of the naturalistic landscape movement was in vogue both in Europe and America. Jefferson made numerous observations of "clumps of trees" in the notes on his tour of English gardens in 1786. In America, tree and shrub clumps were part of William Hamilton's landscape at The Woodlands, and in his *American Gardener's Calendar,* Bernard McMahon discussed this style of planting in the chapter for January, under "The Pleasure or Flower-Garden."

On April 18, a wide selection of spring-flowering annuals, perennials, and bulbous roots, primarily from Bernard McMahon, were planted, including entire oval flower beds of dianthus (China pink, single carnation, and sweet William), yellow horned poppy, blackberry lily, twinleaf, everlasting pea, mallows, Columbian lily (from Lewis and Clark), scarlet cardinal flower, scarlet lychnis, double corn poppy, European winter cherry, ranunculus, double anemone, and Formosa amaryllis and a West Front oval bed with double pink, yellow, white, and blue hyacinths.

By the early summer, Jefferson had concluded that more space was needed for his ambitious flower garden. He wrote to his granddaughter Anne Cary Randolph from Washington,

> I find that the limited number of our flower beds will too much restrain the variety of flowers in which we might wish to indulge, & therefore I have resumed an idea, which I had formerly entertained, but had laid by, of a winding walk surrounding the lawn before the house, with a narrow border of flowers on each side. This would give us abundant room for a great variety. I inclose you a sketch of my idea, where the dotted lines on each side of the black line shew the border on each side of the walk. The hollows of the walk would give room for oval beds of flowering shrubs.[7]

Jefferson sketched his idea on the back of the letter, showing his plan for a walk bordered by flower beds along the perimeter of the leveled West Lawn of Monticello.

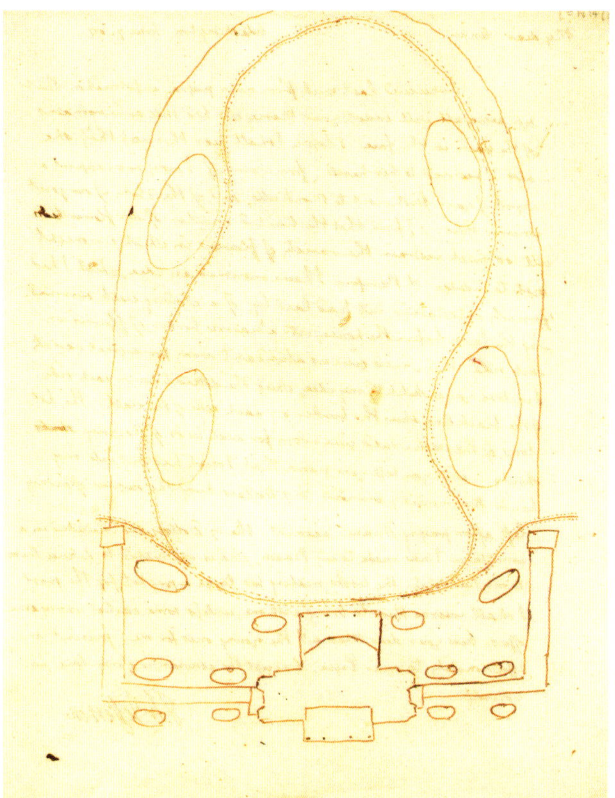

Plan of the winding walk with borders and beds, drawn by Thomas Jefferson on the back of a letter to Anne Cary Randolph, June 7, 1807 (Courtesy of the Massachusetts Historical Society)

This design diverged from Jefferson's previous idea, which is believed to date to the early 1790s. The contour of the walk was changed, and the number of oval-shaped beds in the hollows was reduced from five to four. These large oval-shaped areas were to be planted with flowering shrubs; however, no details of these planned shrubberies exist, and it is not known if they were ever installed.

Reports on the flower gardens during Jefferson's absences from Monticello often came from his correspondence with Anne Cary Randolph, offering a captivating view of their shared gardening endeavors. Writing from Washington, Jefferson addressed his letters to her at Edgehill, the Randolph family home near Monticello. Some letters reported not only successes but also failures, as in Anne's letter from

Edgehill on November 9, 1807: "The tuberoses & Amaryllises are taken up we shall have a plenty of them for the next year. The tulips & Hyacinths I had planted before I left Monticello they had increased so much as to fill the beds quite full. The Anemonies & Ranunculuses are also doing well. fourteen of Governor Lewes's Pea ripened which I have saved." Her report then shifted to a list of the many seeds "which you got from Mr. McMahon," all of which had failed.[8]

The following spring, Anne was anxious to learn of the progress of the flower gardens at Monticello. She wrote to Jefferson from Edgehill on March 18 that she heard about the gardens "once or twice a week" from Monticello's enslaved domestic butler, Burwell Colbert. Colbert's main duty was to run the Monticello household and direct the work of enslaved housemaids, waiters, and porters—and he was Jefferson's personal servant when he was in residence—but he generously responded to Anne's request for reports on the flower gardens. Anne's letter continued: "The last news was that they were all coming up very well particularly the tulips of which he [Colbert] counted at least forty flourishing ones." Anne regularly alluded to her close relationships and reliance upon Colbert and the enslaved gardener Wormley Hughes regarding the condition and care of the Monticello flower gardens. Jefferson likewise often revealed these interdependent relationships.

Jefferson's enthusiasm for the new flower garden and his confidence in Anne's abilities are evident in his letter of February 16, 1808, to "My dearest Anne," where he wrote, "I shall not attempt to get any more flower roots & seeds from Philadelphia this season, and must rely entirely on you to preserve those we have by having them planted in proper time. This you will see from McMahon's book, & mr Bacon will make Wormley [Hughes] prepare the beds whenever you let him know, so that they may be ready when you go over to set out the roots."[9] Two months later, on April 15, Anne reported an update to her grandfather: "I have been twice to Monticello . . . the hyacinths were in bloom, they are superb ones. The Tulips are all bud[d]ing." But then she noted that "neither the hyacinths nor Tulips grow as regularly this spring as they did the last." She added that Hughes had left some of the small bulbs in the ground when taking them up, resulting in a haphazard display of the flowers that were originally planted in rows. This occurrence of errant bulbs is common and happens annually when today's Monticello gardeners dig and replant the flower beds with new hyacinth and tulip bulbs every fall. But Anne's observation reveals a further challenge that the nineteenth-century gardener faced in maintaining rare and costly bulb varieties. If they were to retain their vigor, such bulbs had to be dug and stored during their summer dormancy.[10]

Jefferson arrived at Monticello from Washington on May 11, 1808, for a month-long spring vacation. During this visit he and Hughes laid out the winding walk and flower borders that he had sketched the previous year. He further modified the drawing to better fit the contour of the lawn. In July, Jefferson was writing to McMahon from Washington with assurances of his planned retirement the following spring, confirming, "I shall be at home early in March for my permanent residence, and shall very much devote myself to my garden. . . . I have the tulips you sent me in great perfection, also the hyacinths, tuberoses, amaryllis, and the artichokes."[11]

Jefferson's cherished gardening relationship with his eldest granddaughter, Anne, would change following her marriage to Charles Lewis Bankhead. Anne's sister, Ellen Wayles Randolph, would assume some of the garden oversight going forward. Shortly after her marriage, Anne wrote to her grandfather with assurances about the flowers at Monticello: "on coming from Edgehill I left all the flowers in Ellens care, however I shall be with you early enough in march to assist about the border, which the old French Gentlemans present if you mean to plant them there, with the wild & bulbous rooted ones we have already, will compleatly fill." Anne was referencing the "700 species of seeds" that Thoüin, director of the Jardin des Plantes and a friend of Jefferson's from his Paris days, had sent earlier that fall. The following year Jefferson would write to Anne, "What is to become of our flowers? I left them so entirely to yourself, that I never knew any thing about them, what they are, where they grow, what is to be done for them. You must really make out a book of instructions for Ellen, who has fewer cares in her head than I have. Every thing shall be furnished on my part at her call."[12] Ellen would prove to be an equally diligent reporter of the condition of the tender bulbs from the garden, writing to her grandfather in December that "there are at least a peck of Tuberose and 12 or 14 Amaryllys roots all packed in bran" dug from the flower beds for winter storage.[13]

Jefferson left Washington on March 11, 1809, after completing two terms in the presidency, for the abundant life promised by "those scenes of rural retirement after which my soul is panting."[14] Upon his arrival at Monticello, his attentions turned immediately to his flower and extensive vegetable garden. Spring and summer were busy seasons. He returned to his Garden Book with three and a half pages of lengthy, detailed entries of plantings in the gardens, nurseries, and orchards, including his first vegetable garden "Kalendar," which he continued to chart for fifteen years (through 1824). Seeds of the golden rain tree (*Koelreuteria paniculata*), a gift from Madame de Tessé, were planted in boxes and pots, as well as sweet acacia, a sour orange, and a lime in boxes in the greenhouse.[15] The circular and oval beds around the house were planted with chaste tree (*Vitex agnus-castus*) and star jasmines (*Jasminum officinale*); jujube trees (*Ziziphus jujuba*) were added to the shrubbery clumps in the four angles of Monticello.

For the next several years, McMahon continued sending plants, seed, and bulbs to Monticello. During this period the flower borders outlining the winding walk reached their perfection. In early 1812 McMahon sent roots of belladonna amaryllis and Atamasco lily, auriculas, polyanthus primroses, tulips, double hyacinths, and roots of the Turk's-cap lily. Additionally, he sent cuttings of a species of shrub that Jefferson had forwarded to McMahon from the Lewis and Clark Expedition several years earlier. McMahon named it *Symphoricarpos albus* and described it as a beautiful shrub "from the River Columbia, the flower is small but neat, the berries hang in large clusters are of a snow white colour and continue on the shrubs, retaining their beauty, all the winter; especially if kept in a Green House. The shrub is perfectly hardy; I have given it the trivial english name of Snowberry-bush."[16]

That following October Jefferson reported to McMahon that the plants sent in the spring had been "remarkably successful" and "one only of the cuttings of the

Snowberry

Snowberry failed. The rest are now very flourishing and shew some of the most beautiful berries I have ever seen." Jefferson's success with this western species, which he also sent to Madame de Tessé in Paris, was confirmed on several occasions.[17]

He had just received another large shipment from McMahon of new and unusual bulbs and seeds. The most intriguing bulbs included roots of rare crown imperial lilies, one with two tiers of flowers and one variegated with silver-striped foliage. Additionally, McMahon sent twelve roots of a hardy gladiolus (which he considered fit for the open ground); double hyacinths; parrot tulips variegated red, green, and yellow; several tender greenhouse bulbs; and a number of seeds of annuals and perennials. McMahon's sources for some of these species are a matter of speculation, especially considering the "sweet-scented Marvel of Peru," *Mirabilis longiflora.* Although a relative of the more familiar four o'clock (*M. jalapa*), this native perennial with tubular, pure white, highly fragrant flowers is indigenous to the southwestern regions of United States into Mexico, where it grows in brushy canyons and banks and is rare in the wild.

Originally the winding walk flower borders were continuous on either side of the path. But Jefferson's April 8, 1812, entry in his Garden Book suggested a new planting scheme: "Flower borders. Laid them off into compartmts of 10. f length each. In the N. [North] borders are 43. In the S. [South] borders are 44 ½ compartmts. the odd compartments are for bulbs requird. taking up, the even ones for seeds and permanent bulbs. denote the inner borders (i) and the outer (o)."[18] This new arrangement created an easy shorthand for organizing and locating the plantings and for keeping track of perennial bulbs, such as daffodils, and the more precious bulbs that required digging and storing each year, such as tulips and tuberoses. It also indicated that seedlings of perennials and hardy annuals alike were relegated to the "even" compartments. This simple method, requiring two letters and a number, is still used by Monticello gardeners. In Jefferson's day, the process of digging bulbs for proper storage was an annual exercise that was well understood; in 1812, Jefferson followed Bernard McMahon's instructions from *The American Gardener's Calendar* (1806) to take up and separate offsets and replant lily bulbs. An exchange between Jefferson and his daughter Martha in 1816 clearly reveals this essential process. Writing from Poplar Forest on November 10, Jefferson asked that she have Wormley Hughes bring "some of the hardy bulbous roots" divided from the Monticello collection: "would it be possible for you so to make up some of the hardy bulbous roots of flowers as to come safely on the mule? daffodils, jonquils, Narcissuses, flags & lillies of different kinds, refuse hyacinths E[t]c. with some of the small bulbs of the hanging onion." He then added the instructions, "I think if wrapped & sowed up tight in two balls, one to come in each end of a wallet with nothing else in it to bruise them, they would come safe." Ten days later Martha responded that it was already too late to send all that he listed because the roots were actively growing, but she sent instead "a number of offsets of tulips and hyacinths . . . the smaller ones are not blooming roots yet, but will be in a year or 2. the tulips & hyacinths are mixed but Cornelia knows them all."[19]

Jefferson's interest in bulbs extended to native species as well. He grew the spectacular American Turk's-cap or spotted Canada martagon (*Lilium superbum*), received from McMahon in 1812. Because Jefferson predated the great wave of Japanese introductions by about fifty years, nursery lists such as McMahon's offered a combination of only North American and European species. Thus, the various lilies he ordered included not only the European Turk's-cap (*L. martagon*) but also possibly any number of native species, such as the Canada martagon (*L. canadense*). The white lily (*L. candidum*) of Europe, which became known as the Madonna Lily later in the Victorian period, was at Monticello. More unusual were the Atamasco lily (*Zephyranthes atamasca*), a southeastern US species of rain lily like the *Zephyranthes candida,* and the "Columbia Lily." The latter is believed to be a western species of fritillaria (*Fritillaria pudica*) collected during the Lewis and Clark Expedition and planted at Monticello in 1807 as "Lilly. the yellow of the Columbia. it's root a food of the natives."[20] While this diminutive, bell-like yellow flower is prolific throughout the Northwest, it has proven impossible to grow in central Virginia. Jefferson and McMahon continued their correspondence for several years, but after 1812 the Garden Book is silent about the flowers and flower gardens.

"Belles of the Day"

IN AN 1811 letter to Anne Cary Randolph Bankhead, Jefferson wrote a provocative reflection: "The houses & trees stand where they did. The flowers come forth like the belles of the day, have their short reign of beauty and splendor, & retire like them to the more interesting office of reproducing their like. The hyacinths and tulips are off the stage, the Irises are giving place to the Belladonnas, as these will to the Tuberoses etc."[21] By using flowering bulbs as a fitting metaphor, Jefferson was instructing his granddaughter on the ephemeral nature of beauty, the normal transitions in life, and the inevitable passage of time. Jefferson often looked to the natural world for descriptive inspiration, and bulbs, through their unfolding transformations, compress the stages of a human lifetime into a single season.

Years later, fond memories of the heyday of flower gardening during Jefferson's early retirement were shared by his granddaughter Ellen Randolph Coolidge, who wrote the following lengthy and detailed account to Jefferson's biographer Henry Stephens Randall:

> I remember well when he first returned to Monticello, how immediately he began to prepare new beds for his flowers. He had these beds laid off on the lawn, under the windows, and many a time I have run after him when he went out to direct the work, accompanied by one of his gardeners, generally Wormley [Hughes], armed with spade and hoe, whilst he himself carried the measuring line.[22] I was too young to aid him, except in a small way, but my sister, Mrs. Bankhead [Anne Cary Randolph], then a young and beautiful woman . . . was his active and useful assistant. I remember the planting of the first hyacinths and tulips, and their subsequent growth. The roots arrived, labelled with a fancy name. There was Marcus Aurelius, and the King of the Gold Mine, the Roman Empress, and the Queen of the Amazons, Psyche, the God of Love, etc., etc., etc. Eagerly and with childish delight, I studied this brilliant nomenclature and wondered what strange and surprisingly beautiful creations I should see rising from the ground when spring returned, and these precious roots were committed to the earth under my grandfather's own eyes, with his beautiful grand-daughter Anne, standing by his side, and a crowd of happy young faces, of younger grandchildren, clustering round to see the progress, and inquire anxiously the name of each separate deposit. Then, when spring returned, how eagerly we watched the first appearance of the shoots above ground. Each root was marked with its own name written on a bit of stick by its side, and what joy it was for one of us to discover the tender green breaking through the mould, and run to grandpapa to announce, that we really believed Marcus Aurelius was coming up, or the Queen of the Amazons was above ground! With how much pleasure compounded of our pleasure and his own, on the new birth, he would immediately go out to verify the fact, and praise us for our diligent watchfulness. Then, when the flowers were in bloom, and we were in ecstasies over the rich purple and crimson, or pure white, or delicate lilac, or pale yellow of the blossoms, how he would sympathize in our admiration, or discuss with my mother and elder sister new groupings and combinations and contrasts. Oh, these were happy moments for us and for him! It was in the morning, immediately after our early breakfast, that he used to visit his flower-beds and his garden.[23]

Ellen Randolph's sentimental remembrance conjures an intimate, bucolic scene, where the family gathered to admire the display and discuss the intricacies of garden design and color coordination. We learn about the sophistication of tulip varieties available to Americans during this period. While the tulips in the Monticello borders were named for classical figures, William Faris (1728–1804), a silversmith, clockmaker, and gardener in Annapolis, Maryland, was cultivating, selecting, and breeding thousands of tulips and other bulbs in his modest city lot. In the spring of 1804, Faris counted 2,339 tulips in his garden, some named after statesmen such as President Washington and James Madison, which he invited his neighbors to view.[24] Faris marked his tulips with a coded stick, and similarly, each bulb at Monticello was carefully labeled with "a bit of stick by its side."

At the same time, Ellen Randolph's lengthy recollection also reveals much about the unacknowledged garden dynamics and family associations below the surface. Jefferson's close bond with the children of his daughter Martha stands in contrast with his role overseeing the manual labor of enslaved gardener Wormley Hughes. Still, their unspoken relationship also shows the basic understanding and trust Jefferson had in Hughes's knowledge and abilities as his principal gardener.

The domestic scene that Ellen Randolph Coolidge described dissolved relatively quickly when, after Jefferson's death in 1826, curiosity- and souvenir-seekers came in droves for mementos of the Sage of Monticello. In 1827 another of Jefferson's granddaughters, Virginia Randolph Trist, reported to her sister Ellen:

> It will grieve you both very much to hear of the depredations that have been made at Monticello by the numerous parties who go to see the place. Mama's choicest flower roots have been carried off, one of her yellow jessamines, fig bushes . . . , grape vines and every thing and any thing that they fancied. N [her husband Nicholas Trist] consulted with Mr. Garrett and put a notice in the papers requesting the visitors to desist from such trespasses, but Burwell [Colbert] says that they have been worse *since* than they were before. As it appears to be entirely useless to do any thing in that garden, Wormley [Hughes] is planting every thing down here [Tufton].[25]

In this, the conclusion of Jefferson's 1811 "belles of the day" letter to Anne Cary Randolph Bankhead seems all the more poignant as he himself accepts the inevitable: "As your Mama has done to you, my dear Anne, as you will do to the sisters of little John, and as I shall soon & chearfully do to you all in wishing you a long, long, goodnight."

Poplar Forest, Jefferson's Occasional Retreat

BEGINNING IN 1806, at the same time Jefferson was planning and executing his vision for flower gardens at Monticello, he simultaneously conceived of a house and landscape that was a radical departure from his Albemarle County home. Jefferson had inherited a 4,819-acre tract in Bedford County from his father-in-law, John Wayles, in 1773. Jefferson began making annual spring visits to this retreat beginning in the 1790s, when he would leave his little mountaintop in search of "the solitude of a hermit." Working from Jefferson's designs, a combination of free white and enslaved African American craftsmen and laborers began building Poplar Forest, a one-story octagonal brick house, in 1806. Construction was nearing completion in 1809, when Jefferson's presidency ended. In an 1811 letter to his good friend Benjamin Rush, he shared: "I write to you from a place, 90. miles from Monticello, near the New London of this state, which I visit three or four times a year, & stay from a fortnight to a month at a time. I have fixed myself comfortably, keep some books here, bring others occasionally, am in the solitude of a hermit, and quite at leisure to attend to my absent friends."[26]

Aerial photo of Poplar Forest with a view to the Blue Ridge Mountains, August 19, 2025

By the final decade of his life, Jefferson made at least three annual pilgrimages to his Bedford County villa, often with his granddaughters Ellen and Cornelia Randolph, to retreat from Monticello's busy scene at the height of spring, late summer, and early winter. Jefferson would describe his house as "the best dwelling in the state, except that of Monticello, perhaps preferable to that, as more proportioned to the faculties of a private citizen."[27]

While Jefferson's design for Poplar Forest's ornamental landscape, based on Roman and Palladian traditions, was a significant departure from Monticello's scheme, it evolved over a lifetime of study and firsthand experience of English, French, Italian, and German gardens and landscapes.[28] He interpreted and modified the fundamental design elements from Italian architect Andrea Palladio by substituting the two wings and pavilions that flanked the central house with landscape elements: two earthen mounds replacing the pavilions to the east and west of the house and a double row of paper mulberry trees on the west.[29] In Europe, Jefferson had observed mounds placed away from houses to serve as vantage points, but at Poplar Forest he placed the mounds close to the house. The mounds, representing the end pavilions, were originally circled with willow trees on top and ringed with aspens at the base.[30]

Jefferson's planting memoranda for Poplar Forest left specific details for his ornamental landscape. During 1812, a year of remarkably ambitious gardening activities at Monticello, Jefferson also recorded an impressive landscape for areas around Poplar Forest. Many shrubs and trees were brought from already established plantings at Monticello. In December, Jefferson directed that a variety of flowering shrubs be placed on the slopes of the sunken lawn, or bowling green, to the south of the house: "Plant on each bank, right & left, on the S. side of the house, a row of lilacs, Althaeas, Gelder roses, Roses, dianthus."[31]

Another detailed memorandum written on November 1, 1816, defined the contents he wished for the tree and shrub clumps and oval flower beds on the north lawn:

planted large roses of difft. kinds in the oval bed in the N. front.
Dwarf roses in the N.E. oval. Robinia hispida in the NW. [ditto].
Althaeas, Gelder roses, lilacs, Calycanthus, in both mounds.
Privet round both Necessaries.
White Jessamine along NW. of E. offices.
Azedaracs opp. 4 angles of the house. Aug. 17. 5 livg.[32]

Jefferson reimagined this new landscape for Poplar Forest using the same species of flowering trees, shrubs, and perennials he had known throughout his lifetime. These were the common plants that grew in the familiar landscapes at Shadwell, in the early shrubbery and grove concepts he described for Monticello's north slope, and in the spiraling shrub clumps and oval beds around the house itself: lilacs, sweet shrub, althaeas, white jasmine, viburnum, and roses. Poplar Forest gave him an opportunity to imagine anew what he had learned over a lifetime.

7

THE FLOWER GARDEN RESTORED

AS JEFFERSON GREW OLDER, his attention focused more on his vegetable garden and farms as well as "the hobby of my old age": the design and construction of the University of Virginia. The care of the flower gardens gradually fell to other members of the household. But the granddaughters—Anne Cary and Ellen Wayles—married and moved away from Monticello, while Cornelia lived nearby at Tufton. Thus, his daughter Martha Jefferson Randolph, who remained at Monticello, assumed most of the responsibility, with enslaved gardener Wormley Hughes doing most of the work.

Signs of the flower garden's demise were evident in paintings of Monticello during the final years of Jefferson's life. The 1825 painting by Jane Braddick Peticolas shows many mature trees near the West Front of the house, but the flowers and flower garden beds are either absent or ill-defined. Samuel Whitcomb, a visiting book peddler from Cohasset, Massachusetts, interviewed Jefferson in 1824 and (perhaps gratuitously) reported that the house was "old and going to decay" and that the gardens and lawns were "slovenly."[1]

On July 4, 1826, the fiftieth anniversary of the signing of the Declaration of Independence, Jefferson died at Monticello, surrounded by his family and with Burwell Colbert tending to his final needs. He was buried at 5:00 PM the following day in a wooden coffin, likely made by John Hemmings in the Monticello joinery. It fell to Wormley Hughes, who intimately understood the rhythm of the spade, to dig

< *Tulipa gesneriana* 'Absalon' (Rembrandt tulip)

View of the West Front of Monticello and Garden by Jane Braddick Peticolas, watercolor on paper, 1825

Jefferson's grave. It was raining, and Jefferson's coffin was carried to the burial site by family, friends, and enslaved workers.[2]

Four months after his death, Cornelia Randolph wrote to her sister, Ellen Wayles Randolph Coolidge, in Boston, Massachusetts, sending a package of plants, which she called "little remembrances" of Monticello.

> First on the top of the box is a collection of trees for Mrs. Storer. I did not know what you had carried & lost, but thought I would make a collection according to my own taste; I chose then my favorite snowberry [*Symphoricarpos albus*], so light & elegant in its form & foliage, and its berries so beautiful & pure, but most valued by me because it most flourishes when all other flowers have faded. The pyracantha [*Pyracantha coccinea*] which besides being very ornamental makes as you know a low hedge so thick that nothing can get

> through it. The yellow currant [*Ribes aureum*] which for its fruit is of no value but it bears a quantity of beautiful yellow very fragrant flowers. The Halesia [*Halesia carolina*] or snow drop tree which is so beautiful that I send it though I am afraid it will not bear the winter at fresh pond but it is worth trying. And the fringe tree [*Chionanthus virginicus*] which I know will not bear cold below zero but as old madame Coolidge, I observed, cultivated green house plants, I thought I might send her this little acknowledgement of her kind attentions to me last summer, and in truth this tree is as well worthy a place in any green house as most of the most esteemed exotics. Nothing can be more beautiful than one particular plant that we have growing in our meadow here, behind a rock over which it bends & dips its long pendant graceful branches covered with fringe like flowers into the branch below; you know I love flowers and must excuse my dwelling so long on the beauties of one of the prides of our meadows & woods.[3]

Cornelia's intention to share significant plants as mementos of their grandfather foreshadows what would become of the gardens at Monticello, detailed in Virginia Randolph Trist's letter to Ellen Randolph Coolidge describing souvenir-seekers ransacking the landscape. As noted above, the "choicest flower roots" had been among the plants carted off.[4]

Jefferson left the property to his daughter Martha Randolph, but his enormous debt at the time of his death left the family little choice but to hold a public auction. In mid-January 1827, Monticello's furnishings, kitchenware, farm equipment, and livestock were sold—and, most tragically, 130 enslaved men, women, and children who stood on the West Front portico, looking out upon what had become a diminished and degraded landscape.

The 1827 sale was not the last effort to settle Jefferson's estate and debts. Ultimately, by 1831, the house and 522 acres of surrounding property were sold to a Charlottesville apothecary, James Turner Barclay, for $7,000. Existing reports of Barclay's respect for Jefferson's landscape vary widely. Barclay's descendants maintained that he preserved trees planted by Jefferson as gardeners pruned shrubs, cultivated the flower gardens, and maintained the winding walks. Martha Randolph heard a different account, writing to her daughter Ellen Coolidge on October 27, 1833, that Barclay had "cut down the grove and ploughed up the yard to the very edge of the lawn and planted it in corn." Following his visit in August 1832, William Barry, the US postmaster general, offered a more nuanced opinion: "All is dilapidation and ruin, and I fear the present owner, Dr. Barclay, is not able, if he were inclined, to restore it to its former condition." The only congruent account from both sides, and substantiated by a report written by Barclay himself, was that the greenhouse had been converted into a space for raising silkworms.[5]

Barclay's failure at these enterprises forced him to put Monticello up for sale. Fortunately, Uriah Phillips Levy (1792–1862), a US naval officer, became the third owner of Monticello. In May 1836 Levy completed the purchase of 218 acres of overgrown fields surrounding the dilapidated, almost empty house for $2,700. He began purchasing land around Monticello, and by 1837 he had enlarged his property to 2,700 acres. Renovation of the house and grounds began under Levy's supervision, and in the spring of that year, he brought his mother, Rachel Phillips Levy, to live at Monticello. His duties as a US naval officer required extended absences, resulting in his hire of Charlottesville lawyer George Carr in 1838 to act as superintendent of his property. His mother continued in residence until her death on May 1, 1839, and was buried at Monticello.[6]

Following the outbreak of the American Civil War, Captain Levy was in Washington by November 1861 to take charge of the Navy's Court Martial Board. But he died of pneumonia on March 22, 1862, and did not live to see his country home confiscated by the Confederacy under its Alien Enemies Act and eventually auctioned. During the war, no significant fighting took place near Monticello, though many soldiers, both Confederate and Union, took the opportunity to visit the home of Thomas Jefferson and write their names on the walls of the dome room.[7] Sarah Strickler, a young diarist who visited Monticello during the summer of 1865, reported, "The place was once very pretty but it has gone to ruin now. . . . There are some roses in the yard that have turned wild, and those are the only flowers."[8]

After the Civil War, all properties confiscated by the Confederacy were returned to their previous owner. The Monticello property became complicated, however, as Uriah Levy—though childless—had forty-nine heirs with claims to his estate. This resulted in almost seventeen years of litigation that left Monticello at the mercy of the elements and an indifferent public. In 1870 a visitor described the house as "moss-covered, dilapidated, and criminally neglected."[9] It was not until 1879 that Uriah Levy's nephew, Jefferson Monroe Levy (1852–1924), was able to buy out the other heirs and take possession of the property. In 1889 Levy hired the highly competent and dedicated Thomas L. Rhodes. The two men effected a thorough rehabilitation and restoration of the house, purchasing Jefferson's furniture wherever they could find it and even adding three hundred acres to the property.

In the depression following World War I, Jefferson Levy found it necessary to put his property on the market. On April 13, 1923 (the 180th anniversary of Thomas Jefferson's birth), Monticello was purchased and formed into the nonprofit Thomas

Jefferson Memorial Foundation by an alliance of New York lawyers and businessmen associated with the Woodrow Wilson administration. Under the leadership of Stuart Gibboney, a New York lawyer of Virginia ancestry, the organization negotiated with Jefferson Levy for the purchase of the property at a cost of $500,000. Gibboney continued to serve as president of the Foundation for twenty years and supported the tradition of preservation established by the Levy family.

The Garden Club of Virginia's Restoration

HARVARD-EDUCATED ARCHITECTURAL historian Sidney Fiske Kimball (1888–1955) had a long and influential association with the Thomas Jefferson Memorial Foundation. From 1924 until his death, he served as chair of the Foundation's restoration committee and was elected to the board of directors in 1939. Prior to these appointments, he was chairman of the School of Architecture at the University of Virginia from 1919 to 1923. Notably, he is credited as the first scholar to identify Jefferson as a skilled architect through his folio titled *Thomas Jefferson, Architect* (1916). Serving as chair of the Monticello restoration committee, Kimball set a precedent for restoration, relying on documentary evidence, and he spearheaded the restoration of the house through the mid-1950s.

In the mid-1920s, Kimball began soliciting support from garden clubs to restore the gardens and landscape immediately surrounding Monticello. He initially appealed to the Garden Club of America and sought the services of Amy Cogswell of Connecticut, one of the first female landscape architects in the United States. Cogswell was known for designing colonial revival gardens, a style that was in vogue during the early twentieth century, and she was considered an expert in old-fashioned flowers. Cogswell had an initial idea for a revival-style flower garden around the house, which was not based on historical documentation. These plans were met with strong resistance, especially from members of the Albemarle Garden Club. (Ultimately, Cogswell willingly withdrew from the landscape project, writing to Kimball about her frustrations with the pace of the work and the unpleasant attitude toward her.)

The Albemarle Garden Club, which was both a founding member of the Garden Club of Virginia (GCV) and the Garden Club of America (GCA), offered the strongest response to Kimball's plan. Susanne Williams Massie (1861–1952) was president at the time and had been engaged with the process of garden restoration at Monticello since 1924.[10] Hazlehurst Bolton Perkins (1881–1981), another Albemarle Garden Club member, would ultimately lead the GCV's involvement in restoring the Monticello flower gardens. By 1926 Massie and Perkins had already invested in preserving the neglected trees around the house. With the aid of a $7,000 donation, the Foundation hired a New York–based tree surgeon, George Van Yahres, to treat and preserve the Jefferson-era trees. As a result, the Van Yahres Tree Company relocated and established its headquarters in Charlottesville, Virginia.[11]

By May 1938, Kimball had embraced the ideal of restoring the gardens as Jefferson intended, writing to Massie, "I think today we all feel more kindly to the ideal of putting things back the way they were, irrespective of whether we ourselves wanted to do them just that way or not."[12] Massie concurred. In November, Hazlehurst Perkins was placed in charge of the flower garden restoration with the intention, as she stated, to work in Jefferson's "original plans."[13]

Kimball recommended that Dr. Edwin Morris Betts (1892–1958), professor of biology at the University of Virginia, work with Perkins to provide academic expertise. Betts was a rigorous scholar and tireless documentary historian, and his meticulous scholarship was a critical factor in the success of the restoration. Betts would coauthor *Thomas Jefferson's Flower Garden at Monticello* (1941) with Perkins and he would go on to edit his landmark book, *Thomas Jefferson's Garden Book, 1766–1824* (1944), a comprehensive work that remains a significant reference today. Betts's research at the Pennsylvania Horticultural Society brought to light a critical document showing Jefferson's 1807 plan for the oval flower beds drawn in his own hand: "planted and sowed flower beds as above April 15, 16, 18, and 20." This dramatic discovery, along with the sketch Jefferson made on the back of a letter to his granddaughter Anne Cary Randolph for the winding walk beds, confirmed the plan the garden club would use for the layout of the flower garden.

The GCV's 1939–41 restoration of Monticello's flower gardens relied on the primary documentation found in Jefferson's letters, diary entries, sketches, and directives to his family and overseers. In addition, early twentieth-century analysis by landscape archaeologists provided more information. Encouraged by Fiske Kimball, Morley Jeffers Williams (1886–1977), a landscape architect and garden archaeologist, visited Monticello in 1932 with the initial goal to survey the property and to locate and record evidence of the roundabout roads that Jefferson designed for the mountain. During this survey he was able to locate the walking path and several planting beds on the West Lawn. Williams, who was an early pioneer in the field of garden archaeology, also spearheaded restoration projects at Mount Vernon and Stratford Hall in Virginia and Tryon Palace in New Bern, North Carolina. Williams surveyed Monticello's West Lawn by laying out a grid and taking elevation levels at five-foot intervals. He searched for evidence of the oval shrubbery beds in Jefferson's 1807 drawing along the West Lawn winding walk, but his findings were inconclusive. He surmised that it was probable that the ovals "were to have been planted with a variety of flowering shrubs and small flowering trees to outline the walk [but that] no sign of planting remained."[14] Williams also attempted, without success, to locate possible evidence of rectangular flower beds near the house based on a Jefferson drawing from 1772 that was revised in 1779.[15]

It is possible that the decision not to explore the existence of the oval shrubbery beds on the West Lawn was made quite early. Williams suggested that with the addition of the oval shrubberies, along with a background of trees, the lawn "would change in character from an open space permitting an unrestricted view to that of a hollow thing looked into, and the rival hill [Montalto] would become much less dominate."[16] Perkins likewise expressed the advantages of having a broad, open lawn on the West Front. Jefferson, however, may have held differing ideas. In a letter to William Hamilton of Philadelphia from 1806, he suggested the advantages of shifting perspectives and of opening and closing vistas: "Of prospect I have a rich profusion and offering itself at every point of the compas, mountains distant & near, smooth & shaggy, single & in ridges. . . . to prevent a satiety of this is the principal difficulty. it may be successively offered, & in separate different portions through vistas, or which will be better, between thickets so disposed as to serve for vistas, with the advantage of shifting the scenes as you advance on your way."[17]

According to Perkins, it was Williams who first observed evidence of sunken depressions of a walkway and raised contours of narrow border beds by shining his automobile headlights across the lawn. Perkins's diary went on to state that she later repeated this experiment. She reported, "The curves and width [of the walks] were even more distinctly visible. A gravel path was located by not only a definite mound and side depression, but in the early spring was outlined by clumps of bulbs (hyacinths and narcissus) coming up in the sod."[18] While the conclusions drawn from shining car headlights across the lawn at night may be questionable, Perkins added that the committee also physically dug cross sections into the sod to reveal the winding walk gravel. Williams, however, contradicted the GCV's findings of a gravel path, noting in his 1932 survey that he had found no evidence of gravel under the sod for the walks.[19]

In May 1938, Stuart Gibboney formally requested that the Garden Club of Virginia restore Monticello's gardens, "following the original designs and planting lists delineated by Jefferson."[20] Actual work on the club's restoration project began in March 1939. According to Perkins, their first step was "grubbing honeysuckle, [which] had encroached upon the west lawn and had taken possession of an entire side of the east lawn." Perkins further described lilacs in "thickets too closely to bloom . . . [and that] iris, hyacinths, and narcissus came up every spring in the lawn but produced only foliage." She further described that English ivy, "giving an atmosphere of charm and age, clung to the walls of the house but threatened, by its weight and dampness, to destroy both the brickwork and the cornices."[21]

The restoration committee hired Garland A. Wood from Richmond, Virginia, to prepare the scale drawing for the beds, borders, and walks on the West Front of Monticello. The final design, with drawings by architect Floyd E. Johnson, included numerous concessions to the impact anticipated by thousands of visitors to the gardens. Breaks in the continuous winding walk flower border were strategically added. The oval flower beds and winding walk were edged with brick. A local gardener, Lawrence Kelly, was hired by the Foundation and, under Perkins's direction, his work to prepare planting beds and gravel walkways began on November 15, 1939, and was completed in 1940. In addition to the West Lawn plantings, there was much discussion about the treatment of features such as the fishpond, setting stones,[22] the East Front beds and walks, and the post and chain planting also on the East Front. The Garden Club of America eventually granted funds for the re-creation of the East Front post and chain planting of intermittent weeping willows and flowering shrubs, including Persian lilacs, euonymus, Cape jasmine, and daphne. The addition of brick walkways and flower beds on the East Front was completed by 1941.[23]

The restoration of Monticello's flower gardens was heralded at the GCV's annual meetings. Before the meeting on October 23–24, 1940, in Hampton Roads, Virginia, then restoration committee chair Hetty Cary Harrison (1871–1943) reported: "Spring bloom in the Monticello garden was very encouraging for such new beds, especially the old-fashioned dwarf hyacinths, the unusual botanical tulips, *Scilla nutans* (The bluebells of English gardens), and many other spring bulbs. Even in mid-June the borders were lovely, and our Committee was pleased to have the following words of approval from Mr. Fiske Kimball, 'I was at Monticello with Stuart Gibboney on June 15. He said the place never looked so well, and of course this is chiefly the result of your garden work.'"[24]

Hazlehurst Perkins would also report to the garden club in the "Garden Gossip" column, April 1944, on "Monticello Today":

> What is to be seen today? Gravel roundabout walks which are constantly raked, hedges trimmed, flower beds full of bloom from April to frost, a fishpond which reflects colors and fascinates photographers, white gates, posts and chains, and brick steps easy to ascend. . . . Disappointments there are, of course; horticultural casualties, ants in the tulip bed, wallflowers that just won't live, ice plants that expire after looking "perfectly healthy," yuccas

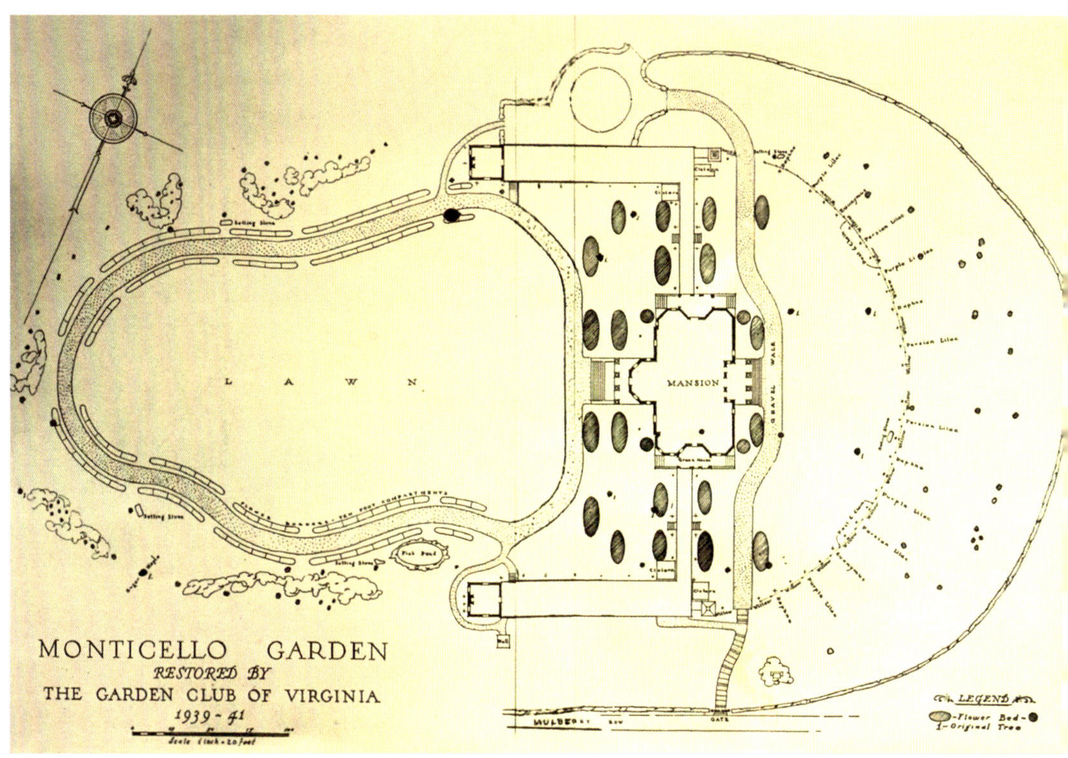

Drawing of the Monticello garden restored by the Garden Club of Virginia, 1939–41

that refuse to be transplanted. But why tell more of these stories familiar to every gardener? . . . On a setting stone at the side of the roundabout walk is a bronze plaque on which is inscribed, "The Gardens of Thomas Jefferson were restored and presented to Monticello by The Garden Club of Virginia, 1940." The work is done; may it mellow through the years and be enjoyed by posterity.[25]

EPILOGUE

JEFFERSON'S FLOWER GARDEN LEGACIES

THE GARDEN CLUB OF VIRGINIA succeeded in reestablishing much of Jefferson's original landscape design surrounding Monticello. The historical accuracy of the club's work, under the leadership of Albemarle Garden Club member Hazlehurst Perkins, relied upon Jefferson's extant drawings, notes, and letters along with instructions given to others. Jefferson-era trees were preserved, and many of the original flower gardens around the house were returned. Through the garden clubs' diligent work, the basic elements were reestablished, to be further enhanced and refined.

The flower gardens underwent continued assessment and revisions over the coming decades. Hazlehurst Perkins served as chair of Monticello's restoration committee until her resignation in 1949. The Foundation then engaged Colonial Williamsburg landscape architect Alden Hopkins (1905–1960) in 1954 to prepare detailed plans for planting revisions and landscape improvements. Hopkins disagreed with the assumption that Jefferson would want to maintain his original ideas and theorized that he would likely have discarded his plans for something showier after he saw their "poor value in the landscape." Monticello's grounds were given a more twentieth-century look when Hopkins added beds with mounded evergreens—including Japanese yews, Pfitzer junipers, rhododendrons—and Lombardy poplars flanking the West Front portico.

For the next two decades, the flower gardens were maintained with many of Hopkins's changes to the GCV's initial restoration. In 1974, following twenty years of service, Curtis Thacker retired from his position as Superintendent of Gardens and Buildings, whereupon the position was divided and John Randolph Crawford became Supervisor of Gardens until 1977. During this period the GCV engaged University of Connecticut professor and landscape architect Rudy J. Favretti, a role in which he served until 1998. Favretti's academic and professional experience in historic landscape preservation launched a new era of horticultural accuracy in garden restorations. His books, cowritten with his wife, Joy Putman Favretti, became seminal references and essential guides for determining historically accurate plant choices for period gardens.[1] Following Favretti's retirement, William D. Rieley

< *Vigna caracalla* (Caracalla bean)

served as GCV landscape architect from 1998 to 2021, continuing Monticello's restoration priorities based on scholarship and archaeological research. It was upon Favretti's recommendation that Monticello hired Peter J. Hatch as its first professional horticulturist in December 1977. Hatch joined Monticello as a senior staff member and was responsible for all aspects of Monticello's landscape restoration mission, including restoring the massive, thousand-foot-long vegetable garden and the grove at Monticello.

As part of the renewed focus on scholarship, it became imperative to research appropriate historic plants and reassess the existing planting program. The collection of flowers was reviewed and scrutinized, and decisions were made to replace many modern hybrids with the species or the early cultivated forms of ornamental flowers. Determining the appropriate period flowers became paramount. A decision was also made to supplement and expand the Jefferson-documented list with flowers available through contemporaneous sources known to Jefferson, such as Bernard McMahon's Philadelphia seed house and nursery. McMahon's 1802–3 broadside seed list, considered one of America's first seed catalogues, included over 720 species and varieties of seeds, from native and ornamental flowers to vegetables and herbs. This landmark index, along with the hundreds of flowers included in the extensive appendix of *The American Gardener's Calendar* (1806), enhanced the plantings selected for the flower gardens. Additionally, species associated with the plants documented by the Lewis and Clark Expedition were added as a means of telling the story of the botanical collections made by the Corps of Discovery.

The annual show-stopping display of thousands of tulips in bloom every spring has become a popular departure from an otherwise strict adherence to authenticity. Tulips in Jefferson's day were extremely difficult to obtain and rare in gardens, but the present-day parade of colorful blossoms preserves a tradition established by the GCV. Nonetheless, historic tulips have been added to the selection each year, replacing more modern varieties with authentic seventeenth- and eighteenth-century ones, including the oldest tulip still in cultivation: Duc van Tol 'Red and Yellow', dating to 1592.

Poplar Forest, Jefferson's "Occasional Retreat"

IN HIS seminal essay "Thomas Jefferson's Poplar Forest: The Mathematics of an Ideal Villa," landscape historian C. Allan Brown articulated Jefferson's idealized vision of "a place of harmonious order expressed in architecture and landscape through pure geometry."[2] The ongoing restoration of the ornamental landscape at Poplar Forest, which began in 1989, has been based on archaeological confirmation of features documented by Jefferson. Archaeologists excavated the remains of planting beds for shrubs and an area of densely planted trees on the north side of the house and determined the exact location of the west allée of original paper mulberries, which have been replanted to provide the shade that Jefferson envisioned. Jefferson also had designed ornamental clumps of trees and shrubs intended to frame views of the house. Two clumps on the north have been replanted with a spiraling configuration of trees and shrubs, including redbud, dogwood, tulip poplar, sweet shrub, and Kentucky coffee trees.

Poplar Forest's archaeologists, with direction from consulting landscape historians and architects, confirmed the location of clearly defined flower beds on the north front of the house. Further analysis revealed that the dimensions and shape of the oval beds were originally laid out with the thirty-three-foot, two-pole metal chain that Jefferson used in his surveying.[3] Oval beds of roses and moss or prickly locusts (*Robinia hispida*) have been planted on the north front of the house. The selection of roses was based on the varieties that were already growing at Monticello and could easily have been divided and transplanted to Poplar Forest. Research has determined that the ancient European alba roses (*Rosa alba plena* and *R. alba semiplena*) and the European musk rose (*R. moschata plena*) are likely candidates for the large white roses. The dwarf roses could include *R. centifolia* 'Pompon de Bourgogne' and the *R. gallica* varieties (apothecary's rose, Rosa Mundi, and 'Tuscany').

Seed-Saving Program

COLLECTING THE seed directly from Monticello's flower gardens was a program already in place by the late 1970s. This effort has expanded dramatically over the ensuing decades. Additionally, the search for species and early garden varieties of flowers connected Monticello with gardens and gardeners around the world, from Hatfield House in Britain, where seed of the species snapdragon (*Antirrhinum majus*) was obtained, to a remote rural garden in south Texas, where the elusive scarlet mallow (*Pentapetes phoenicea*) was spotted by an eagle-eyed horticultural historian. Seed preservation has become part of the overall garden interpretation. Visitors to Monticello are often surprised to learn that seeds are collected on site in much the same way they were two hundred years ago. The seed pods and capsules of most annual, biennial, and some perennial flowers are allowed to mature in the gardens throughout the growing season. Seed collecting, cleaning, and packaging is done by hand and is an important and often labor-intensive winter occupation for Monticello's gardening staff. This basic, centuries-old process, tactile and organic, is the very essence of the gardener's work.

Thomas Jefferson Center for Historic Plants

BOTANISTS, ACADEMIC extension agents, landscape architects, historic site professionals, and amateur gardeners have contributed to Monticello's quest for appropriate period plants. The formation of the Thomas Jefferson Center for Historic Plants (CHP), which was launched in 1986 under Peter Hatch's leadership, facilitates these connections among a community of like-minded historic plant preservationists. The Center, which supports the Thomas Jefferson Foundation's twin mission of preservation and education, is headquartered at Tufton Farm, one of Jefferson's original land holdings adjacent to Monticello and still owned by the Foundation. The program focuses on Thomas Jefferson's horticultural interests but includes plants documented through the nineteenth century. The work of the CHP has been inspired by British nurserymen David Stuart and James Sutherland, who authored the 1987 landmark book *Plants from the Past.* They state, "Hundreds of plant genera which play important roles in the garden scene have long and fascinating histories. The gorgeous antiques of the garden are every bit as important as are more obvious antiques like furnishings, paintings, even houses, and they are just as much part of our past. Yet many are in danger of extinction."[4] The Center embraced this compelling argument, agreeing that there is an urgent need not only to conserve endangered native species but also to preserve horticultural varieties of previous eras, which are just as much in danger of extinction.

By collecting, preserving, propagating, and making available historic plant varieties, the Center strives to educate the public about the importance of garden history in America. Through the Center's efforts, significant collections of roses, iris, and peonies have been added to the CHP nursery and headquarters at Monticello's Tufton Farm. The restored flower gardens at Monticello and Poplar Forest have benefited from the plant collections preserved by CHP. Both sites now display rare and, in some cases, endangered roses rescued from historic sites and cemeteries, including the nearly extinct European musk rose (*Rosa moschata plena*), which was brought back to cultivation in the late twentieth century.

"Flowers All Over the Place": The Legacy of Flower Gardening at Monticello

SOME OF the most compelling legacies of the flower gardens come from the descendants of the enslaved people who cared for them. The African American History Department's Getting Word project has helped transform and expand Monticello's interpretive experience since its inception in 1993. Oral histories of descendants of Wormley Hughes, Monticello's principal enslaved gardener, are particularly revealing of the family's gardening legacy.[5] In 1996, four generations of the Hughes family of Fauquier County, Virginia, came to Monticello soon after learning of their descent from the Reverend Robert Hughes of Union Run Baptist Church. Robert Hughes (1824–1895), son of Wormley Hughes, was born at Monticello. Along with his mother and several of his siblings, he lived in slavery until the end of the Civil War at Edgehill, the plantation of Thomas Jefferson's grandson, Thomas Jefferson Randolph. After the war, Hughes, who was a blacksmith, acquired over a hundred acres of Albemarle County land. He was the founding minister of Union Branch Baptist Church near Charlottesville, Virginia, where he served for three decades. In their interviews, Karen Hughes White and Angela Hughes Davidson shared memories of their ancestors that revealed an intrinsic reverence for gardening and the sense of pride that a beautiful yard instilled in the family. When Karen White visited Monticello and looked out at the flower beds, she recognized the same flowers that her Aunt Ethel grew in her gardens and on her porch in Asheville, Virginia. White went on to reflect, "You go down to Aunt Ethel's and there [were] flowers all over the place."[6]

Strolling along the winding flower garden walk today can evoke strong memories and reflections of what may have been there two hundred years ago. Today the garden continues to have a comforting effect, as much as it did for Jefferson soon after his retirement to Monticello in 1809, when he wrote to Étienne Lemaire, his former butler at the President's House, "I am constantly in my garden or farms, as exclusively employed out of doors as I was within doors when at Washington, and I find myself infinitely happier in my new mode of life."[7]

Monticello flower garden by Pat Brodowski, oil on canvas

APPENDIX A

FLOWERS JEFFERSON DOCUMENTED AND FLOWERS GROWN AT MONTICELLO

The following descriptive list of flowers includes the herbaceous annuals, perennials, and significant flowering shrubs mentioned in the Garden Book, Weather Memorandum Book, letters, and memoranda of various sorts. Additionally, this list includes period flowers documented by contemporary sources, such as Bernard McMahon's *The American Gardener's Calendar* (Philadelphia, 1806), and others documented in the "Southern Plant Lists" compiled by the Southern Garden History Society with the Colonial Williamsburg Foundation (southerngardenhistory.org). The plants are arranged alphabetically according to their botanical genus, and entries includes the following: family name; common names, with the exact names used by Jefferson in quotation marks; the year when Jefferson mentioned them; a brief discussion of the flower; the hardiness zones in which it grows; and a chronological list of other sources documenting it.

SYMBOLS

◊	Plant documented by Thomas Jefferson
◊+	Plant listed in *Notes on the State of Virginia* and native in the Monticello woodlands
+	Native species common in the Monticello woodlands

< *Dictamnus albus* (fraxinella)

CONTEMPORARY SOURCES

BGB Bartram's Garden Broadside Catalogue, Philadelphia, 1783. See Joel T. Fry, "Bartram's Garden Catalogue of North American Plants, 1783," *Journal of Garden History* 16, no. 1 (1996).

BM Bernard McMahon, *The American Gardener's Calendar* (Philadelphia, 1806).

BMB Bernard McMahon Broadside Catalogue, Philadelphia. The catalogue was published across multiple years beginning in 1802. List compiled by Larry Griffith and submitted by Barbara Sarudy.

GF George French Seeds, Fredericksburg, VA, 1799–1800. French's seed list appeared in the *Virginia Herald* (Fredericksburg) in January 1799. Submitted by Peter Hatch.

HM Henry Middleton Charleston, SC, 1800. Plant list compiled by Dawson Hodges, Middleton Place Foundation, and submitted by Carolyn Harrington.

JC/PC John Custis and Peter Collinson, Williamsburg, VA, 1734–46. The Custis and Collinson correspondence between 1734 and 1746 is compiled in *Brothers of the Spade* by E. G. Swem (American Antiquarian Society, 1949). Submitted by Peter Hatch.

JS Jean Skipwith, Prestwould plantation, Clarksville, VA, 1793. Jean Skipwith (1748–1826), wife of Sir Peyton Skipwith, documented her garden at Prestwould plantation in south central Virginia's Mecklenburg County. Her extensive garden library included Philip Miller's *The Gardeners Dictionary,* 8th ed. (London, 1768). Her "Garden Notes of 1793," published by the Garden Club of Virginia in *Garden Gossip* 10, nos. 2, 4, and 6 (1935), was submitted and annotated by Peggy Cornett.

JT John Townley, Lexington, MA, 1760. Townley advertised seed in the *Boston Evening-Post in* 1760.

L&C Plants documented by the Lewis and Clark Expedition between 1803 and 1806.

MC Minton Collins, Richmond, VA, 1792–93. Collins offered seed and bulbs just imported from London through his Richmond store; see the *Virginia Gazette and Richmond Daily Advertiser* from November 1792.

MGB Moravian Gardens at Bethabara, North Carolina, 1753–72. See Flora Ann L. Bynum, "Old World Gardens in the New World: The Gardens of the Moravian Settlement of Bethabara in North Carolina, 1753–72," *Journal of Garden History* 16, no. 2 (1996): 70–86.

O&L William Owens & G. L. Leckie, "Garden & Flower Seeds," Lynchburg, VA, 1826. Owens and Leckie offered seed received from New York in *The Virginian* (Lynchburg).

PC See JC/PC above.

PC&Co Peter Crouwells, Philadelphia, and *Virginia Journal and Alexandria Advertiser,* 1786. Peter Crouwells and Co., Gardeners and Florists, in Philadelphia advertised "rare bulbous flowers, roots and seed" in the *Virginia Journal and Alexandria Advertiser* in 1786.

S&M Sinclair & Moore Catalogue, Baltimore, 1825. Submitted by Barbara Sarudy.

WB William Booth, Baltimore, 1810. Booth had a "Catalogue of Kitchen Garden Seeds and Plants."

WBII William Byrd II, Westover, Charles City County, VA, 1736. William Byrd II (1674–1744) was a wealthy Virginia planter at Westover, his inherited plantation on the James River in Charles City County. *William Byrd's Natural History of Virginia* (Dietz Press, 1940) was translated by Richard Croom Beatty and William J. Mulloy from a German edition printed in 1737.

WF William Faris, Annapolis, MD, 1790. Faris kept a plant list of his middle-class garden from 1792 to 1804. Submitted by Barbara Sarudy.

ABELMOSCHUS MANIHOT (L.) MEDIK.

MALLOW FAMILY

Syn. Hibiscus manihot L.
Sunset Hibiscus, Palmate-leaved Hibiscus

This showy plant is native to the tropical regions of Asia and is in the same genus as okra (*Abelmoschus esculentus*). It was introduced into Europe from East India, under the name *Hibiscus manihot,* by 1712. The common name "Ketmia" was often used in the eighteenth and nineteenth centuries for hibiscus- or mallow-like flowers. Jefferson documented numerous mallows and hibiscus in correspondence and in *Notes on the State of Virginia,* but this species is inconclusive. Virginia's Jean Skipwith, who gardened at her home, Prestwould, from 1785 until 1805, grew both an "Indian Ketmia" and an "Esculent Syrian Mallow," which could be the sunset hibiscus. The edible leaves are high in protein and can be eaten raw or cooked.

HARDINESS ZONES 8 TO 10

1793: JS, "Indian Ketmia," "Esculent Syrian Mallow"

ACANTHUS SPINOSUS L. AND ACANTHUS MOLLIS L.

ACANTHUS FAMILY

Spiny Bear's Breeches, Bear's Breeches

This handsome perennial, native to Italy through western Turkey, was first documented in British herbals by 1629, although it was grown much earlier by the Romans and Greeks. The distinctive, jagged foliage inspired the stylized architectural motif on the capitals of Corinthian columns in fifth-century Greek temples, echoed in the Corinthian capitals on Monticello's West Front. *Acanthus spinosus* and its cousin *A. mollis* were commonly cultivated in American gardens by the mid-nineteenth century. The British garden writer William Robinson revived interest in the acanthus by extolling its virtues in his classic book, *The Wild Garden* (1870). New Jersey nurseryman Peter Henderson admired both species as "stately" and remarkably beautiful ornamentals in his *Handbook of Plants and General Horticulture* (1890). The plant's large, dramatic flowers are attractive to bees, and the plant is deer resistant.

HARDINESS ZONES 5 TO 9

ACTAEA RACEMOSA L.

BUTTERCUP FAMILY

Formerly Cimicifuga racemosa
◊ "Black Snake-root," Black Cohosh
TJ 1781 (Notes)

Black cohosh, or snakeroot, is a North American herbaceous perennial that has been cultivated in American gardens since the late eighteenth century. Thomas Lamboll sent three kinds of snakeroot from his botanical garden in Charleston, South Carolina, to the Philadelphia nurseryman and plant explorer William Bartram during the late 1700s, and one is believed to be this species.

Thomas Jefferson included "Black snake-root" in a list of native medicinal plants in *Notes on the State of Virginia*. Although it is not known whether this species was cultivated in the gardens at Monticello, it is abundant in the Monticello woodlands, where it produces tall spires of snow-white flowers that tower above the rich, broad mounds of astilbe-like dark green foliage in early summer. Black cohosh is a long-lived perennial and is grown today in Monticello's East Front oval flower beds.

HARDINESS ZONES 3 TO 8

AGAVE AMICA (MEDIK.) THIEDE & GOVAERTS

ASPARAGUS FAMILY

Syn. Polianthes tuberosa
◊ "Double Tuberose," Tuberose
TJ 1786, 1807

This tender perennial bulb is native to Mexico. It bears highly scented single and double white flowers in summer; the double tuberoses are the most fragrant. The Quaker Peter Collinson, a London woolen merchant, was a financial supporter and patron of North American plant exploration. In 1736 he sent Williamsburg's John Custis roots of tuberose, but Custis replied that they were already common in Virginia and that he need not send any more. Jean Skipwith also recorded growing single and double tuberoses at Prestwould. While in Paris in 1786, Thomas Jefferson first noted "Tuberose." In a February 25, 1807, letter responding to Jefferson's January 6 request posted from Washington, Bernard McMahon mentioned that he would delay sending double tuberose roots because they "are extremely impatient of frost" and thus "it would be hazardous to send them at present." Jefferson included an entire West Front oval bed of tuberose in his 1807 plan for the oval and round flower beds at Monticello, and twenty double tuberoses were planted that spring. They flowered on August 12, and after the roots were dug, Jefferson's granddaughter Anne Cary Randolph reported on November 9 that "we shall have a plenty of them for the next year."

HARDINESS ZONES 9 TO 10

1792, 1793: MC, "Do. Tube roses"
1793: JS, "3 tuberose"
1799: GF, "Tuberose"
1802, 1806: BMB and BM, "Double Tuberose"
1810: WB, "Tuberose, double and single"

ALCEA ROSEA L.

MALLOW FAMILY

Formerly Althaea rosea

◊ "Holly hock," Hollyhock

TJ 1767, 1782

Thomas Jefferson observed this centuries-old biennial flowering on June 10, 1767, and recorded it in his Garden Book. Later, in 1782, he made a chart titled "Calendar of the bloom of flowers" for that year, showing that the hollyhocks flowered at Monticello from mid-June to mid-July. Hollyhocks were considered old-fashioned garden flowers. Philip Miller, whose *The Gardeners Dictionary* Jefferson owned, was already referring to both the single and double forms of hollyhocks as "old-fashioned flowers." A century and a half later, in her book *Old-Time Gardens Newly Set Forth* (1901), Alice Morse Earle proclaimed, "I think we may safely affirm that the Hollyhock is the most popular, and most widely known, of all old-fashioned flowers."[1] During the late nineteenth and early twentieth centuries, the "Grandmother's Garden" became a style reflective of a nostalgia for a simpler, preindustrial time when the garden resembled impressionistic paintings celebrating domestic life. Landscape artists of this period often indulged in adding hollyhocks as floral accents to their pastoral landscapes and romantically illustrated flower borders, a process called "hollyhocking." In a sense, no Grandmother's Garden could be depicted without an exuberant, towering plant such as the hollyhock, whether it grew there or not. Hollyhocks were once naturalized in the Monticello vegetable garden.

HARDINESS ZONES 2 TO 10

1735: PC to JC, *Alcea rosea,* "Hollihocks"
1760: JT, "Holly-hock"
1790: WF, "Hollyhocks"
1793: JS, *Alcea rosea* varieties, "Variety of Hollyhocks"
1802, 1806: BMB and BM, *Alcea chinensis,* "China Hollyhock" and *Alcea rosea,* "Double Hollyhock"
1810: WB, "Alcia . . . Hollyhocks, in varieties . . . Chinese painted lady ditto"
1826: O&L, "Hollyhock, Double black hollyhock, Double mixt hollyhock"

ALLIUM MOLY L.

AMARYLLIS FAMILY

Golden Moly, Lily Leek, Golden Garlic

Golden moly is native to southern Europe and was first described by John Gerard in the 1633 edition of his *Herball or Generall Historie of Plants.* While this species is one of the most common grown today, Gerard grew nine different "mollies," and John Parkinson grew fourteen. Williamsburg's John Custis first received bulbs of "white moley" from his British patron, Peter Collinson, in 1737. Bernard McMahon listed "Yellow Garlick or Molly" in his *Calendar* (1806).

HARDINESS ZONES 3 TO 9

1806: BM, "Yellow Garlick or Molly"

AMARANTHUS CAUDATUS L.

AMARANTH FAMILY

◊ "Prince's feather," "Amarenths," Love-lies-bleeding

TJ 1767, 1806

Thomas Jefferson recorded "Amarenths" and "Prince's feather" on several occasions, including at

Shadwell and Monticello. He was likely referencing members of the amaranth family, which are tender, heat-loving, summer-flowering annuals native to Mexico and tropical regions across Asia and South America and long cultivated in early American gardens. On April 2, 1767, Jefferson noted in his Garden Book that seeds were sowed of a variety of flowers, including "Cockscomb, a flower like the Prince's feather." Though Edwin M. Betts, editor of *Thomas Jefferson's Garden Book,* identified Jefferson's prince's feather as *Amaranthus hybridus hypochondriacus,* it could more likely be what is commonly known as love-lies-bleeding (*A. caudatus*). The name "prince's feather" was used in America as early as 1709, when John Lawson described "Prince's feather very large and beautiful" in his *A New Voyage to Carolina.* Love-lies-bleeding gets its unusual common name from its tiny, blood-red petal-less flowers that bloom in narrow, drooping, tassel-like, terminal and axillary panicles throughout the growing season. The panicles, twelve to twenty-four inches in length, typically hang straight down. The first commercial mention of this flower occurred in the 1760 edition of John Townley's advertisement in the *Boston Evening-Post,* in which he offered seed for "love lies bleeding" and "princess feathers."

1802, 1806: BMB and BM, "Love-lies bleeding"

AMARANTHUS TRICOLOR L.

AMARANTH FAMILY

◊ "Three-coloured Amaranth," Joseph's Coat

TJ 1786

In his *New Voyage to Carolina* (1709), John Lawson documented Joseph's coat (*Amaranthus tricolor*). Jefferson's "three-coloured Amaranth," which he included in a shipment of seeds to his brother-in-law Francis Eppes from Paris in 1786, was most certainly the flower described by Lawson. Joseph's coat is one of the most dramatic flowers in the summer display at Monticello. The large, voluptuous plants produce multicolored foliage of green, bronze, or purple to brilliant maroon or crimson, which often suffuses with yellow and rose-pink.

1736: WBII, "Tricolor"
1742–43: JC/PC, "Amaranthus Tricolor"
1790: WF, "Amaranthus tricolor"
1799: GF, "Amaranthus"
1802, 1806: BMB and BM, *A. bicolor,* "Bicolor Amaranthus"

AMARYLLIS BELLADONNA L.

AMARYLLIS FAMILY

◊ Belladonna Lily, Cape Belladonna, Jersey Lily, Naked-lady Lily, March Lily

TJ 1812

The *Amaryllis belladonna,* or Cape belladonna, is a tender, fall-flowering perennial bulb native to the Cape Province of South Africa. It was first introduced into Britain by way of Portugal in 1712 but was not likely available through American nurseries until after 1800. By the nineteenth century, it was cultivated abundantly in Italy and exported to northern Europe. Linnaeus gave it the species name *belladonna,* or "beautiful lady," for the "exquisite blending of pink and white in that flower, as in the female complexion."[2] Following the rhythms of the southern hemisphere, the foliage grows throughout the winter months and dies to the ground by late summer, when the leafless, bronzy green flower stalks emerge, giving the bulb its common name of naked-lady-lily. In the southwestern Cape Province, these heavily scented blossoms burst suddenly in just a few days during early spring. A package of flowering roots and bulbs sent to Jefferson from Philadelphia nurseryman Bernard McMahon on February 28, 1812, included "2 Roots Amaryllis Belladonna." When McMahon, aware of the bulb's dormancy cycle, sent a second parcel of three more "roots" of the "Belladonna Lily" in October, his directions noted that "if their strong succulent fibres or roots retain their *freshness* on receipt of them, do not have them cut off, but let them be planted with the bulbs in pots of good rich mellow earth; the flowers are beautiful and fragrant; their season of flowering is Septr. & Octr.," indicating that the fleshy roots were still actively growing and that they had likely just finished flowering. Belladonna lily is one of two members of the Amaryllis species. Other bulbs commonly called "naked ladies" are members of the genus *Lychoris.*

HARDINESS ZONES 7 TO 10

1792: MC, "Bella-donna lilies"
1800: HM, "Belladonna Lily"

ANEMONE CORONARIA L.

BUTTERCUP FAMILY

Syn. Anemone hortensis L.
◊ "Double Anemone," Poppy Anemone
TJ 1807

This southern European and central Asian native was known in England by 1596, and many named varieties were listed by the mid-1600s. Jefferson ordered tubers of the "double Anemone" from Bernard McMahon in 1807. In his book McMahon not only provided "A Description of the Properties of a fine Double Anemone" but also said the double varieties "being generally extremely beautiful, are particularly deserving of attention."[3]

HARDINESS ZONES 7 TO 10

1806: BM, "*Anemone hortensis* . . . Garden Anemone (many varieties)"

ANEMONE PULSATILLA L.

BUTTERCUP FAMILY

Syn. Pulsatilla vulgaris Mill.
◊ Pasque Flower, Meadow Anemone
TJ 1771, 1811

This European wildflower was sent to Monticello by André Thoüin of the Jardin des Plantes in Paris. It was planted in an oval flower bed near the house in 1811. Jefferson also considered the pasque flower suitable for naturalizing in 1771 when he listed the "hardy perennial flowers" for the "Open Ground on the West." On April 8, 1811, he planted "Anemone pulsatilla. belle plante vivace" in a southwest oval flower bed near the west portico of Monticello. Jefferson likely received seed from Bernard McMahon, who listed *Anemone pulsatilla* as early as 1802. This spring-flowering perennial bears striking, deep royal purple to pale purple (or, rarely, white) flowers followed by silvery plumed seed heads in early summer.

HARDINESS ZONES 3 TO 8

1802, 1806: BMB and BM, "pasque-flower, Anemone pulsatilla"

ANTIRRHINUM MAJUS L.

PLANTAIN FAMILY

◊ "Snap-dragon," "Snapdragon," Calves' Snout, Lion's Mouth

TJ 1767, 1771

This hardy, southern European summer-blooming perennial is commonly grown as an annual. The species bears deep wine-red flowers on upright stems. On May 28, 1767, Jefferson observed "Snap-dragon" blooming at Shadwell. Four years later, he listed it among the hardy flowers to be naturalized in a "shrubbery" at Monticello. This species has been cultivated in American gardens since the mid-eighteenth century, but Jefferson's is the earliest American reference. In *The Gardeners Dictionary* (1768), Philip Miller wrote that "these plants may be placed amongst stones, or they will grow in the joints of old walls, where they may be placed so as to render some abject part of a garden very agreeable."[4] Bernard McMahon's 1802 broadside listed "Red and White Snapdragon," and he included "Common Snapdragon" in his 1806 *Calendar* as a biennial flower. By the mid-1800s snapdragon cultivators had developed many varieties of colors and forms. In 1890, however, Peter Henderson noted in *Henderson's Handbook of Plants and General Horticulture* that "this plant, in its wild state, is very commonly found growing on the tops of old walls."[5] It became a favorite for Victorian bedding schemes. The snapdragon grown in the restored Monticello gardens today was obtained in 1985 through a friendship between Monticello and the gardeners at Hatfield House, a sixteenth-century country estate outside London. The name "Calves' Snout" comes from the shape of the seedpods, which the herbalist John Parkinson compared to "a Calves head, the snout being cut off."[6] The genus name, *Antirrhinum,* is Latin for "rhinoceros's nose."

HARDINESS ZONES 7 TO 10

1790: WF, "Snapdragon"
1802: BMB, "Red and White Snapdragon"
1806: BM, "Common Snapdragon"
1826: O&L, "Scarlet Snapdragon"

AQUILEGIA CANADENSIS L.

BUTTERCUP FAMILY

◊ Wild Columbine, Eastern Red Columbine

TJ 1791

Thomas Mann Randolph Jr., Jefferson's horticulturally astute son-in-law, observed this hardy, spring-flowering North American perennial blooming at Monticello on April 30, 1791, and the species can still be found in the Monticello woodlands. John

Tradescant, a seventeenth-century English plant explorer, introduced this graceful and highly ornamental species into British and European gardens by the 1640s. Bernard McMahon's broadside listed seed of this wildflower as "Feathered Columbine." This was a popular common name, referring to the way the delicate flowers and foliage sway with the slightest breeze, reminiscent of ostrich feathers. The flowers of the Eastern red columbine attract butterflies and hummingbirds, and the seeds provide food for some birds, including finches and indigo buntings. Deer are not typically attracted to this plant.

HARDINESS ZONES 3 TO 8

1792: JS, "Canada columbine"
1800: HM, "American columbine"
1802, 1806: BMB and BM, "Feathered Columbine," "*Aquilegia canadenses* columbine"

AQUILEGIA VULGARIS L.

◊ "COLUMBINES," EUROPEAN COLUMBINE, COMMON COLUMBINE

TJ ca. 1806–9

Both single- and double-flowered forms of the perennial European columbines have a long history in cultivation and were grown in American gardens before 1700. Thomas Jefferson noted "columbines" in a list of flowers for the garden dating from around 1806–9; they were likely intended for the winding walk border beds as part of his retirement flower garden. The genus name derives from the Latin word for eagle, referring to the flower's five spurs, which purportedly resemble an eagle's talon. The common name comes from the Latin word *columba,* meaning "dove-like."

HARDINESS ZONES 6 TO 8

1790: WF, Columbine
1793: JS, "Columbines"
1826: O&L, "Red, purple & white Columbines mixed"

ARGEMONE MEXICANA L.

POPPY FAMILY

Syn. Argemone leicocarpa
◊ "Prickly Poppy," Mexican Prickly Poppy

TJ 1767

Prickly poppy is a tender, summer-flowering annual native to the West Indies, Central America, and Florida and has naturalized worldwide. Discovered by Spanish New World explorers in the early sixteenth century, the prickly poppy was first described by British herbalist John Gerard in 1592. On June 18, 1767, Thomas Jefferson recorded "Argemone put out one flower" in his garden at Shadwell. On July 18 he noted another prickly poppy flower and observed that it was "the 4th this year," a testament to his keen appreciation for the natural world around him. Bernard McMahon sold prickly poppy as "Mexican Argemone" in 1802 and 1804. This tender species produces pale yellow flowers and attractive, deeply lobed, green and white variegated leaves tipped with prickly spines. When broken, the plant exudes bright yellow fluid.

English gardener Philip Miller understood this annual flower's habit of reseeding, writing in *Figures of the Most Beautiful, Useful, and Uncommon Plants* (1760), "For if a few Plants are suffered to scatter their Seeds, they will sufficiently stock the Ground."[7] Plants are tolerant of drought and poor soil and resist most pests.

1802, 1804, 1806: BMB and BM, "*Argemone mexicana* Prickley Argemone"

ARISTOLOCHIA SERPENTARIA L.

BIRTHWORT FAMILY

Syn. Endodeca serpentaria (L.) Raf.

◊+ "Virginia Snake-root," Virginia Snakeroot

TJ 1781 (Notes)

Virginia snakeroot is a perennial North American vine. Its species and common names come from its use by Native Americans and pioneers to cure rattlesnake bites. It was also used to treat fevers, toothaches, coughs, and disorders of the stomach and lung. The genus name is from the Greek for "best" (*aristos*) "delivery" (*lochia*), echoing the plant's ancient use in delivering children. It bears purplish-brown, pipe-shaped flowers held above narrow, heart-shaped leaves on zigzag stems. It is a larval host to the pipevine swallowtail and polydamas swallowtail butterflies.

HARDINESS ZONES 7 TO 10

1810: WB, "Birthwort"

ASARUM CANADENSE L.

BIRTHWORT FAMILY

+ Wild Ginger, Canada Wild Ginger

This hardy, herbaceous, perennial North American wildflower, called wild ginger on account of the ginger-like fragrance and flavor of the roots, was listed by John Clayton (1694–1773) of Williamsburg in the early eighteenth century. The species was introduced to British gardens by 1713 and was reported by Peter Collinson in London. Wild ginger thrives on the wooded slopes of Monticello Mountain, where its thick rhizomes and heart-shaped leaves form dense carpets. It produces a solitary, dark red–brown flower at ground level. Because the flowers resemble decaying flesh, they are attractive to ants, which pollinate them. Native Americans used the plant as a medicinal herb to treat numerous ailments.

During the Corps of Discovery expedition, Meriwether Lewis reported that a specimen of the *Asarum canadense* "was taken the 1st of June at the mouth of the Osage River; it is known in this country by the name of the wild ginger, it resembles that plant somewhat in both tast and effect; it is a strong stomatic stimelent, and frequently used in sperits with bitter herbs—it is common throughout the rich lands in the Western country."[8] He shipped the specimen back east from Fort Mandan in April 1805. The shipment was received by John Vaughan at the American Philosophical Society in November 1805 and forwarded to Benjamin Smith Barton. The specimen, along with about thirty others, disappeared before Frederick Pursh could examine it.

HARDINESS ZONES 4 TO 8

1739: John Clayton, *Flora Virginica,* Williamsburg, VA
1805: L&C

ASCLEPIAS TUBEROSA L.

MILKWEED FAMILY

◊+ "Pleurisy Root," Butterfly Weed

TJ 1781 (Notes)

This striking North American herbaceous perennial is commonly seen blooming in meadows and along roadsides throughout the eastern United States. Thomas Jefferson included "Pleurisy Root" in a list of native medicinal plants in *Notes on the State of Virginia*. The name refers to the historic use of this plant in treating lung ailments. *Asclepias tuberosa* was recommended by Robert Buist in his influential *The American Flower Garden Directory* (1839); he called it one of our finest wildflowers and suitable for dry places.[9] *Asclepias* flowers are an important nectar source for many butterflies, and the monarch butterfly caterpillar feeds on its leaves. This plant is not attractive to deer.

HARDINESS ZONES 3 TO 9

1734: Peter Collinson received from John Bartram "Root of the Swallow-wort or Apocinon w/ narrow leaves and orange coloured fls."
1783: BGB, "Asclepias decumbens" Pleurisy Root
1793: JS, "Apocynum"
1810: WB, "Swallow wort in varieties"

BAPTISIA AUSTRALIS R. BR.

BEAN FAMILY

Syn. Podalyria australis; Sophora caerulea
Blue False Indigo

Blue false indigo, a North American herbaceous perennial, was introduced to Britain by 1724; it was grown in early American gardens as a source of blue dye to substitute for the costly true imported indigo. This species was noted by Williamsburg naturalist John Clayton in the early eighteenth century and listed in the catalogue of Philadelphia nurserymen John and William Bartram in 1783. Once established, this long-lived perennial is drought tolerant, and its attractive blossoms and foliage make it a fine subject for the flower border or wild garden. The showy, inflated black seedpods are used in both fresh and dried flower arrangements.

HARDINESS ZONES 3 TO 9

1783: BGB, "Sophora caerulea"
1806: BM, "*Podalyria australis,* Blue Podalyria, or Sophora," "P. alba, White Podalyria," "Podalyria tinctoria, Yellow Podalyria or Bastard Indigo"
1810: WB, "Sophora tinctora"

BELAMCANDA CHINENSIS (L.) DC.

◊ See *Iris domestica* (L.) Goldblatt & Mabb

BELLIS PERENNIS L.

ASTER FAMILY

◊ English Daisy, "Daisy"

TJ 1771

This hardy, spring-flowering European wildflower, also native to northern Africa and western Asia, was well established as a garden plant in Britain by the time of English herbalist John Parkinson, who described and illustrated several forms in *Paradisi in Sole Paradisus Terrestris* (1629). The variety of common names also attests to its early origins: bone flower, herb Margaret, measure of love, lawn daisy, and March daisy. Brought to America by the early colonists, English daisies were listed by Jefferson in 1771 for planting in the "Open Ground on the West" with ornamental shrubs and other hardy perennials, including everlasting pea, pasque flower, "flower de luce" (fleur-de-lis iris), and gilliflower. Single and double flowers are common in a range of colors from pink to pure white. The genus name *Bellis* is Latin for "pretty."

HARDINESS ZONES 4 TO 8

1802, 1806: BMB and BM, "*Bellis perennis hortensis,* Double Daisy"
1810: WB, "Double Daisy's, in variety; Quilled daisy; Hen and chicken"

BIDENS ARISTOSA (MICHX.) BRITT.

ASTER FAMILY

Syn. Coreopsis aristosa Michx.
+ Tickseed Sunflower, Bearded Beggarticks

This showy, self-seeding, North American annual bears abundant bright yellow, daisy-like flowers on slender stalks from late summer into early autumn. Tickseed sunflower is so named for the appearance of its dark brown, flattened seeds. The robust, bushy plants boast delicate, deeply dissected foliage on green or reddish multibranched stems. The flowers are attractive to butterflies, bees, and other pollinators.

1783: BGB, includes several species of *Bidens* and *Coreopsis*
1806: BM, lists include several species of *Coreopsis*

BROWALLIA AMERICANA L.

NIGHTSHADE FAMILY

Amethyst Flower, Bush Violet

Browallia, also called amethyst flower or bush violet, is a tender tropical perennial grown as an annual and self-sows easily in the garden. Named after Johan Browallius (1707–1755), a Swedish botanist, physician, and bishop, this South American species was introduced into cultivation in 1735 and was recommended by Bernard McMahon in his *Calendar* (1806).

HARDINESS ZONES 9 TO 11

1800: HM, "Bush Violet"
1802, 1806: BMB and BM, "*Browallia scoparia*"

CAESALPINIA PULCHERRIMA (L.) SW.

PEA FAMILY

Syn. Poinciana pulcherrima
◊ "Barbadoes Prickly Flower-Fence," "Pride of Barbadoes," Peacock Flower, Red Bird of Paradise

This tropical ornamental, which is the national flower of the island of Barbados, has a beautiful inflorescence in yellow, red, and orange. Jefferson's granddaughters, especially Ellen Wayles Randolph and Cornelia Jefferson Randolph, inherited their grandfather's devotion to gardening. Writing to her mother from Poplar Forest in July 1819, Ellen

Randolph mentioned "my pride of Barbadoes," and a few months later she wrote to Virginia Randolph, "Thank Aunt M for taking such good care of my pride of Barbadoes." In the appendix of *The American Gardener's Calendar* (1806), Bernard McMahon classified "pride of Barbadoes" as "Barbadoes Prickly Flower-fence . . . *Caesalpinia pulcherrima.*" A member of the bean family, this lanky shrub or small tree with formidable thorns resembles the acacia. Its highly ornamental blossoms, distinguished by long and gracefully curled red stamens, vary in color from scarlet red edged with yellow to rose-colored to pure yellow. In 1807, William Curtis's *Botanical Magazine* described and illustrated the plant under its synonym *Poinciana pulcherrima* and noted that although it was common in the West Indies, it was probably "imported into Barbadoes from the Cape de Verd Islands."[10]

HARDINESS ZONES 9 TO 11

1802: BMB, "*Poinciana pulcherrima*"
1806: BM, "*Caesalpinia pulcherrima* Barbadoes Prickly Flower-fence" (under "Hot-House Trees and Shrubs, &c")

CALENDULA OFFICINALIS L.

ASTER FAMILY
◊ "Marygold," Pot Marigold, Calendula
TJ 1767

When "Marygold" seed was planted at Shadwell in 1767, Jefferson was referring to the pot marigold, or calendula, an Old World tender annual grown for centuries as both a useful and an ornamental plant. It is the marigold of English literature and is still known by that name in Britain. The petals were commonly used to flavor stews and soups, though they were not to everyone's taste. The English essayist Charles Lamb, for instance, abhorred "detestable marigolds floating in the pot."[11] Dutch grocers kept the dried petals by the barrelful, while apothecaries used the whole plant to make a soothing skin ointment. This "marigold" was being grown by gardeners in Virginia by the 1600s.

1806: BM, "Marigold, Pot . . . *Calendula officinalis*" (under "Aromatic, Pot, and Sweet Herbs")
1825: S&M, "Pot Marigold"
1826: O&L, "Pot Marigold"

CALLISTEPHUS CHINENSIS (L.) NEES

ASTER FAMILY
Formerly Aster chinensis
China Aster

China aster seeds were first sent to Paris from China in 1728 by a Jesuit priest. This showy, tender annual flower was cultivated in America as early as 1731 by Williamsburg's John Custis from seed sent by Peter Collinson, and it grew in popularity in European gardens through the eighteenth century. By 1802, 1804, and 1806 Bernard McMahon was selling eleven varieties of *Aster chinensis* in a range of "sorts," including double and quilled forms as well as a "Double Red Bonnet China Aster" and a "Double Red Striped." The genus name comes from the Greek for "beautiful" (*kalli-*) "crown" (*stephos*).

1731: PC to JC, "China Aster"
1760: JT, "Queen margrets"
1790: WF, "Asters"
1799, 1800: GF, "China Asters"
1800: HM, "China Asters, 4 Sorts"
1802, 1804, 1806: BMB and BM, "Double Blue . . . Double Purple . . . Double Purple Striped . . . Double Red Bonnet . . . Double

Red China . . . Double Red Striped . . . Double White . . . Quilled China Aster"
1825: S&M, "China Aster, assorted"
1826: O&L, "Red-striped China Aster"

CAMASSIA QUAMASH (PURSH) GREENE

ASPARAGUS FAMILY

◊ Camas, Quamash

The camas—or quamash, as it was known to the Nez Perce—is native to the western United States and British Columbia. It was first collected on June 11, 1806, by Meriwether Lewis on the Camas Plains of Idaho's Lolo Trail as the Corps of Discovery traveled across the American continent. In the wild, the bulbs bloom in such profusion that from a distance they appear to form lakes. In his journals, Lewis described this illusion upon seeing them on the Weippe Prairie, writing that the color of the multitude of light-blue flowers from a short distance resembled a "lake of fine clear water." The German botanist Frederick Pursh noted that the root, which was an essential food for the Native Americans, was "an agreeable food to Governor Lewis's party" but caused indigestion among members of the expedition.[12] An illustration of this attractive lily, first published in William Curtis's *Botanical Magazine* in 1813 as *Scilla esculenta,* was made from specimens that the plant explorer Thomas Nuttall collected, shipped to England in 1812, and made available through John Fraser's Nursery in Sloane Square, London.

HARDINESS ZONES 4 TO 11

1806: L&C, "quamash"

CAMPANULA AMERICANA L.

BELLFLOWER FAMILY

◊ "Campanula Americana of Millar," American Bellflower, Tall Bellflower

TJ 1786

This eastern North American annual or biennial plant bears tall, upright, three- to five-foot flower stems in elongated clusters of light blue to violet flowers, which are flattened rather than bell-shaped. The genus, by some authorities, has been reassigned to *Campanulastrum americana.* On January 27, 1786, while in Paris, Jefferson wrote to John Bartram Jr. with a long list of plants and seeds, which he requested to be sent "from America for a friend here whom I wish much to oblige." His friend was Madame de Tessé, and his request included "Campanula perfoliata and Campanula Americana of Millar."

HARDINESS ZONES 4 TO 8

CAMPANULA MEDIUM L.

BELLFLOWER FAMILY

◊ "Bellflower," Canterbury Bells

TJ 1812

On April 8, 1812, Jefferson recorded "Bellflower along with White Poppy and African Marigold seeds" planted on both the north and south side of the winding walk flower border. Philadelphia nurseryman Bernard McMahon offered seed for blue and white Canterbury bells in his 1802 and 1804 broadside catalogues and listed the plant in *The American Gardener's Calendar* (1806). This species is native to the Pyrenees and southern Europe, where it has been in cultivation since at least the sixteenth century. Canterbury bells were among the first imported flowers grown in colonial American gardens, and the earliest American citation was in 1760 from the J. Townley Seed Company in Boston.

HARDINESS ZONES 3 TO 9

1760: JT, "canterbury bells"
1799, 1800: GF
1802, 1804, 1806: BMB and BM, "Campanula Medium Canterbury Bells"
1826: O&L

CAMPANULA PERFOLIATA L.

BELLFLOWER FAMILY
Syn. Triodanis perfoliata (L.) Nieuwi.
◊ Clasping Bellflower, Clasping Venus' Looking-Glass
TJ 1786

In a letter written to John Bartram Jr. from Paris on January 27, 1786, Jefferson requested a long list of plants and seeds, including seed of "Campanula perfoliata and Campanula Americana of Millar." On August 12, 1786, Jefferson wrote to his fellow Virginian and kinsman Richard Cary, requesting both species of campanula. This North and South American annual species with wheel- or bell-shaped violet blue flowers grows to eighteen inches high and flowers through the summer.

HARDINESS ZONES 3 TO 10

1806: BM, *Campanula speculum* [syn.], Venus's Looking-glass (hardy annual)

CAMPSIS RADICANS SEEM

BIGNONIA FAMILY
Syn. Bignonia radicans L.
◊ "Trumpet Flower," Trumpet Vine, Trumpet Creeper
TJ 1771

In 1771, at the age of twenty-eight, Jefferson made elaborate plans for the grounds of his Little Mountain, in which he specified plant lists for the "Open Ground on the West. A shrubbery," containing "Climbing shrubby plants—Trumpet flower—Jasmine—Honeysuckle." (Jefferson could have been referring to a related species, *Bignonia capreolata.*) This vigorous, woody, multi-stemmed, deciduous clinging vine is native to the southeastern United States but has naturalized in many northern states. Clusters of red trumpet-shaped flowers (to three inches long) appear throughout the summer and are very attractive to hummingbirds. The flowers are followed by bean-like seedpods, three to five inches long, which split open when ripe, releasing numerous two-winged seeds for dispersal by the wind.

HARDINESS ZONES 6 TO 11

1806: BM, *Bignonia radicans*

CELOSIA CRISTATA L.

Amaranth Family
Syn. Celosia argentea var. cristata
◊ Cockscomb
TJ 1767

On April 2, 1767, Jefferson noted planting seeds of a variety of flowers, including "Cockscomb, a flower like the prince's feather." This tender tropical annual is likely the crested form of *Celosia,* with its fascinating scarlet flower heads resembling a rooster's comb. Cockscombs are sun- and heat-loving reseeding annuals that are popular in flower borders during summer.

1738: JC/PC, "tall coxcombs"
1790: WF, "Coxcomb"
1800: HM, "Cockscomb, 2 Sorts"
1802, 1804, 1806: BMB and BM, "*Celosia cristata* Common Cock's-comb; *Celosia argentea* Silvery-spiked Celosia; *Celosia coccinea* Scarlet Chinese Celosia"
1826: O&L, "Crimson coxcombs"

CENTAUREA CYANUS L.

ASTER FAMILY

◊ "French pink bleuette," Bachelor's Button, Cornflower, Bluebottle

TJ, ca. 1806-9

Also known as cornflower, bluebottle, and bleuette, bachelor's button is an easy-to-grow, self-seeding, cool-season annual with bright blue, pink, or white flowers, and it has been popular in America since colonial times. Bernard McMahon offered it in five colors in 1802, and Jefferson included "French pink bleuette" in an undated list of flowers, believed to be written around 1806–9.

1760: JT, "cyanus"
1802, 1806: BMB and BM, "blue, purple, red, striped, white Cyanus"

CENTAUREA MACROCEPHALA MUSS. PUSCHK. EX WILLD.

ASTER FAMILY

◊ Globe Centaurea, Great Golden Knapweed

Globe centaurea is a robust perennial from the Caucasus, introduced to Britain by 1805. Philadelphia nurseryman Bernard McMahon sent seeds to Thomas Jefferson in 1812. The plant forms clumps of basal foliage three to four feet in height with large, thistle-like flowers in early summer. Its chestnut-brown buds open to expose a crown of rich yellow florets.

HARDINESS ZONES 3 TO 8

CHRYSANTHEMUM INDICUM L.

ASTER FAMILY

◊ Chrysanthemum

TJ ca. 1806-9

The chrysanthemum, the "Queen of Flowers," has been cultivated in China since at least 500 BCE. The first to arrive in the West was a simple semidouble form called 'Old Purple'. It was introduced at Kew Gardens in London in 1790 and was illustrated in Curtis's 1796 edition of the *Botanical Magazine*. The William Prince Nursery of Long Island, New York, listed "43 varieties of 'Chinese' chrysanthemums" in its 1820s catalogue. By the mid-nineteenth century, at least fifty varieties had been developed from new strains sent from China. Their forms ranged from single and double to quilled, anemone-flowered, and pompon. The chrysanthemum's popularity increased, and in 1871 Shirley Hibberd's *The Amateur's Flower Garden* listed the "Best One Hundred Chrysanthemums" of the many available. While president, Thomas Jefferson wrote in an undated letter to Mrs. (Anna Maria Brodeau) Thornton, "Th: Jefferson presents his respectful compliments to mrs Thornton and is able now to restore to her the plant of Chrysanthemum she was so kind as to send him the last summer, having taken from it this spring a luxuriant shoot and set it in a box, in which it is growing well. he returns her his thanks for the same."

HARDINESS ZONES 5 TO 9

1790: WF, *Dendranthema indicum*
1793: JS, "*Chrysanthemum Indicum* the latter hardy enough to live in the garden through the winter though the first frost destroy the flower."
1800: HM, "Chrysanthemum"
1802, 1806: BMB and BM, "*Chrysanthemum coronarium*—Double White Chrysanthemum . . . Double White Quilled Chrysanthemum . . . Double Yellow Chrysanthemum . . . Double Yellow Quilled Chrysanthemum"
1810: WB, "Chrysanthemum Sylphium . . . Double yellow, Double white, Double quilled," "Chrysanthemum indicum"
1826: O&L, "White chrysanthemum . . . Tricolour chrysanthemum"
1827: John Skinner, *The American Farmer* (Baltimore) 9 (1827), "43 varieties of 'Chinese' chrysanthemums . . ." from the Prince Nursery

CLARKIA PULCHELLA PURSH

EVENING PRIMROSE FAMILY

Deerhorn Clarkia, Elkhorn, Ragged Robin, Elegant Clarkia

Western North American species often fared better in England than they did in the eastern United States. The elegant clarkia or "elkhorn flower," named for Captain William Clark by the German botanist Frederick Pursh, became widely popular in nineteenth-century British gardens. Accounts of London exhibitions in which clarkias received first-class certificates appeared in American magazines of the 1860s. After traveling to England, James Vick of Rochester, New York, described "immense fields ablaze with bright colors, acres each of pink, red, white, purple, lilac" in Essex. Although he offered a broad selection of both single and double cultivars, he admitted that clarkia was better suited to an English climate: "It suffers with us in hot dry weather."[13] In hot, humid climates, clarkia has been found to perform best when seeds are sown in the fall so that it blooms as the season cools.

HARDINESS ZONES 3 TO 11

1806: L&C

CLEMATIS VIRGINIANA L.

BUTTERCUP FAMILY

◊ "Virgin's Bower," Woodbine, Native Clematis

TJ 1807

This hardy native vine was first introduced to American gardens in 1720. The early nineteenth-century writer Robert Buist described it in the *Directory* has having "profuse and conspicuous flowers." In 1807, as Thomas Jefferson approached retirement from his second presidential term, he noted in his Garden Book on April 27 that seeds for virgin's bower, *Clematis virginiana,* were planted "about the 3. springs on & near the road from the river up to the house & at the Stone spring." It appears that Jefferson hoped to create a scene where the vine tumbles and cascades over the woodland springs with a shower of fragrant, creamy-white flowers, which resonates with Philip Miller's *The Gardeners Dictionary* entry for clematis: "These may also be planted to cover Seats in Wilderness-quarters, that are designed for shade; to which Purpose these Plants are very well adapted."[14] Another native species, curlyhead clematis (*C. ochroleuca*), is a rare occurrence in the woodland on the north slope of Monticello. This species is listed in Bernard McMahon's 1806 *Calendar* as "Yellow-flowered Virgin's Bower."

HARDINESS ZONES 4 TO 8

1783: BGB, "Clematis vitalba" Woodbine
1806: BM, "Yellow-flowered Virgin's Bower"
1810: WB, "Curled virgins bower"

CLEOME HASSLERIANA CHODAT

CLEOME FAMILY

Syn. Cleome houtteana Schltdl. Spider Flower

Spider flower is a self-seeding annual native to southern regions of South America and was introduced to England via the West Indies. Bernard McMahon included "cleome" in his *Calendar* (1806), to be sown in April along with amaranths, balsam, and other tender annuals. Also called spider legs and grandfather's whiskers, it was considered a choice flowering annual by Robert Buist in his 1839 edition of *The American Flower Garden Directory*. Its showy pink and white flowers, large multilobed leaves, and strong growth habit make it a handsome addition to the flower border in summer and fall.

HARDINESS ZONES 10 TO 11

1806: BM, "Cleome"

COLCHICUM AUTUMNALE L.

COLCHICUM FAMILY

Autumn Crocus, Meadow Saffron

This hardy, long-lived bulb is native to Europe and North Africa. Philadelphia nurseryman Bernard McMahon included "Meadow Saffron (double and single)" in *The American Gardener's Calendar* (1806), and Jean Skipwith planted colchicums at Prestwould, according to her Garden Notes of 1793. The dried seeds and corms are the source of medicinal colchicum and colchicines—all parts are highly toxic if ingested. Therefore, these bulbs are deer and rodent resistant. Plants bear showy, lavender-pink flowers in fall after the foliage has died down. Like daffodil leaves, the leaves of autumn crocus should not be removed until they naturally begin to turn yellow in early summer.

HARDINESS ZONES 4 TO 9

1793: JS, "Meadow Saffron, bulbous root a bt size of tulip, flowers in autumn and the lvs green all winter. Called by common people Naked Ladies, great var. obtained from seed."
1800: HM, "Autumn Crocus"
1806: BM, "*Colchicum autumnale* . . . Meadow Saffron (double and single)"

CONOCLINIUM COELESTINUM (L.) DC.

ASTER FAMILY

Syn. Eupatorium coelestinum L. Blue Mistflower, Hardy Ageratum

This handsome North American member of the aster family occurs naturally in low, moist ground, on moist wooded slopes, on savannas, and along streams from New Jersey to Minnesota and the West Indies. The species is listed in the British *Botanical Magazine* in 1730 and appears in Philadelphia nurseryman John Bartram's broadside catalogue in 1783. Also known as hardy ageratum, this species resembles the cultivated annual *Ageratum houstonianum* from Mexico, with deep blue, mist-like flowers in late summer. In 1851, New England garden writer Joseph Breck called it "the most beautiful species in existence."[15]

HARDINESS ZONES 5 TO 9

1783: BGB, "*Eupatorium coelestinum*"
1806: BM, *E. coelestinum,* "Blue-flowered Eupatorium (with many others)"

CONSOLIDA AJACIS (L.) SCHUR

BUTTERCUP FAMILY

Syn. Delphinium ajacis, D. consolida, Consolida ambigua
◊ Larkspur
TJ 1767, 1771, 1810

This European hardy annual species was introduced into cultivation before 1572. The earliest American citation is from J. Townley Seed Company, Boston, in 1760 ("Double Larkspur"). Jefferson noted larkspur blooming at Shadwell in July 1767. He thought it suitable for naturalizing at Monticello in the "Open Ground on the West" in 1771, listing it among "hardy perennial flowers," and he noted that seed was sowed on Monticello's winding walk flower border on April 8, 1810. Larkspur is a self-seeding annual species with blue, pink, and occasionally white flowers in late spring through early summer.

1760: JT, "Double larkin spur"
1800: HM, "Larkspur, 3 Sorts"
1802, 1806: BMB and BM, "Double Blue Rocket Larkspur," "Double Purple," "Double Rose," "Double Striped White," "Tall White Rocket," "Branched Larkspur"
1810: WB, "Larkspur: Double dwarf rocket . . . double tall rocket . . . double variegated branching . . . double rose coloured . . ."

CONVALLARIA MAJALIS L.

ASPARAGUS FAMILY

◊ "Lilly of the Valley," Lily-of-the-Valley
TJ 1771, 1808

This well-known flower, native to Europe, is a universal favorite and has been in gardens since the sixteenth century. Williamsburg's John Custis first mentioned it around 1738, and by 1829, flowers in white, double white, and rose red were known. Thomas Jefferson recorded lily-of-the-valley as early as 1771 in a list of hardy perennial flowers suitable for the "Open Ground on the West" at Monticello and in an undated "list of flowers," believed to be from about 1806–9, in which Jefferson noted "lilly valley plant spring or fall." In 1808 Jefferson's granddaughter Anne Cary Randolph Bankhead wrote that a friend was to give her "a few roots of the Lilly of the valley" in exchange for seed of the ice plant (*Mesembryanthemum crystallinum*). By the late nineteenth century, it had become an important florist flower in America and was produced in immense quantities.

HARDINESS ZONES 3 TO 8

1738: JC/PC, "Lilly of the valley"

1790s: WF
1792: MC, "Lillies of the valley"
1793: JS, "Convallaria"
1810: WB

CROCUS ANGUSTIFOLIUS WESTON

IRIS FAMILY
◊ Cloth-of-Gold Crocus
TJ 1812

Once known as the "Turkey crocus," cloth-of-gold crocus was introduced in 1587 and described in early British herbals, including John Parkinson's *Paradisi in Sole Paradisus Terrestris* (1629). In 1812, Thomas Jefferson was sent a dozen bulbs of this early flowering "herald of spring" from Bernard McMahon, who offered many rare and unusual plants. McMahon described it as golden yellow, striped with brown outside. It is also known as *Crocus susianus.* Cloth-of-gold produces golden yellow flowers in early spring, striped with brown on the outside of the petals. It can readily naturalize in flower beds, lawns, and deciduous woodlands.

HARDINESS ZONES 3 TO 8

1806: BM, "*Crocus susianus* . . . Cloth of Gold Crocus"

CROCUS SATIVUS L.

IRIS FAMILY
◊ Saffron Crocus
TJ 1807

Although in cultivation since Roman times, the saffron crocus is not known to exist in the wild. It is the source of the culinary herb saffron, which is the long, conspicuous, deep red stigma present in each flower. The genus name comes from *krokos,* the ancient Greek name for saffron. Saffron production became a major industry in England after its introduction in the fourteenth century. It has been documented in American gardens since the eighteenth century. In 1807, Jefferson requested "Saffron" roots from Bernard McMahon. This hardy, fall-flowering bulb (corm) bears rich lilac flowers with dark purple veins.

HARDINESS ZONES 6 TO 8

1790: WF, "Saffron"
1800: HM, "Blue Autumnal Crocus," "True Cultivated Saffron"
1806: BM, "*Crocus officinalis* . . . Officinal Crocus or True Saffron"

CROCUS VERNUS (L.) HILL

IRIS FAMILY

◊ Dutch Crocus, Spring Crocus

TJ 1812

Dutch or garden crocus produces purple, blue, yellow, or white flowers in early spring. Native to high alpine areas of Europe and western Russia, garden forms of this bulb (corm) have been in cultivation since the seventeenth century. In 1812 Bernard McMahon sent Jefferson a crocus variety "of very early bloom; flower white inside & beautifully striped outside."[16]

HARDINESS ZONES 3 TO 8

1790: WF, "crocus"
1792, 1793: MC, "Mixed blue and yellow crocus"
1793: JS, "yellow and blue crocus"
1800: HM, "Crocus, 5 sorts"
1806: BM, "*Crocus vernus* . . . Spring Crocus (many varieties)"
1810: WB, "Crocus vernus, or spring, in varieties"

CYCLAMEN HEDERIFOLIUM AITON

PRIMROSE FAMILY

Ivy-leaved Cyclamen

Native to southern Europe, *Cyclamen hederifolium* came into cultivation by the late sixteenth century. The roots, or corms, were used medicinally for ailments in pigs long before the plants came into the garden, and they were commonly called "sowbread," "hogges meat," and "swynes meat." Peter Collinson sent various cyclamens to Williamsburg's John Custis in 1739–40, and Jean Skipwith grew a "great variety" of cyclamen in her garden at Prestwould. This hardy fall-to-winter-flowering perennial can naturalize in the landscape.

HARDINESS ZONES 5 TO 9

1739–40: PC to JC, "Cyclamens" "spring cyclamen" [*C. coum*]
1793: JS, "1. Raised from seed. 4 years to flower. Blooms Dec. to late spring. 2. Raised fr. Seed fr. which a great var. may be obtained—is four yrs from seed before they fl. which is in Dec. and will cont. in beauty until late in the Spring (write to Mrs. S. for seeds)"
1800: HM, "Cyclamen"
1802, 1806: BMB and BM, "*Cyclamen autumnalis* and *C. vernus*"

CYPRIPEDIUM ACAULE AITON

ORCHID FAMILY

◊ "Mockaseen," "Mockasun," Pink Lady Slipper Orchid

TJ 1806, 1809

The English botanist and naturalist John Bradbury (1768–1823) visited Monticello in 1809 and remarked upon several unusual native plants, including three "Cypripedia," or lady slipper orchids. He noted that "some of these are removed into Mr. Jefferson's Garden and others are marked in the Woods & known to Col. R. [Randolph] who has this morning promised to take care of them for me." Jefferson also included the "Mockasun," or moccasin flower, generally considered the rare and beautiful pink lady slipper, on his list of cultivated plants.

HARDINESS ZONES 3 TO 8

1806: BM, "*Cypripedium aucaule* . . . Two-leaved Purple Lady's Slipper"

CYPRIPEDIUM CALCEOLUS L.

ORCHID FAMILY

+◊ Yellow Lady Slipper Orchid

TJ 1791

Jefferson's son-in-law Thomas Mann Randolph Jr. reported that this lovely orchid was flowering at Monticello on April 30, 1791. Although less common than the pink lady slipper in Virginia forests, the yellow lady slipper does exist on the wooded north slope of Monticello. It is not clear whether this wildflower was transplanted into the flower garden, which is considered a questionable practice. Collecting rare native orchids not only threatens the species but also puts the plants at risk, as most wild orchids suffer and usually die after a few years when removed from their native habitat.

HARDINESS ZONES 3 TO 8

1806: BM, "*Cypripedium canadense*. . . . Yellow-flowered Lady's Slipper" or "*Cypripedium Calceolus*. . . . English Lady's Slipper"

DELPHINIUM EXALTATUM AITON

BUTTERCUP FAMILY

◊ "American Larkspur," Tall Larkspur

TJ 1811

This rare native species—sparsely scattered in the rich woodlands of eastern North America, primarily along the Appalachian Mountain chain—was planted on the outer northwest border of the winding walk on March 22, 1811. The source of Jefferson's planting was likely Bernard McMahon, who listed *Delphinium exaltatum* along with four other delphinium species in *The American Gardener's Calendar*. This perennial prefers partial shade in hot, humid climates and bears blue and purple flowers in late summer. It prefers alkaline soil.

HARDINESS ZONES 4 TO 7

1806: BM, "American Larkspur"

DIANTHUS BARBATUS L.

CARNATION FAMILY

◊ Sweet William

TJ 1767, 1782, 1807

Thomas Jefferson first noted "sweet William began to open" in his Garden Book on April 16, 1767—when he still lived at his boyhood home, Shadwell—and he recorded its flowering in May and June in "a Calendar of the bloom of flowers in 1782." Sweet William is one of the oldest of garden flowers and is illustrated in the sixteenth- and seventeenth-century English herbals of John Gerard and John Parkinson. An entire oval flower bed of sweet William was featured in Jefferson's 1807 plan for the gardens around Monticello, which he drew while still living in Washington, DC, during his second term as president. He had ordered seed from Philadelphia nurseryman Bernard McMahon. Numerous forms of sweet William were available in Jefferson's time, including 'Painted Lady' types, with a solid band of color on the petals, and double-flowered forms.

HARDINESS ZONES 3 TO 9

1760: JT, "sweet Williams"
1793: JS, "Sweet William"
1795: JL, "Carnations, Pheasant ey-d pink, and Sweet William"
1799: 1800, GF, "Sweet William"
1806: BM
1807: BGB, "Dianthus barbatus"
1810: WB, "Sweet William, in varieties"

DIANTHUS CARYOPHYLLUS L.

CARNATION FAMILY

◊ "Double Carnation," Carnation

TJ 1767, 1807, 1811, 1812

Carnations are native to the Mediterranean region, and their cultivation dates to ancient Greek and Roman times. In his Garden Book, Jefferson first referenced the sowing of carnations at Shadwell on April 2, 1767, along with seeds of both annual and perennial flowers. Seeds sent from Bernard McMahon were planted in one of the oval flower beds in April 1807, but according to a report from Jefferson's granddaughter the following November, the carnations—along with a long list of flowers "which you got from Mr. McMahon"—failed to come up. Jefferson again ordered double carnation seed from McMahon in 1811 and 1812.

HARDINESS ZONES 6 TO 9

1760: JT, "carnation"
1786: PC&Co, "double carnations, 72 sorts"
1790: WF, "Carnation"
1793: JS, "Picottee Pink or Carnation . . . Prince Picoti or July flower"
1802, 1806: BMB and BM, "Dianthus caryophylus maximus . . . Double Carnation"
1810: WB, "Carnations, fifty sorts by name"
1826: O&L, "Carnation Pink"

DIANTHUS CHINENSIS L.

CARNATION FAMILY

◊ "China Pink," "Indian Pink"

TJ 1807, 1812

This showy, short-lived perennial, often grown as an annual, bears single to semidouble, mixed-color flowers from early June until late fall and has dark green, grass-like foliage. Thomas Jefferson grew China pinks along his winding walk flower border in 1807, along with sweet Williams and carnations. The "Indian pink" planted at Shadwell in 1767 may have been this species or *Dianthus plumarius*, the perennial cottage pink with blue, grass-like foliage. Although the fringed petals of China pink resemble the perennial fringed pink (*D. superbus*), this species has no fragrance.

HARDINESS ZONES 6 TO 9

1738: PC to JC, "Double Flowering China or

India pink," "India pinks"
1760: JT, "india pink"

DIANTHUS PLUMARIUS L.

CARNATION FAMILY

◊ "Pinks," Garden Pinks, Cottage Pinks, Grass Pinks
TJ 1767, 1811

The perennial dianthus is a compact, evergreen perennial garden plant of unknown origin. The common name "pink" was first used in reference to a "pale rose-colored flower" by the 1680s. "Grass pink" refers to its blue-green, grass-like foliage, which forms a low-growing mat. Highly fragrant single or double flowers emerge in spring in shades of rose pink, white, and red. Pinks enjoyed their greatest development and history in Britain; single and double forms were commonly available at least by the sixteenth century. Pinks were very popular and highly developed florists' flowers by the late eighteenth century, and many forms were available in Europe and America. When Jefferson mentions a pink blooming at Shadwell in 1767, or the planting of "pinks. in locks of fence N. & W." at Poplar Forest in 1811, he was likely referring to one of these types.

HARDINESS ZONES 4 TO 10

1760: JT, "pink"
1786: PC&Co, "pinks of all sorts"
1793: JS, "pinks of various kinds, very fine," "double Charlottes pink"
1806: BM, "Dianthus glaucus Mountain Pink"
1810: WB, "pink"
1826: O&L, "Pheasant's eye pink"

DIANTHUS SUPERBUS L.

CARNATION FAMILY

Fringed Pink

Fringed pink is a native European and Asian perennial with flowers in shades of pale pink to white in early summer. Its flowers have a spicy fragrance and deeply cut petals, thus the common name "pink" (for pinking shears). Although recorded in European gardens by the seventeenth century, it remained uncommon in both Europe and America until the early nineteenth century.

HARDINESS ZONES 4 TO 8

1806: BM, "Superb Pink"

DICTAMNUS ALBUS L.

RUE FAMILY

◊ "Fraxinella," Gas Plant, White Dittany, Burning Bush
TJ 1807

This handsome, long-lived perennial, native from southern Europe to northern China, has been cultivated in American gardens since the early eighteenth century. Thomas Jefferson noted planting "Fraxinella in center of NW shrub circle" at Monticello on April 16, 1807. He received the plant from his friend Thomas Main, a Washington, DC, nurseryman. It is also called "gas plant" because it emits a volatile vapor that can be ignited on a still evening. In his 1831 nursery catalogue, William Prince exclaimed that "this plant exhales inflammable gas!" The name "fraxinella" refers to its foliage, which resembles the leaves of ash trees (genus *Fraxinus*). A reddish-purple variety, *D. albus* var. *purpureus,* was available through a Philadelphia nursery in 1796. Gas plants take several years to become well established in the garden, forming a dense clump with many showy flowering stalks.

HARDINESS ZONES 3 TO 8

1741–43: PC to JC, "White and Red Fraxinelloes"
1806: BM, "*Dictamnus albus* White Fraxinella" and "*Dictamnus albus* v. *flore rubro* Red-flowered ditto"

DIGITALIS FERRUGINEA L.

PLANTAIN FAMILY
Rusty Foxglove

Rusty foxglove is native to southeastern Europe, Turkey, and Lebanon and is documented to the sixteenth century in the early British herbals of Parkinson and Gerard. While there is no direct evidence that Thomas Jefferson cultivated this species, it was available on Bernard McMahon's broadside and listed in *The American Gardener's Calendar* under the common name "Iron-coloured Fox-glove." The plant often begins to flower in the second season after it becomes well established in the garden, where it will also reseed if allowed.

HARDINESS ZONES 4 TO 8

1804, 1806: BMB, BM, "Iron-coloured Fox-glove"

DIGITALIS PURPUREA AND DIGITALIS PURPUREA ALBA L.

PLANTAIN FAMILY
Foxglove and White Foxglove

Foxglove, a showy biennial bearing spires of deep pink tubular flowers in late spring and early summer, was grown in American gardens by 1735 and likely became more common after its medicinal properties were discovered in the late eighteenth century. Bernard McMahon listed both the pink and white forms in his broadside catalogue.

HARDINESS ZONES 4 TO 8

1738: PC to JC, "White Foxglove," "rose colored foxglove"
1800: HM, "Foxglove, 2 sorts"
1802, 1806: BMB and BM, "Purple Fox-glove and White-flowered Fox-glove"
1810: WB, "White, Purple, Yellow foxglove"

DIONAEA MUSCIPULA ELLIS

DROSERA FAMILY
◊ Venus Flytrap
TJ 1786, 1787, 1789, 1796, 1800, 1804, 1809

Thomas Jefferson, like many others, was fascinated by the plant called the Venus flytrap and, after numerous requests, was able to acquire seeds in 1804. He likely was never successful in growing the flytrap, however. This unusual carnivorous species is native to coastal bogs of the Carolinas and was known by its Indigenous American name, Tippitiwitchet. It was first taken to England by William Young in 1768, six years after its discovery by John Bartram and his son William. British botanist John Ellis named it *Dionaea* after the Greek goddess of beauty. In *The American Gardener's Calendar* (1806), Bernard McMahon described it as "one of the most extraordinary productions of nature . . . the lobes close, like the teeth of a rat-trap."[17]

Insects that touch the leaf's hairs are caught in the trap-like structure, where they are digested, providing the plant with nutrients. The Venus flytrap is a North American perennial with rosettes of five-inch leaves and small white flowers.

HARDINESS ZONES 7 TO 10

1806: BM, "*Dionaea Muscipula,* or Venus's fly-trap"

DOLICHOS LABLAB L.

BEAN FAMILY
Syn. Lablab purpureus (L.) Sweet
◊ Hyacinth Bean
TJ, possibly 1812

This tender vine is native to the tropical regions of Africa and is cultivated extensively in Asia and North Africa for its edible fruit pods, which, like the flowers, are highly ornamental. The hyacinth bean, also known as Egyptian and Indian bean, was introduced to European gardens by the early 1700s and was sold by American nurserymen by the early nineteenth century. In 1812, Thomas Jefferson recorded planting "Arbor beans white, scarlet, crimson, purple. at the trees of the level on both sides of the terrasses, and on long walk of [kitchen] garden." Although Jefferson does not specifically cite this species, hyacinth bean was sold by Philadelphia nurseryman Bernard McMahon and listed as a tender annual in his 1806 *Calendar.* It is possible that Jefferson's "purple" bean was the *Dolichos lablab.*

HARDINESS ZONES 10 TO 11

1804, 1806: BMB and BM, "*Dolichos purpurea,* Purple Dolichos; *D. Lablab,* Black-seeded Dolichos"
1810: WB, "*Dolichos lablab* . . . Egyptian Kidney-bean," "*Dolichos alba* . . . White dolichos"
1826: O&L, "Purple hyacinth bean"

ECHINACEA ANGUSTIFOLIA DC.

ASTER FAMILY
Syn. Rudbeckia angustifolia
"Mad Dog Plant," Narrow-leaved Cone-flower

Also known as mad dog plant because the Plains Indians prized it as a remedy for rabid dog and rattlesnake bites, this species was likely included in an 1805 shipment of plants sent to Thomas Jefferson by the Lewis & Clark Expedition. Narrow-leaved coneflower is a drought-tolerant, summer-blooming perennial bearing daisy-like, rosy-pink flowers with reflexed petals. It is attractive to butterflies and is deer resistant. Like the common purple coneflower (*Echinacea purpurea*), this species is native to the midwestern United States. The genus name derives from the Latin *echinos,* meaning "hedgehog," referring to the bristly cone of disk florets in the center of the large composite flower.

HARDINESS ZONES 3 TO 8

1805: L&C
1806: BM, "*Rudbeckia angustifolia* Narrow-leaved Rudbeckia"

ECHINACEA PURPUREA (L.) MOENCH

ASTER FAMILY
Purple Coneflower

Native to the central and southeastern United States, this showy herbaceous perennial was first sent to Europe by the Reverend John Banister, an English chaplain sent to Virginia by Bishop Compton in 1678. Banister was not only a clergyman but also a notable plant collector and naturalist. In the nineteenth century, Thomas Fessenden, an important American garden writer, commented that coneflowers produce "many flowers, which are very durable and much admired."[18] This coneflower has many landscape benefits: the flowers attract butterflies, birds consume the seeds, and it is drought- and deer-tolerant.

HARDINESS ZONES 4 THOUGH 9

1783: BGB, "*Rudbeckia purpurea*"
1806: BM, "*Rudbeckia purpurea* Purple Rudbeckia"

ECHINOPS RITRO L.

ASTER FAMILY
Globe Thistle

Globe thistle, a hardy, herbaceous Mediterranean species, long cultivated throughout Europe, is an undemanding perennial suitable for the border or the wild garden. Williamsburg's John Custis might have received this—or its more vigorous cousin, *Echinops sphaerocephalus*—from his English patron Peter Collinson in 1738. Both are listed in Parkinson's early seventeenth-century herbal and Philip Miller's eighteenth-century botanical dictionary.

HARDINESS ZONES 3 TO 9

1760: JT, "globe thistle"
1806: BM, "*Echinops sphaerocephalus* . . . Great Globe Thistle," "*Echinops Ritro* . . . Small Globe Thistle"

ERANTHIS HYEMALIS (L.) SALISB.

BUTTERCUP FAMILY

Winter Aconite

This tiny harbinger of spring is native to France, Italy, Yugoslavia, and Bulgaria. Winter aconite is a hardy bulb that has been in cultivation since the late 1500s in Europe and Britain, where it has naturalized extensively. British merchant Peter Collinson sent "spring Acconite" bulbs to Williamsburg's John Custis in the 1700s. Bernard McMahon listed winter aconite as "*Heleborus hyemalis,* Winter Helebore or Aconite" in *The American Gardener's Calender* (1806). Lemon-yellow flowers are borne on short stems nestled in green, collar-like, leafy bracts.

HARDINESS ZONES 4 TO 7

1739–40: JC/PC, "spring Acconite"
1806: BM, "Winter Helebore or Aconite"

ERYSIMUM CHEIRI (L.) CRANTZ

MUSTARD FAMILY

Syn. Cheiranthus cheiri
◊ "Wall Flowers," Wallflower
TJ 1771, 1806, 1807

The ancient garden wallflower has been in cultivation for so long that its origin is uncertain. While serving as president, Thomas Jefferson sent his daughter Martha a "bundle of Wallflowers" on November 27, 1806. The flowers were transported by David "Davy" Hern Jr., an enslaved wagoner. Jefferson ordered wallflower seed from Philadelphia nurseryman Bernard McMahon in 1807. Wallflowers are divided into two genera, *Cheiranthus* and *Erysimum,* and there is much debate as to the differences between the two. The name *Cheiranthus* derives from the Latin for "hand flower," referring to this fragrant flower's use in nosegays and tussiemussies. The Siberian wallflower, *Erysimum* × *allionii,* bears bright orange-yellow flowers through the season.

HARDINESS ZONES 6 TO 9

1760: JT, "wall flower"
1790: WF, "Wallflower"
1792, 1793: MC, "Widow wall flower"
1793: JS, "Wall Flower . . . Widowed Wall Flower . . . Bloody Wall Flower"
1799, 1800: GF, "Yellow Wallflower . . . Bloody Wallflower," "White and Yellow Double Wallflower . . . Single Yellow Wallflower"
1800: HM, "Wallflower"
1806: BM, "Bloody . . . Yellow . . . White Wallflower"
1810: WB, "Double bloody wall-flower, Double yellow wall flower, Single wall-flower, Single bloody wall-flower"
1826: O&L, "Bloody wall flower"

EUPATORIUM COELESTINUM L.

ASTER FAMILY

Syn. Conoclinium coelestinum (L.) DC.
Hardy Ageratum, Mist Flower

This handsome North American member of the aster family is a hardy, herbaceous perennial that occurs naturally in low moist ground, on moist wooded slopes, on savannas, and along streams from New Jersey to Minnesota and the West Indies. The species is listed in the British *Botanical Magazine* in 1730 and appears in Philadelphia nurseryman John Bartram's broadside catalogue in 1783. Also known as hardy ageratum, this species resembles the cultivated annual *Ageratum houstonianum* from Mexico. In 1851, New England writer Joseph Breck called it "the 'most beautiful' Eupatorium."[19]

HARDINESS ZONES 5 TO 10

1783: BGB, "*Eupatorium coelestinum*"
1806: BM, "*E. coelestinum* . . . Blue-flowered Eupatorium (with many others)"

EUPATORIUM PURPUREUM L.

ASTER FAMILY

Syn. Eutrochium purpureum (L.) E. E. Lamont

Joe-pye Weed

This hardy, herbaceous North American perennial aster occurs naturally in low moist ground, on moist wooded slopes, on savannas, and along streams from New Hampshire to Minnesota, Iowa, and Nebraska south to Florida and Georgia. The species was introduced to Europe by 1640 and listed in Philadelphia nurseryman John Bartram's catalogue in 1783. Also known as gravel root, purple boneset, and hempweed, Native North Americans used it as a diaphoretic to induce perspiration and break a fever, and early settlers quickly adopted this practice. Sweet Joe-pye has large leaves in whorls around the stem, and its late-season blooms attract swallowtail butterflies. This plant is not attractive to deer.

HARDINESS ZONES 3 TO 8

1783: BGB, "*Eupatorium dentatum*"

EUPHORBIA MARGINATA PURSH

SPURGE FAMILY

◊ Snow-on-the-Mountain

On July 28, 1806, William Clark, co-captain of the Lewis and Clark Expedition, collected this curious plant while exploring Montana's Yellowstone River. Although its natural distribution is along the west side of the Missouri River in North Dakota, it proved adaptable to a wide range of soil types and growing conditions and likely escaped from cultivation into farmlands from Minnesota to Texas and New Mexico. German American plant hunter and botanist Frederick Pursh named this species, which was new to science, and called it a "very handsome species" in his *Flora Americae Septentrionalis* (1814), which described many plants collected by Lewis and Clark. Snow-on-the-mountain, which is distinguished by white-edged and veined upper leaves, is now popular in cutting gardens. It tolerates deer, drought, and poor soils. *Euphorbia marginata* became a common annual in nineteenth-century seed catalogues.

HARDINESS ZONES 2 TO 11

1806: L&C

FRASERA CAROLINIENSIS WALTER

GENTIAN FAMILY

Syn. Swertia caroliniensis (Walter) Kuntze
◊ "American Columbo," Green Gentian
TJ 1810

A Garden Book entry on April 18, 1810, noted that this rare North American perennial was planted in a southwest oval flower bed, but Jefferson does not reveal the source. Peter Collinson, an early English botanist and sponsor of plant explorer John Bartram, described this plant as the "pyramid of Eden" because of its stately, two-foot panicle of purple-spotted, light green to white flowers. American columbo is a monocarpic perennial, meaning that it dies after flowering; however, the attractive basal rosette of leaves will persist for up to fifteen years before a purple flowering stalk shoots up. It is found in calcareous grasslands and savannas and is considered threatened or endangered in certain northern states.

HARDINESS ZONES 4 TO 8

FRITILLARIA IMPERIALIS L.

LILY FAMILY

◊ "Crown Imperials," Crown Imperial Lily
TJ 1786, 1807, 1809, 1810, 1811, 1812, 1816

The crown imperial lily was brought to western Europe from southern Turkey and Kashmir as early as 1576. By 1770, Dutch bulb growers had developed thirteen distinct varieties. Thomas Jefferson first mentioned this bulb as "Couronne Imperial. Crown imperial" in a list of plants he sent from Paris to Francis Eppes in 1786. He would order this lily from Bernard McMahon five times before receiving three "roots" of the orange-red variety (*Fritillaria imperialis rubra*). In September 1812 McMahon sent a rare "silver striped" form and a small box with three roots of "Crown Imperial which ca[r]ry two tiers of flowers *when in very luxuriant growth.*"[20] The crown imperial lily is also called "stink lily" and "old stinky" because of its foxy odor. Today the Monticello gardens also display the yellow fritillaria (*F. imperialis lutea*) and occasionally the variegated and unusual double forms of crown imperial lilies.

HARDINESS ZONES 4 TO 8

1737: PC to JC, *F. imperialis lutea* "lemon colord crown imperiall," "yellow ones"
1738: PC to JC, *F. imperialis* cv. "striped"
1739: PC to JC, *F. imperialis rubra* "orange ones"
1790: WF, "Crown Imperial"
1800: HM, "Crown Imperial"
1802, 1806: BMB and BM, "Crown Imperial (many varieties)"
1810: WB, "Fritillaria, in varieties"

FRITILLARIA MELEAGRIS L.

LILY FAMILY

Checkered Lily, Guinea Hen Flower, Snake's-head Fritillary

This delightful bulb is native to English meadows and was grown in American gardens before 1700. In 1806 Philadelphia nurseryman Bernard McMahon included it in *The American Gardener's Calendar* as "Chequered Lily." If well situated in moist ground, it can persist for many years, naturalizing in lawns or beds rich in leaf mold. Guinea hen flower is known by several names, including snake's-head lily, Madam Ugly, and drooping tulip. The 1597 edition of John Gerard's *Herball* lists it as "Checkered Daffodil" and "Ginnie Hen Flower" and describes the flowers as "checkered most strangely . . . surpassing . . . the curiest painting that Art can set down."[21] The specific epithet *meleagris* means "spotted like a guinea fowl."

HARDINESS ZONES 4 TO 8

1800: HM, "Fritillaria"
1806: BM, "Chequered Fritillary"

FRITILLARIA PERSICA L.

LILY FAMILY

Persian Fritillary

The Persian fritillary was introduced into English gardens in the late sixteenth century, but at the time it did not capture the same attention as its cousin, the crown imperial lily. Both deep violet and white forms are cultivated today in the Monticello flower borders. Bernard McMahon listed the *Fritillaria persica* in *The American Gardener's Calendar* (1806) and on his 1810 broadside catalogue.

HARDINESS ZONES 4 TO 8

1806, 1810: BM and BMB, "Persian Fritillary or Lily"

FRITILLARIA PUDICA (PURSH) SPRENG.

LILY FAMILY

◊ "Columbian Lily," Yellow Fritillary

TJ 1807

In 1807 Thomas Jefferson noted that seed of the "Lilly. the yellow of the Columbia. it's root a food of the natives" was planted in an oval flower bed at Monticello. The yellow fritillary, or *Fritillaria pudica,* is a bulbous plant with edible roots and was collected by the Lewis and Clark Expedition near the headwaters of the Missouri River. It grows throughout the Pacific Northwest in well-drained, dry, sunny sites, and today it is a valued rock garden species for its nodding, golden-yellow flowers and dwarf habit. Jefferson's seeds failed to germinate, according to his granddaughter, and it is generally difficult to grow in humid climates.

HARDINESS ZONES 3 TO 8

1802, 1806: BMB and BM, "Persian Fritillary"

GAILLARDIA ARISTATA PURSH 1813

ASTER FAMILY

+ Blanket Flower

As the Lewis and Clark Expedition crossed the Continental Divide on July 6, 1806, this showy native species was collected. Philadelphia botanist Frederick Pursh, who first published descriptions of new species from the expedition's collection in 1813, noted that it was found "on dry hills on the Rocky-mountains." This showy species is a common perennial found in open, sunny habitats on prairies and hillsides from western British Columbia to western Arizona and New Mexico. Blanket flower blooms from summer through autumn, with yellow ray florets, sometimes tinged red at the base, and reddish-orange central disk florets that are attractive to pollinators.

HARDINESS ZONES 3 TO 10

1806: L&C

GALANTHUS NIVALIS (L.) KUNTZE

AMARYLLIS FAMILY

◊ Snowdrop

TJ 1806, 1808

Ellen Wayles Randolph wrote her grandfather in 1808 from Edgehill, her family's neighboring plantation home: "The third of April snow drops bloomed, you have none but I will give you mine if you want them, and have them set out in your garden when we go to Monticello." April 3 is very late for this white-blossoming bulb, often the first flower of the season, and it seems possible that Ellen's "snow drops" were instead what we now call "snowflake" (*Leucojum* sp.). Jefferson, however, also included "snowdrop" on an undated list of flowers from about 1806–9, possibly in anticipation of his retirement garden.

HARDINESS ZONES 3 TO 8

1793: JS, "Large Snowdrop"
1802, 1806: BMB and BM, "Single and Double Spring Snowdrop"
1810: WB, "common snow drop"

GLADIOLUS COMMUNIS L.

IRIS FAMILY

◊ Hardy Gladiolus, Sword Flag, Corn Flag

TJ 1812

This winter-hardy species of gladiolus, native to the Mediterranean region, is more delicate than modern hybrids, bearing small, purple flowers on two-foot stalks about sword-like, fan-shaped foliage. British botanist John Parkinson, writing in *Paradisi in Sole Paradisus Terrestris* (1629), provided the first description and commented on its aggressive habit of growth: "If it be suffered any long time in a Garden, it will rather choake and pester it, than be an ornament unto it."[22] It was growing in American gardens by 1800. Thomas Jefferson received twelve hardy *Gladiolus communis* bulbs from Philadelphia nurseryman Bernard McMahon in 1812. Colonies of this species persist in several of the winding walk flower beds at Monticello. *G. communis byzantinus,* a showier, wild-occurring subspecies with larger, magenta-red flowers, was illustrated in Curtis's *Botanical Magazine* in 1805.

HARDINESS ZONES 6 TO 9

1735: BGB
1793: JS, "Corn Flag"
1806: BM, "European Corn-flag"

GELSEMIUM SEMPERVIRENS (L.) J. ST-HIL. 1805

GELSEMIUM FAMILY

Syn. Gelsemium nutidum and Bignonia sempervirens L. 1753
◊ "Jesamine," "Yellow Jessamine," Carolina Jessamine, Evening Trumpet Flower
TJ 1771, 1781 (Notes)

In 1771 Jefferson made elaborate plans for the open grounds of his Little Mountain, in which he specified that "Jesamine, honeysuckle [*Lonicera sempervirens*], sweetbriar [*Rosa eglanteria*], and even hardy flowers which may not require attention" should be interspersed throughout the landscape. His fanciful idea for a grotto at the North Spring included "an abundance of Jesamine, Honeysuckle, sweet briar, etc." And his plant lists for the shrubbery on the "Open Ground on the West" contained "Climbing shrubby plants—Trumpet flower [either *Campsis radicans* or *Bignonia capreolata*]—Jasmine—Honeysuckle." Jefferson included "Yellow Jessamine" in his list of ornamental plants in *Notes on the State of Virginia*. This evergreen, twining native vine was named the official state flower of South Carolina in 1924.

HARDINESS ZONES 7 TO 10

1783: BGB, "Bignonia Semper Virens, Yellow Jasmin"

GENTIANA VILLOSA L.

SYN. SAPONARIA VILLOSA

Striped Gentian
TJ 1781 (Notes)

The striped gentian is a hardy, fall flowering perennial native to the southeastern regions of the United States. It bears clusters of bottle-shaped white flowers with an intricate network of green striping. It is an extremely rare species that grows in grasslands, barrens, and dry open woods. In his 1806 *Calendar,* Bernard McMahon lists eight species of perennial gentian.

HARDINESS ZONES 6 TO 9

1806: BM, "*Gentiana vollosa* Hoary Gentian"

GERANIUM MACULATUM L.

GERANIUM FAMILY

◊ Wild Geranium, Spotted Cranesbill
TJ 1786

In his *New England Rarities* (1672), John Josselyn called the wild geranium "Raven's-Claw," and in 1814 Frederick Pursh noted the name "Alum-root, on account of the astringent taste of the roots." Its name derives from *geranos,* the Greek word for crane, alluding to the long beak of the seed. While in France in 1786, Thomas Jefferson requested plants of this species from the nursery of Quaker botanist John Bartram Jr. to share with his many Parisian friends. Wild geranium grows abundantly in the forests of Monticello today and is not attractive to deer.

HARDINESS ZONES 3 TO 9

1806: BM, "Spotted Crane's-bill"

GILLENIA TRIFOLIATA (L.) MOENCH

ROSE FAMILY

Syn. Spiraea trifoliata L.; Porteranthus trifoliatus (L.) Britton
◊ "Indian Physic," "Spiraea trifoliata," Bowman's Root, American Ipecac, Indian Physic, Mountain Indian-physic
TJ 1781 (Notes)

This deciduous, herbaceous perennial is native to the eastern United States and Canada and spans from southern Ontario to Georgia. The late seventeenth-century naturalist John Banister collected this plant in Virginia and sent dried specimens to England in 1688. He later introduced it into the gardens at Fulham in 1690. It was identified then as *Spiraea opulifolia* and known commonly as "Trifoliate Virginia Meadow-sweet." Virginia-born aristocrat William Byrd II wrote of the curative properties of Indian physic, or "Ipecacuaha," to his colleague Sir Hans Sloane of England's Royal Society during the early 1700s. Thomas Jefferson listed this choice, long-lived native perennial as a medicinal plant in *Notes on the State of Virginia*. It is also known as Bowman's root.

HARDINESS ZONES 4 TO 8

1736/37: JC to PC, "Ipacacuana"
1783: BGB, "Spirea Foliis Ternatis, Ipecacuaha"
1806: BM, "*Spiraea trifoliata* Three leaved Spiraea"

GLAUCIUM FLAVUM CRANTZ

POPPY FAMILY

◊ "Glaucium Yellow Horned Poppy," Yellow-horned Poppy
TJ 1807

This unusual, short-lived yet self-seeding perennial—native to the coastal regions of North Africa, Europe, Britain, and western Asia—was observed naturalized along the New England coast as early as the seventeenth century. The eighteenth-century botanist John Clayton included this species in his *Flora Virginica* (1739). Thomas Jefferson noted that the seed of yellow horned poppy was planted at Monticello in an oval flower bed southeast of the house in 1807. It has attractive, bluish-gray foliage and bears bright golden-yellow, poppy-like flowers followed by long, curious, "horned" seedpods.

HARDINESS ZONES 5 TO 9

1806: BM, "*Glaucium luteum* Yellow Horned Poppy"

GOMPHRENA GLOBOSA L.

AMARANTH FAMILY

◊ Globe Amaranth, Bachelor's Buttons, Everlasting, English Clover
TJ 1767

Globe amaranth seeds were first planted at Shadwell, Thomas Jefferson's boyhood home, on April 2, 1767. The species was introduced into Europe from India in 1714. Apparently, Pennsylvania gardeners were the first in the colonies to bring the plant to bloom. According to Joan Parry Dutton in *Plants of Colonial Williamsburg* (1979), John Custis, who received seeds repeatedly from Peter Collinson, wrote triumphantly to him in 1742 that one seed came up—"shot into multitude of branches and bore more than 100 flowers; came out daily till the frost stopt them; I esteem it one of the prettyest things I ever saw." Peter Collinson responded, "It is a Real and I may say perpetual Beauty. If the flowers are gather'd in perfection and hung up with their Heads Downwards in a Dry shady Room, they will keep thear Colours for years and will make a pleasant Ornament to Adorn the Windows of your parlor or study all the Winter. I Dry great Quantities for that purpose and putt them in flower potts and China basons and they make a fine show all the Winter."[23] The clover-like flowers bloom from summer through fall in shades of magenta, pink, and occasionally white. Globe amaranth thrives in hot, dry weather, and the long-lasting flowers are superb for fresh or dried arrangements.

HARDINESS ZONES 9 TO 11

1737: PC to JC, "Amarantheodes," "Amaranthoides"
1760: JT, "globe amaranthus"
1790: WF, "Globe Amaranthus"
1800: HM, "Globe Amaranthus"
1802, 1806: BMB and BM, "*Gomphrena globose* Globe Amaranth (purple, spiked, white, and striped)"
1826: O&L, "Purple"

HELIOTROPIUM ARBORESCENS L.

BORAGE FAMILY

Syn. Heliotropium peruvianum L. and H. corymbosum Ruiz & Pav.
◊ Heliotrope, Garden Heliotrope, Cherry-pie
TJ 1786

This tender perennial flower was first discovered in Peru and brought to France sometime between 1735 and 1757. There, it was a novelty much appreciated for its blue flowers, which have a pleasant, sweet fragrance. In 1786, while he was living in Paris, Jefferson sent seed of this species to his brother-in-law Francis Eppes of Eppington plantation in Chesterfield County, Virginia, commenting that it was "to be sowed in spring. A delicious flower, but I suspect it must be planted in boxes & kept in the house in winter. The smell rewards the care." It was likely not widely cultivated in America before 1800. There are popular, modern cultivars, but the species form of the plant is cultivated at Monticello.

HARDINESS ZONES 10 TO 11

1806: BM, "*Heliotropium peruvianum* Peruvian Heliotropium" (under "Hot-House Trees and Shrubs, &c")

HELLEBORUS NIGER L.

BUTTERCUP FAMILY

Christmas Rose

This is an ancient garden plant reputed to have strong curative powers. The Greeks believed it cured insanity, and John Gerard wrote in 1597 that it was "good for mad and furious men, for melancholike, dull, and heavie persons . . . and briefly for all those that are troubled with blacke choler, and molested with melancholie."[24] It was grown in the colonies before 1700. When well situated, Christmas rose—also known as black hellebore owing to the color of its roots—is a long-lived perennial. *Helleborus niger* ssp. *maximus* and *H. niger* ssp. *macranthus* are both European strains with large flowers; however, the maximus flowers remain pure white, while the subspecies macranthus flowers mature to pink.

HARDINESS ZONES 4 TO 9

1806: BM, directions for September: "divide and transplant the roots of the Helleborus niger, or Christmas rose."

HELLEBORUS X HYBRIDUS.

LENTEN ROSE

Jean-Baptiste Lamarck, a French naturalist and botanist, first described a species of hellebore in 1789. The true Lenten rose (*Helleborus orientalis*), native to Asia Minor, Greece, and Turkey, crosses easily with other hellebore species and thus has become increasingly rare; it has been mostly supplanted by *H.* × *hybridus,* which is largely derived from *H. orientalis.* Bernard McMahon described several species in his 1806 *Calendar,* including "green, purple, stinking, black, and Ranunculus-leaved" hellebores.

HARDINESS ZONES 4 TO 9

1806: BM, "Helleborus viris, H. lividus. H. garidus, H. niger, H. ranunculinus"

HEMEROCALLIS FULVA (L.)

LILY FAMILY

Tawny or Orange Daylily

Daylilies are tough, long-lived, tuberous-rooted perennials originating primarily from Asia. The orange or tawny daylily has naturalized throughout Europe and North America and is considered invasive in some situations. Although not documented by Thomas Jefferson, this species is found in various areas of the Monticello landscape and may be associated with the gardens and gravesites of the enslaved.

HARDINESS ZONES 3 TO 9

1793: JS, "Common Tawny Daylily"
1806: BM, "Orange Day-Lily"

HEMEROCALLIS LILIOASPHODELUS L.

LILY FAMILY

Syn. Hemerocallis flava
Lemon Lily
TJ ca. 1820

Although likely native to Asia, as are all the other daylily species, the lemon lily was once thought to be native to the foothills of the southern Alps. It was widely cultivated and "common in every country garden" in Britain by the 1660s. It immigrated to America by the 1800s and was often found in Victorian flower arrangements. Bernard McMahon listed *Hemerocallis flava* as the "Yellow Day-Lily" in *The American Gardener's Calendar* (1806), and Jean Skipwith mentions the "Common Yellow and Tawny Day Lily" for her late eighteenth-century garden.

HARDINESS ZONES 4 TO 10

1793: JS, "Common Yellow Daylily"
1806: BM, "Yellow Day-Lily"

HEXAGLOTTIS LONGIFOLIA (L.F.) SWEET

IRIS FAMILY
Syn. Moraea flexuosa Goldblatt

This iris-like, tender South African bulb, formerly called *Morae flexuosa,* was sent by Bernard McMahon in 1812 as a plant suitable for the greenhouse. It has bright yellow flowers in May and was a recent introduction to Europe from the southwestern region of the Cape of Good Hope. It is unlikely that Jefferson was successful in maintaining this unusual bulb in his Monticello greenhouse.

1806: BM, "*Moraea flexuosa* Flexuous Moraea"

HIBISCUS COCCINEUS (MEDIK.) WALTER

HIBISCUS FAMILY
Great Red Hibiscus, Scarlet Hibiscus

This southeastern US native was first named in the late eighteenth century and was soon being grown by avid American gardeners of the day—notably William Bartram, George Washington, and Jean Skipwith. In London, Peter Collinson saw a painting of the flower done by Bartram and asked for seeds to be sent from Charleston, South Carolina. Despite its early popularity and its use in hybridizing modern hibiscus cultivars, there is little evidence that this species was ever widely grown in American gardens. Also known as star of Texas, this showy perennial is suitable for border plantings, rain gardens, or as an accent plant, and the flowers attract hummingbirds and butterflies.

HARDINESS ZONES 6 TO 9

1768: John Bartram (Philadelphia) to Peter Collinson (London), "Hibiscus, Great Crimson flower'd St. John Rose"
1793: JS, "Crimson Mallow"

HIBISCUS LEAVIS ALL.

HIBISCUS FAMILY
Syn. Hibiscus militaris All.
Halberd-leaved Hibiscus, Soldier Rose Mallow, Military Rose Mallow

This large perennial occurs naturally in low and wet places over much of North America. It was first introduced into Great Britain around 1800, and Bernard McMahon listed it in his *Calendar.* A halberd was a fifteenth-century weapon consisting of battle-ax and pike mounted on a six-foot handle. The name "halberd-leaved hibiscus" was given to describe the spear-shaped, triangular leaves on the plant's tall, straight stems. Other common names include soldier or military rose mallow. In 1851, Boston-based garden writer Joseph Breck recommended it as a "fine species."[25]

HARDINESS ZONES 4 TO 9

1763: BGB, "*Hibiscus militaris,* Soldier Rose Mallow"
1806: BM, "*Hibiscus militaris*—Halbert-leaved Hibiscus"

HIBISCUS MOSCHEUTOS L.

HIBISCUS FAMILY

◊ "Musk-smelling Hibiscus," Rose Mallow, Syrian Mallow

TJ 1781 (Notes)

This robust herbaceous perennial is native to low, marshy sites in eastern North America. John Bartram sent seeds to England in the mid-1700s, and it was recommended for American gardens by Bernard McMahon in *The American Gardener's Calendar* (1806). Thomas Jefferson mentioned several hibiscus and mallows, including "Hibiscus moschentos," in *Notes on the State of Virginia.* The midsummer flowers are five to eight inches in diameter with deep rose (sometimes white) petals and often a reddish-purple to maroon eye.

HARDINESS ZONES 5 TO 9

1806: BM, "Musk-smelling Hibiscus"

HIBISCUS SYRIACUS L.

HIBISCUS FAMILY

Syn. Althaea frutex
◊ "Althaea," Rose of Sharon

TJ 1767, 1771, 1794, 1812, 1816

Rose of Sharon is a deciduous shrub native to south-central and southeast China and is the national flower of South Korea. It was introduced to the West before 1600 and first cited in America by John Custis, who received seed of "althea" from Peter Collinson in 1736. Also known as Syrian ketmia, shrub althea, and rose mallow, this shrub produces flowers that are most commonly single or double white or purple. The short-lived flowers only last a day but are produced abundantly in late summer. Jefferson first documented it in his Garden Book on April 4, 1767: "Planted suckers of Roses, seeds of Althaea & Prince's Feather" at Shadwell. In 1771 he included it in his scheme for the "Open Ground on the West," where shrubs "not exceeding a growth of 10 ft" were planted along with small trees, climbing shrubby plants, evergreens, and hardy perennial flowers. Jefferson later included "Althaeas" in his planting memoranda for Poplar Forest in 1812 and 1816.

HARDINESS ZONES 5 TO 8

1734–36: PC to JC, "althea"
1790: WF, "Althea"
1793: JS, "Double white and common Althea"
1802, 1806: BMB and BM, "Althaea Frutex, Syrian"
1810: WB, "Double flowering red althea; Double flowering white althea, Silver striped leafed althea; Single althea in variety"

HOSTA VENTRICOSA STEAM

ASPARAGUS FAMILY
Blue Plantain Lily, Hosta

The blue plantain lily is an Asian species introduced into European gardens in 1790. It was believed to be an exotic species of daylily and was illustrated by Pierre-Joseph Redouté under the name *Hemerocallis caerulea* for his book *Les liliacées* in 1805. They were soon recognized as a different genus and named *Funkia* for the German cryptogamist Henry Funk. *Hosta ventricosa* was in American gardens by 1820, and in 1858 Joseph Breck listed the "Blue Day Lily" as *Funkia caerulea* in his *Flower-Garden.* This genus name persisted throughout the 1800s until it was changed again, early in the twentieth century, to honor Nicholaus Host, an early nineteenth-century physician to the emperor of Austria.

HARDINESS ZONES 3 TO 8

HYACINTHUS ORIENTALIS L.

ASPARAGUS FAMILY
◊ "Purple Hyacinth," "Double Pink, Yellow, White, Blue Hyacinths"
TJ 1766, 1807, 1812

Describing the garden at Shadwell, his birthplace, Jefferson opened his Garden Book on March 30, 1766, with the observation, "Purple hyacinth begins to bloom." By the time he returned to Monticello after his term as president, the hyacinth was one of the more prominent flowers in the gardens. Bernard McMahon made four shipments of hyacinth bulbs between 1807 and 1812, when he wrote that "they are of the *first-rate* kinds, and nearly of as many varieties as roots."[26] In 1807, President Jefferson recorded that one of the oval flower beds at Monticello was planted with double hyacinths in four colors—pink, yellow, white, and blue, probably following the checkered planting plan sketched by McMahon in his book. Jefferson's granddaughter described them the following spring, when they were in flower, as "superb ones." So successful was this early and fragrant flower that excess bulbs were forwarded from Monticello to Poplar Forest in 1816.

An early flowering strain native to the south of France, *Hyacinthus orientalis albulus,* commonly known as the French or French Roman hyacinth, bears small, slender spikes of highly fragrant white, pink, or blue flowers. Garden hyacinths became very popular in the eighteenth century for both their fragrance and their range of colors. More than two thousand distinct varieties were being produced by Dutch growers in the mid-1700s.

HARDINESS ZONES 4 TO 8

1786: PC&Co, "Hyacinths, 600 sorts"
1790: WF, "Hyacinth"
1792, 1793: MC, "Fine large hyacinths" "Red, White, & Blue Hyacinths"
1793: JS, "Double blue and blush coloured hyacinths"
1799, 1800: GF, "Purple blue Hyacinth" "Rose coloured Hyacinth"
1800: HM, "hyacinths-dble. & single"
1802, 1806: BMB and BM, "double hyacinth"
1810: WB, "Oriental, double, and a great variety of colours"

HYPOXIS HIRSUTA (L.) COVILLE

LILY FAMILY

◊ "Yellow . . . Star of Bethlehem," Eastern Yellow Star-grass, Common Goldstar

TJ, ca. 1806–9

This low, tufted, grass-like, spring-flowering perennial is native to the United States, Canada, and northeastern Mexico. In an undated memorandum of flowers, likely written between 1806 and 1809, Jefferson described a "little yellow [flower from woods] star of Bethlehem." The Eastern yellow star-grass is a spring-flowering perennial that can be found on the northern slope of the Monticello woodlands. It grows three to eight inches tall from a rosette of basal leaves that emerge from a hard, hairy corm. Star-shaped flowers are formed on slender, thread-like flowering stems below the top of the leaves.

HARDINESS ZONES 3 TO 9

IMPATIENS BALSAMINA L.

BALSAM FAMILY

◊ Balsam, Garden Balsam, Touch-me-not

TJ 1767, 1812

This is the traditional garden balsam popular in old-fashioned gardens. Thomas Jefferson planted double-flowering balsam seeds at Shadwell in April 1767 and received seeds from Philadelphia nurseryman Bernard McMahon in 1812. McMahon considered the balsam to be among the "more valuable and curious sorts of tender annuals,"[27] and he gave detailed instructions for raising young plants in beds heated by decomposing manure. The double and striped varieties were highly esteemed in Jefferson's time.

1760: JT, "balsam"
1790: JF
1791: MC
1793: JS, "double Balsam" [ordered by Peyton Skipwith, according to Ann Leighton]
1799: GF
1802, 1806: BMB and BM, "Double Purple Striped Balsam, Balsmine," "Double Red," "Double Red Striped," "Double White," "Immortal Eagle Flower"

IPOMOEA QUAMOCLIT L.

MORNING GLORY FAMILY

◊ Cypress Vine

TJ 1791, 1808

The first citation documenting this species in North America is attributed to Thomas Jefferson. While in Philadelphia in December 1790, he sent a collection of seeds to Monticello that included "some seed of the Cypress vine for Patsy" (his eldest daughter, Martha). The following March, Martha wrote back that she and "Polly" (Jefferson's daughter, Maria) had "planted the cypress vine in boxes in the window," perhaps to serve as houseplants. This tender annual vine, native to tropical America and noted in Italy in the 1500s, was known among eighteenth-century Virginia gardeners. Philadelphia nurseryman Bernard McMahon offered seed in 1804, calling it "Wing'd leaved Ipomoea." The cypress vine is a morning glory relative, with star-shaped scarlet and white flowers that provide a vivid contrast to the plant's lacy green foliage. Like the morning glory, cypress vine will twine up a trellis, pole, young tree, fence, or woven branches used to stake pea vines. It is a summer-flowering annual vine and is considered invasive in some regions.

1802, 1804, 1806: BMB and BM, "Wing'd leaved Ipomoea"

IRIS CRISTATA AITON

IRIS FAMILY

◊ "Dwarf Flag," Dwarf Crested Iris

TJ 1766

This woodland iris is native to the eastern North American deciduous forest, where it often grows on rocky slopes. Peter Collinson, an English patron and regular correspondent of John Custis from Williamsburg and the Bartrams of Philadelphia, grew this plant from roots sent to him during the mid-eighteenth century. In 1766 Jefferson began his Garden Book with observations of wildflowers along the Rivanna River, including the "Dwarf flag" flowering May 4 "in our woods." Dwarf crested iris spreads slowly, creating large mats of handsome light green foliage that deer do not find attractive. A white form, *Iris cristata* 'Alba', also occurs in the wild.

HARDINESS ZONES 4 TO 8

IRIS DOMESTICA (L.) GOLDBLATT & MABB

IRIS FAMILY

Syn. Belamcanda chinensis L.; Ixia chinensis L. ◊ "Chinese Ixia," Blackberry Lily, Leopard Lily

TJ 1807

This Asian perennial, which Thomas Jefferson called "Chinese Ixia," is a member of the iris family. Jefferson first received seed from nurseryman Bernard McMahon in 1807, during his second term as President of the United States. These were sown in an East Front oval flower bed at Monticello. Today the blackberry lilies that are found naturalized around Monticello are believed to be descendants of Jefferson's original plantings. The common name "blackberry lily" describes the shiny black seeds that "must fool even the birds," as the early twentieth-century American garden writer Elizabeth Lawrence put it. But Lawrence also called it by another name, leopard flower, for the ephemeral leopard-spotted flowers that open throughout the morning and close at dusk, "neatly furling themselves into a minute and almost invisible red and yellow striped barber pole."[28] This relates to a fourth Latin name used through the last century, *Pardanthus chinensis,* which derives from *pardos,* meaning leopard.

HARDINESS ZONES 7 TO 10

1793: JS, "Bermudian Ixia, 2. Blackberry Lily, 3. Ixia Bermudiana, perhaps the blackberry lily in the garden."
1800: HM, "Ixia chinensis"

IRIS GERMANICA L. AND *IRIS PALLIDA* L.

IRIS FAMILY

◊ "Flag," German or Bearded Iris, Sweet Iris
TJ 1771, 1782

German or bearded iris have been cultivated since 1000 BCE and are first cited in American literature in 1672. Jefferson referred to iris as "flags," a term still used today. The development of bearded iris varieties began in the nineteenth century and continues to this day. The "beard" is the patch of hairs extending down the three lower petals ("falls"), below the three upper petals ("standards"). Purple bearded iris and blue sweet iris, *Iris pallida,* are naturalized in the Monticello landscape and, although they could date to Jefferson's period, their origin is uncertain. Orris root, *Iris* × *germanica* 'Florentina,' is a white to pale blue-gray iris used to manufacture a powder to add fragrance to perfume or flavor chianti.

HARDINESS ZONES 4 TO 9

1793: JS, "Sweet Iris, Florentine Blue Iris"
1810: WB, "White Florentine"

IRIS PERSICA L.

IRIS FAMILY

◊ "Dwarf Persian Iris"
TJ 1812

Six bulbs of this unusual species were sent by Bernard McMahon in 1812. A native of Iran and Turkey with greenish-blue flowers and a yellow keel, the Persian iris has a reputation of being difficult to grow. McMahon, however, found it most suitable for forcing in February with the aid of a greenhouse or hot bed.

HARDINESS ZONES 5 TO 9

1793: JS, "3 Persian Iris"
1793: MC
1800: GF
1800: HM, "Persian Iris, Mourning Iris"
1802, 1806: BMB and BM, "Dwarf Persian Iris"
1810: WB, "Dwarf purple"

IRIS PSEUDACORUS L.

IRIS FAMILY

◊ "Flower-de-luces," Fleur de Lis Iris, Yellow Flag, Yellow Iris, Water Flag

TJ 1767

This native of Europe, northern Asia, the Middle East, and northern Africa is the fleur-de-lis that King Clovis I adopted as his emblem in the sixth century. Backed to the Rhine River by the Goths, Clovis noticed that yellow flags grew far out into the water and realized his army could cross and escape. The early colonists brought this plant to America by the end of the seventeenth century. Today it grows abundantly in wet meadows throughout much of the northeast and can become invasive. Thomas Jefferson noted "Flower-de-Luces just opening" in his boyhood garden at Shadwell on May 28, 1767.

HARDINESS ZONES 3 TO 9

1790: WF, "Fleur-de-Lis"
1810: WB, "Flower-de-luce"

IRIS SIBIRICA L.

IRIS FAMILY

◊ Siberian Iris (possibly TJ's "Iris bicolor")

TJ 1782

The Siberian iris was first introduced into Britain from central Europe and Russia during the late sixteenth century. White, light blue, and double white flowering forms were cultivated by this period.

HARDINESS ZONES 3 TO 8

1800: HM, "Siberian Iris"
1806: BM, "Siberian Iris"
1810: WB, "Persian Iris"

IRIS VERSICOLOR L.

IRIS FAMILY

Blue Flag, Harlequin Iris

This water-loving iris is native to eastern Canada and the northeastern and north central United States. It was introduced into Europe from North America in 1732. The Philadelphia nursery of John Bartram & Son offered the wild blue flag along with four other native iris species in 1807. Another prominent Philadelphia nurseryman, Bernard McMahon, listed it as "Various-coloured iris" in the appendix of his *Calendar* (1806).

HARDINESS ZONES 2 TO 7

1806: BM, "Various-coloured Iris"
1810: WB, "Variegated Iris"

IRIS VIRGINICA L.

IRIS FAMILY

Southern Blue Flag

This delicate iris is native to wetland coastal plain regions of the United States and Canada from the East Coast to the middle states as far west as Texas. The plants grow to two feet high and bear nonfragrant, violet blue flowers with falls that are crested with yellow and white.

HARDINESS ZONES 5 TO 9

1806: BM, "Virginian Iris"
1810: WB, "Virginian Iris"

IRIS XIPHIUM L.

IRIS FAMILY

◊ Spanish Iris

TJ 1812

Bernard McMahon sent this species to Jefferson in 1812 and described it as "*a new & fine variety.*"[29] This is a parent of the Dutch iris and a good example of one of the many newly introduced species relayed by McMahon to Monticello.

HARDINESS ZONES 6 TO 8

1810: WB, "Spanish bulbous iris"

JASMINUM OFFICINALE L.

IRIS FAMILY

◊ "White Jasmine," "Star Jasmine," Poet's Jasmine

TJ 1794, 1807

Native to the Caucasus, northern Persia, the Himalayas, and China, poet's jasmine is a hardy, semievergreen vine that was known to all ancient civilizations. It was common in England before 1548 and was grown in North America by the eighteenth century as "Jasmine of India." In 1794, Thomas Jefferson noted "White Jasmine" in his list of "Objects for the garden this year" and planted "Star Jasmines. 2 in each of the oval beds" surrounding Monticello on November 6, 1809. In 1839 Robert Buist commented that "its white, delicate and lovely fragrant flowers render it a great acquisition."[30]

HARDINESS ZONES 7 TO 10

1793: JS, "White Jasmine"
1810: WB, "Common white jasmine"

JEFFERSONIA DIPHYLLA (L.) PERS.

BARBERRY FAMILY

Formerly *Jeffersonia binata*

◊ Twinleaf

TJ 1792, 1807

This rare and desirable native woodland perennial was named to honor Thomas Jefferson in 1792 by the "Father of American Botany," Benjamin Smith Barton. Jefferson grew the plant at Monticello in one of the oval flowerbeds in 1807. The attractive flowers last only a few days in early spring, often near the time of Jefferson's early April birthday. This ephemeral species bears small, pure white flowers that resemble bloodroot blossoms. The deeply divided foliage inspired the common name "twinleaf."

HARDINESS ZONES 4 TO 9

LANTANA CAMARA L.

VERBENA FAMILY

Common Lantana, Shrub Verbena

The multicolored flowers of the lantana have endeared it to American gardeners since at least the beginning of the nineteenth century. Jean Skipwith of Prestwould described it as "Prickly Lantana (house plant) very brilliant, seldom without flowers." Bernard McMahon suggested lantana as a greenhouse plant, to be moved outdoors in summer. Robert Buist, an influential garden writer of the early nineteenth century, wrote of lantana: "these are very handsome growing plants, and will even keep in a good green-house; but in such case will only bloom in summer."[31] Common lantana is a shrubby, woody perennial native to the subtropical regions of Central and South America but has spread in southern areas of North America.

HARDINESS ZONES 9 TO 11

1793: JS, earliest American citation, "Prickly Lantana"
1806: BM, "*Lantana camara* Various-coloured Lantana" (under "Hot-House Trees and Shrubs, &c")

LATHYRUS LATIFOLIUS L.

PEA FAMILY
◊ "Everlasting Pea," Perennial Pea
TJ 1771, 1807

Perennial pea (*Lathyrus latifolius*) is a vigorous, long-lived, summer-flowering vine. It was an established garden plant in America before 1720, when the annual sweet pea, *L. odoratus,* was introduced. Unlike the sweet pea, the flowers of *L. latifolius* are not fragrant. Jefferson first noted the everlasting pea in a 1771 Garden Book entry under a list of plants for the "Open Ground on the West." The inclusion of several perennial vines, which can grow six to nine feet or more, suggests that he planned for them to climb on the shrubs and trees in this designed landscape. The everlasting pea in Jefferson's shrubbery likely reflected the style of the British wilderness garden. Philip Miller wrote: "These Plants are very proper to plant against a dead Hedge, where they will run over it, and if they be kept train'd up, will cover it in the Summer."[32] In 1807, prior to his retirement from the presidency, Thomas Jefferson noted in his Garden Book that seed of "Everlasting pea" was sowed in an East Front oval flower bed at Monticello. Although European in origin, it has naturalized in many parts of the United States, especially along roadsides and fence lines.

HARDINESS ZONES 4 TO 9

1793: JS, "Perennial Pea"
1802, 1806: BMB and BM, "Everlasting Pea"

LATHYRUS ODORATUS L.

PEA FAMILY
◊ "Sweet-scented Pea," Sweet Pea
TJ 1767 (?), 1811

This tender annual vine with delightfully fragrant flowers was first brought into cultivation by a Franciscan monk, Francis Cupani, who sent seed to England from Sicily in 1699. The name "Cupani Sweet Pea" is often applied to the species form, which has sweetly fragrant, dark bluish-purple to light blue bicolored flowers. By 1730, several color forms were known, including the lovely pink and white 'Painted Lady', which is also maintained in the Monticello flower gardens today. Sweet peas were very popular in early American gardens, and Thomas Jefferson, who desired "fragrant or beautiful flowers" for his gardens, planted "Lathyrus odoratus. sweet scented pea" in an oval flower bed near the southwest portico of Monticello in 1811.

1760: JT, "sweet scented pease"
1806: BM, Painted Lady Sweet Pea

LAVANDULA ANGUSTIFOLIA MILL.

MINT FAMILY
◊ English Lavender
TJ 1794

Thomas Jefferson included "lavender" in a 1794 list of "Objects for the garden this year." Lavender is one of the most well known of the traditional aromatic herbs and has been used since at least the twelfth century. In Jefferson's time, lavender water for the bath was popular, and Mary Randolph gave "receipts" for lavender water in *The Virginia Housewife* (1824). She also recommended preparing "cosmetic soap for washing hands" using oil of lavender. This hardy dwarf shrub is native to southern Europe and northern Africa. It is a traditional edging plant for geometric beds, especially for roses, but is also very effective in mixed borders. The flowers attract bees and butterflies. This plant is deer and drought tolerant.

HARDINESS ZONES 4 TO 9

1767: MGB
1802, 1806: BMB and BM, "lavender"
1810: WB, "lavender"
1825: O&L, "lavender"

LAVATERA OLBIA L.

MALLOW FAMILY
◊ "Shrub Marshmallow," Tree Lavatera
TJ 1807

Seeds of this short-lived shrub, considered an herbaceous perennial by many, were planted in the Monticello nursery at the southeastern end of the vegetable garden terrace. They were sent in 1807 by Doctor Gouan of Montpellier, France, and if they were ever transferred to an oval flower bed, they would have provided a striking display in midsummer with their hollyhock-like purple flowers. The tree lavatera is a plant native to the Mediterranean and is as rarely cultivated in the United States now as it was in Jefferson's day.

HARDINESS ZONES 4 TO 9

LAVATERA THURINGIACA (L.) VIS.

MALLOW FAMILY
Syn. Malva thuringiaca; possible syn. for Lavatera olbia
◊ Garden Tree Mallow
TJ 1807

This European mallow-like perennial with purplish-pink flowers was planted in an oval bed at Monticello on April 18, 1807. Later that year, however, Jefferson's granddaughter wrote to him that it and the "pinks Carnations Sweet Williams Yellow horned Poppy Ixia Jeffersonia everlasting Pea . . . Columbian Lilly Lobelia Lychnis double blossomed Poppy & Physalis failed, indeed none of the seeds which you got from Mr. McMahon came up."

HARDINESS ZONES 7 TO 10

1760: JT, "lavatera" ("*Lavatera trimestris*")
1800: HM, "Mallow"
1806: BM, "*Lavatera thuringiaca,* Great-flowered Lavatera"

LIATRIS ELEGANS OF MICHAUX (WALTER) MICHX.

ASTER FAMILY

◊ Gayfeather, Dense Blazing Star, Pink-scale Blazing Star
TJ 1805

Benjamin Smith Barton wrote to Jefferson from Philadelphia on June 12, 1805, with a list of plants that Jefferson had forwarded to him, which included "*Liatris elegans* of Michaux" among other native species. This tall and elegant North American species was first recorded in the botanical notes of the French botanist André Michaux. It grows in dry, sandy soils in prairie and pineland habitats found in the southeastern United States as far west as Texas and Oklahoma. *Liatris* are members of the aster family whose flowers open from the top of the inflorescence downward. The pale lavender to white flowers attract bees, butterflies, and hummingbirds, and they are good for cutting.

HARDINESS ZONES 6 TO 8

LILIUM CANADENSE L.

LILY FAMILY

◊ "Canada Martagon," Canada Lily, Meadow Lily
TJ 1786, ca. 1806-9

While in Paris, Jefferson wrote to Anthony Giannini with a request for seeds, including "Lilly of Canada. This is the lilly which [enslaved gardener] George found for me in the woods near the stone spring. I think that before I left home we took up some roots and planted them in the flower borders near the house. Send all the seed you can get, and some roots."[33] This reference confirms the existence of the flower borders Jefferson documented in 1782. In an undated list of flowers from around 1806–9, Jefferson noted cultural instructions for plant care and included "Canada Martagon," noting, "July or Aug. take & replt." These instructions may have been taken from Bernard McMahon's *The American Gardener's Calendar* (1806). The Canada lily has nodding yellow flowers with chocolate-spotted throats and yellow anthers. It was introduced to Europe from America by the French about 1620 and was first described by John Parkinson in his *Paradisus in Sole Paradisus Terrestris* (1629). It was frequently called "martagon," and Mark Catesby painted it for his *Natural History of Carolina* . . . (1747), calling it "Martagon Canadense, Le Lis de Canada or Martagon," from roots sent from Pennsylvania to Peter Collinson in England.[34] It is distinguished by the petals that flare out like bells rather than the recurved petals of the true martagon.

HARDINESS ZONES 3 TO 8

1793: JS, "spotted Canada Martagon Lily . . . much admired"
1810: WB, "Canada martagon"

LILIUM CANDIDUM L.

LILY FAMILY

◊ "White Lily," Madonna Lily

TJ 1782

Lilium candidum is a rare species native to the eastern Mediterranean and Balkans. It was commonly known as the white lily until the end of the eighteenth century, when other white lilies began to be imported into England. It forms bulbs at ground level and grows a basal rosette of leaves during the winter. The extremely fragrant flowers are pure white, tinted yellow in the throat. In the nineteenth century, when there was much interest in recovering the traditional folklore of plants, it became known instead as the "Madonna Lily," since it was often depicted in paintings of the Virgin Mary. This lily is considered endangered because it is often collected from wild populations; therefore, it is not advised to purchase this species.

HARDINESS ZONES 5 TO 9

1793: JS, "large White Lily"
1802, 1806: BMB and BM, "Jacobaea Lily"
1810: WB, "common white lily"

LILIUM CHALCEDONICUM L.

LILY FAMILY

◊ "Fiery Lily," "Scarlet Martagon Lily," Scarlet Turk's-cap Lily

TJ 1782

This species is believed to be the "Fiery" lily Jefferson noted flowering in late May in "a Calendar of the bloom of flowers in 1782." This species is native to Tuscany, Greece, and Albania, and it bears brilliant, fiery red flowers that resemble a turban. It is prominently listed in Bernard McMahon's *Calendar* (1806). It should not be confused with the North American Turk's-cap lily (*Lilium superbum*).

HARDINESS ZONES 3 TO 9

1806: BM, "Scarlet Martagon Lily"

LILIUM SUPERBUM L.

LILY FAMILY

◊ "Alleghany Martagon," American Turk's-cap Lily, Spotted Canada Martagon

TJ 1809, 1812

This spectacular native lily grows from New York and New Hampshire south to Alabama and Georgia. It is said that soil could not possibly be too rich for this species. Also known as the spotted Canada martagon, this lily has been in cultivation since the late 1700s. On November 28, 1809, Jefferson wrote to Judge William Fleming, a lifelong friend in Richmond, thanking him for the foliage of the "Alleghaney Martagon," adding that "a plant of so much beauty & fragrance will be a valuable addition to our flower gardens. should you find your roots of it I shall be very thankful to participate of them, and will carefully return you a new stock should my part succeed & yours fail."[35] On February 28, 1812, Bernard McMahon sent a box of plants including "4 roots Lillium superbum L." Jean Skipwith grew a spotted martagon in her garden at Prestwould, which could be either *Lilium superbum* or *L. canadense.* The magnificent, red-flushed orange flowers with maroon spots form on stately five- to ten-foot stalks.

HARDINESS ZONES 4 TO 9

1783: BGB, "Lillium martagon"
1793: JS, "Spotted Canada Martagon Lily . . . much admired"

LINUM PERENNE LEWISII PURSH

LINUM FAMILY

◊ Lewis's Prairie Flax

In 1806, near the end of their great expedition, Meriwether Lewis and William Clark observed this western North American perennial in the valleys of the Rocky Mountains and along the Missouri River. It was named *Linum lewisii* after Captain Lewis. Bernard McMahon was offering the plant in his catalogue by 1815. This subspecies, which is more robust than the common European blue flax, is desirable in the perennial border or sunny wildflower garden for its airy texture and sky-blue flowers. Although the individual flowers last only one day, they are produced in such profusion that the plant is in continuous bloom.

HARDINESS ZONES 5 TO 9

1806: L&C
1815: BMB

LOBELIA CARDINALIS L.

CAMPANULA FAMILY

◊ "Scarlet Cardinal's Flower," "Cardinel," Cardinal Flower

TJ 1807

The brilliant, scarlet-colored blossom of this North American species was considered the finest red in nature upon its introduction to Europe in 1629. Linnaeus named the genus *Lobelia* in honor of Matthias de l'Obel (1538–1616), a Flemish botanist who became physician to James I of England. Native Americans once made tea from the roots for the treatment of stomachaches, typhoid, and other ailments. William Byrd II documented this species in his *Natural History of Virginia* (ca. 1736), and eighteenth-century botanists and nurserymen listed various native lobelias among their offerings, including John and William Bartram in 1783. Cardinal flowers grow in moist woodland areas of Monticello, but in 1807 the seed Thomas Jefferson sowed in an oval bed was probably obtained from Bernard McMahon. Although a short-lived perennial, the species will persist in the garden if allowed to reseed each year.

HARDINESS ZONES 3 TO 9

1783: BGB
1800: HM, "Cardinal Flower"
1806: BM, "Scarlet Cardinal's-flower"
1810: WB, "Scarlet cardinal flower"

LOBELIA SIPHILITICA L.

CAMPANULA FAMILY

Great Blue Lobelia

This native wildflower has been grown in American flower gardens since at least the beginning of the nineteenth century. At one time it was thought to be a cure for venereal disease, thus the botanical name. Philadelphia nurserymen John and William Bartram sent the cardinal flower (*Lobelia cardinalis*) and great blue lobelia (*L. siphilitica*) seed to Europe in 1784. In his 1806 *Calendar*, Bernard McMahon named "Lobelias of various kinds" first among the "beautiful ornamental plants [that] may now be collected from the woods, fields, and swamps . . . [to] embellish the Flower-garden and Pleasure-grounds."[36] McMahon advertised seeds of this species in his broadside, and the William Prince Nursery on Long Island offered it in 1818. Bees, butterflies, and hummingbirds are attracted to the tubular flowers, but deer typically avoid this plant because of its toxicity.

HARDINESS ZONES 4 TO 9

1783: BGB, "Blue Cardinal Flower"
1806: BM, "Blue Cardinal's-flower"
1818: William Prince Nursery, Long Island, NY

LONICERA SEMPERVIRENS L.

HONEYSUCKLE FAMILY

◊ "Honeysuckle," "Trumpet Honeysuckle"

TJ 1771, 1781 (Notes), 1791

Trumpet or coral honeysuckle, native to the eastern and southern United States, is evergreen in the south but deciduous in the north. The clusters of showy scarlet flowers attract hummingbirds and butterflies but are not fragrant. The species was introduced to Europe in 1686, and Bartram's Nursery in Philadelphia first offered it in 1783. Jefferson first listed honeysuckle in 1771 for shrubs and trees to be planted in the "Open Ground on the West" at Monticello. He later considered trumpet honeysuckle as an ornamental native plant in *Notes on the State of Virginia* (1781). In 1791, on the reverse of a plant order from the William Prince Nursery, Jefferson penned planting instructions for various trees and shrubs and concluded that the honeysuckle should be planted "at the roots of the weeping willows."

HARDINESS ZONES 4 TO 8

1793: JS, "Red-trumpet Honeysuckle"
1800: HM, "Trumpet Honeysuckle"
1810: WB, "Scarlet trumpet honeysuckle"
1806: BM, "*Lonicera sempervirens* Carolina Trumpet Honeysuckle"

LUNARIA ANNUA L.

MUSTARD FAMILY

◊ Honesty, Money Plant, Satin Flower

TJ 1767

Money plant, or honesty, is a self-seeding biennial named for its showiest feature—its two-foot stalks of silvery, coin-shaped seedpods, which are attractive in dried arrangements. It was among the first European flowers grown in American gardens and was valued for its seedpods and edible roots. Seeing the small purple flowers on April 25, 1767, Jefferson remarked, "Lunaria still in bloom, an indifferent flower."

HARDINESS ZONES 5 TO 9

1790: WF, "Satin Flower"
1802, 1806: BMB and BM, "Honesty, Satin Flower"
1810: WB, "Honesty"

LUPINUS TEXENSIS HOOK

PEA FAMILY

◊ "Lewis' Pea," "Arkansas Pea," Texas Bluebonnet

TJ 1807

Bernard McMahon, who was caretaker of the initial collection of plants brought east by the Lewis and Clark Expedition, sent seeds of "the flowering pea of the plains of Arkansas, a Lupinus," to Monticello in 1807.[37] This was likely the species known as the Texas bluebonnet, which Jefferson subsequently had planted in an oval flower bed at Monticello. Years later, seeds were even planted in the vegetable garden. Jefferson also included the *Lupinus perenne,* or wild lupine, in *Notes on the State of Virginia.* Lupines are an important nectar source for bees and butterflies, and the plant is the sole host of the Karner blue butterfly, native to the Great Lakes region, and is also a host of the frosted elfin butterfly, which ranges across the eastern United States. Blue, pea-like flowers are held on upright spikes above palmately divided leaves with seven to eleven leaflets.

HARDINESS ZONES 4 TO 8

LYCHNIS CHALCEDONICA (L.) E. H. L. KRAUSE

CARNATION FAMILY

◊ "Scarlet Lychnis," Maltese Cross

TJ 1807

Maltese cross was an early import to the American colonies and was listed in Bernard McMahon's 1804 broadside as "Scarlet Lychnis." Thomas Jefferson's 1807 sketch of the flower beds at Monticello included "Lychnis chalcedonica. Scarlet Lychnis" in an oval flower bed on the West Front. According to Anne Cary Randolph's report to her grandfather on November 9, 1807, none of the many seeds sent by McMahon that spring came up. A native of Russia, Maltese cross is thought to have been introduced to European gardens by Louis IX on his return from the Holy Land, where it was already being grown as an ornamental garden plant. It subsequently became a popular ornamental for English gardens, as the many common names testify: Jerusalem cross, campion of Constantinople, nonesuch, flower of Bristow, knight's cross, scarlet lightning, and Bridget-in-her-bravery. The striking scarlet-red flowers attract butterflies and hummingbirds.

HARDINESS ZONES 3 TO 10

1800: HM
1802, 1804: BMB, "Scarlet Lychnis"
1806: BM, "Scarlet Lychnis"

LYCHNIS CORONARIA (L.) CLAIRV.

CARNATION FAMILY

Syn. *Silene coronaria*
◊ "Catchfly," Rose Campion
TJ 1767, 1791

When Thomas Jefferson noted the "Lychnis bloom" at Shadwell in 1767, he was probably referring to the woolly-leaved, self-seeding rose campion, a biennial or short-lived perennial popular in early American gardens. It has attractive magenta or white flowers in early summer as well as ornamental, silver foliage that resembles lamb's ears (*Stachys byzantina*). Rose campion was sold by Bernard McMahon, the Philadelphia nurseryman, in 1804. In a 1791 letter, Thomas Mann Randolph Jr. reported to Jefferson that *Silene* and *Fragaria vesca* bloomed on April 4 at Monticello.

HARDINESS ZONES 3 TO 8

1826: L&O, "rose campion"

LYCORIS RADIATA (L'HÉR.) HERB

AMARYLLIS FAMILY

Red Spider Lily

This showy, perennial bulb is native to China, Japan, Korea, and Nepal, where it is found in shady, moist areas along slopes and rocky streams. The bright red flowers appear in late summer on naked flower stalks soon after the foliage has gone dormant. Although it is often found in abandoned homesites and fields, the red spider lily was not documented in American gardens until the mid-1800s.

HARDINESS ZONES 7 TO 10

MALVA SYLVESTRIS L.

MALLOW FAMILY

◊ "French Mallow," Common Mallow, High Mallow
TJ, ca. 1806-9

When Thomas Jefferson noted "French mallow" on an undated list of flowers, he was probably referring to *Malva sylvestris,* a European, Asian, and

North African native with handsome, hollyhock-like, purplish-pink flowers with dark purple veins. The perennial French mallow is similar in appearance to its more familiar mallow cousin, the hollyhock. Another common name is cheeses mallow, a reference to the shape of the seed clusters.

HARDINESS ZONES 4 TO 8

MATTHIOLA INCANA (L.) W. T. AITON

MUSTARD FAMILY

◊ "Gilliflower," Common Stock, Stock Gillyflower

TJ 1771

This is likely the "Gilliflower" Jefferson found suitable for naturalizing in the "Open Ground on the West" in 1771, although the garden carnation was also called by this name. It would be extremely difficult to naturalize either flower in the Central Viriginia climate and growing conditions. The Elizabethans called these plants "stock gillyflower" for their stock (or thick stems) and their carnation- or gillyflower-like fragrance.

HARDINESS ZONES 7 TO 10

1760: JT, "purple Stock" "Brompton stock" ("*Matthiola incana v. coccinea*"), "ten-week stock" ("*Matthiolten-week annua*")
1793: JS, "Queens Stock" "Red 10-week stock"
1793: MC, "Stock July flower"
1799: GF, "Red Brompton Stock"
1800: HM, "Brompton Stocks, 4 Sorts"
1826: O&L, "White wall leav'd stock gilli . . . Scarlet Brompton [ditto] . . . purple [ditto] . . . Queens [ditto] . . . Ten week [ditto] . . . Virgins [ditto] . . . Mixt biennial [ditto]"

MERTENSIA VIRGINICA (L.) PERS. EX LINK, 1829

BORAGE FAMILY

◊ "Bluish-coloured, funnel-formed flower in the low grounds," "Mountain Cowslip," Virginia Bluebell

TJ 1766

The Virginia bluebell is a hardy, North American, early spring–flowering perennial with delicate, terminal clusters of light pink buds, which open to flared, long, tubular, sky-blue to purple flowers. On April 16, 1766, in one of the earliest observations in his Garden Book, Thomas Jefferson noted "a bluish-coloured, funnel-formed flower in the low grounds in bloom." Long before Jefferson's observation, this North American wildflower had been introduced to Britain. According to Philip Miller's 1754 edition of *The Gardeners Dictionary,* the Reverend John Banister sent seeds from Virginia to England in the 1600s, but the plants produced from Banister's seeds eventually died out. In the 1730s, Williamsburg's John Custis sent roots of the "beautiful out of the way plant and flower" to his patron, Peter Collinson in London. On April 21, 1808, Ellen Wayles Randolph wrote to her grandfather, "I found in the woods a great many mountain cowslips and wild Ranunculus besides other wildflowers."

HARDINESS ZONES 3 TO 9

1734–36: JC to PC, "mountain cowslip"
1793: JS, "Pulmonaria officinalis . . . P. virginica. Lung-wort. What I call blue funnel flower"
1806: BM, "Pulmonaria virginica Virginian Lung-wort"

MESEMBRYANTHEMUM CRYSTALLINUM (L.) N.E. BR

FIG-MARIGOLD FAMILY

◊ Ice Plant

TJ 1808-9

This tender plant, also known as fig marigold, is a South African species that was introduced to Britain before 1732; it was considered a greenhouse annual there. According to the Reverend William Hanbury in *A Complete Body of Planting and Gardening* (1771), this curious plant was cultivated "for the singular and beautiful oddness of its appearance, it being a large succulent plant, lying prostrate on the ground, and bespangled all over with silvery particles, glittering gems, and pellucid icy pimples or bubbles. . . . [W]hen the sun shines on the plant, it appears like one that is adorned by the piercing severity of a sharp frosty night. . . . They will display their bespangled pride, and shine with their icy brilliancy until the first frost happens, to which the Ice Plant immediately gives way."[38] On December 19, 1808, Anne Cary Randolph Bankhead wrote to her grandfather from Port Royal, "I would be much obliged to you if you will send me in a letter some of the ice plant seed a Lady here has Lost it & is to give me a few roots of the Lilly of the valley & a beautiful pink [Dianthus] for it I know it is to be had in Washington Mr Burwell got some there for Ellen." One month later, on January 19, 1809, Jefferson wrote Charles L. Bankhead from Washington, "I have waited till I could execute Anne's commission as to the seed of the ice-plant, before acknoleging the reciept of her letter of Dec. 19. and your's of the 20th. I now inclose the seed, in the envelope of a pamphlet for Doctr. Bankhead's acceptance. . . . mr Lomax writes me he has given Anne a small plant of the Acacia for me, with which I hope I shall meet you both at Monticello in March." Jefferson's efforts to obtain this plant met with dubious success. In his February 6, 1809, letter to Anne's sister Ellen Randolph, he wrote, "Ice-plant. not entirely dead, but I suppose it's seeds shed on the earth & will come up."

HARDINESS ZONES 8 TO 11W

1793: JS, "Ice Plant (see Mesembryanthemum) should be raised in pots—I must get some seed if I can"
1800: HM, "Ice Plant"
1810: WB, "Dimond Ficoides"
1806: BM, "Diamond Fig-Marigold, or Ice-Plant"
1826: O&L, "Ice Plant"

MIMOSA PUDICA L.

PEA FAMILY

◊ Sensitive Plant

TJ 1767, 1811

Jefferson first recorded "sensitive plant" among a great variety of ornamental annuals and perennials sowed in his flower garden at Shadwell on April 2, 1767. Over four decades later, in the gardens at Monticello, seeds of "Mimosa pudica. Sensitive plant" were planted in an oval flower bed in the corner of the "N.W. Piazza & covd. way" on March 22, 1811. This species has been grown as a curiosity for centuries and was included in many early nineteenth-century seed lists. A favorite feature of a child's garden, the unusual leaves fold together when touched. The shrubby plants produce pink, mimosa-like pompon flowers in midsummer. In *The American Gardener's Calendar* (1806), Bernard McMahon described them as plants with sensibilities, a notion that intrigued Jefferson: "The sensibility of this plant is worthy of admiration . . . with the least touch . . . the leaves just like a tree a dying, droop and complicate themselves immediately . . . so that a person would be induced to think they were really endowed with the sense of feeling."[39]

HARDINESS ZONES 10-12

1790: WF, "Sensitive Plant"
1799, 1800: GF, "Sensitive Plant"
1800: HM
1800: WB, "Mimosa, Humble Plant"
1806: BM, "Sensitive and Humble Plant"

MIRABILIS JALAPA L.

FOUR-O'CLOCK FAMILY

◊ "Mirabilis," "Marvel of Peru," Four o'clock
TJ 1767, 1811

On July 18, 1767, Thomas Jefferson observed: "Mirabilis just opened, very clever." On April 3, 1811, he noted planting seed of "Mirabilis tota varietas, plante vivace d'ornement," sent by his Parisian friend André Thoüin of the Jardin des Plantes, in an oval flower bed on the northwest corner of the southwest portico and dining room at Monticello. The four-o'clock, or marvel of Peru, has long been cherished for the simple miracle of its flowers, which only open during low light periods, such as in the late afternoon and on cloudy days. The plants bloom in a range of flower colors: red, purple, white, and yellow.

HARDINESS ZONES 7 TO 10

1802, 1806: BMB and BM, "Gold Striped . . . Purple Striped . . . Red . . . White . . . White Striped . . . Yellow Marvel of Peru"

MIRABILIS LONGIFLORA L.

FOUR-O'CLOCK FAMILY

◊ "Sweet-scented Marvel of Peru," Sweet Four o'clock
TJ 1812

In 1812 Bernard McMahon sent Jefferson seed of the "Sweet-scented Marvel of Peru." This cousin of the *Mirabilis jalapa* is native to the arid regions of the southwest United States and Mexico. This tuberous-rooted perennial has the curious habit of flowering at dusk, when the fragrant, tubular, pure white blossoms unfurl. It is as rare in gardens today as it was in 1812. In the late 1980s Dr. William C. Welch, extension horticulturist at College Station, Texas, and Dr. Michael Powell, professor of biology at Sul Ross State University in Alpine, Texas, located two populations of this Texas native along rural roadways and shared seed with Monticello gardeners.

HARDINESS ZONES 7 TO 10

1806: BM, "Sweet-scented Marvel of Peru"

MOMORDICA BALSAMINA L.

CUCUMBER FAMILY

◊ Balsam Apple

TJ 1810

Balsam apple was cultivated in Europe as early as 1542, as illustrated by the German physician and botanist Leonhard Fuchs (1501–1566) in *De Historia Stirpium,* and was used medicinally to treat wounds. The English herbalist John Gerard included a lengthy account of its medicinal virtues, and as late as the mid-nineteenth century, American garden writers were proclaiming its healing properties when applied to fresh wounds. On April 18, 1810, Thomas Jefferson noted that seeds of this curious vine were sowed in his flower borders at Monticello along with larkspur, poppies, and nutmeg plant. The balsam apple, a tropical vine native to Africa, Asia, and Australia, is grown as a garden annual with glossy green foliage and bright yellow, deeply veined flowers followed by curious, orbicular, yellow-orange warty fruits, or "apples." The fruits burst open when ripe, revealing numerous seeds covered with a brilliant scarlet, extremely sticky coating. Young, immature fruits are used in Asian cooking and are known as bitter melon.

1790: WF
1793: JS, "Balsam Apple, see Momordica"
1806: BM, "Male Balsam Apple"
1826: O&L, "Balsam Apple"

MOMORDICA CHARANTIA L.

CUCUMBER FAMILY

◊ Bitter Melon, Balsam Pear

This unusual vine from the Old World tropics has been cultivated for its edible fruits since the early 1700s. The vine grows twelve to fifteen feet long and bears attractive, glossy green foliage and bright yellow flowers followed by curious, oblong, yellow-orange warty fruits that burst open when ripe. Thomas Jefferson grew the balsam apple (*Momordica balsamina*), a related species with round, bright orange fruits. Philadelphia nurseryman Bernard McMahon listed both species as "tender annual flowers" in *The American Gardener's Calendar* (1806), an important reference manual that Jefferson owned and often consulted. The balsam pear can be grown as an ornamental annual on trellises, fences, or arbors.

1806: BM, "Hairy Balsam Apple"

MONARDA DIDYMA L.

MINT FAMILY

Bee Balm, Oswego Tea, Bergamot, Scarlet Sage

This vigorous native perennial was recognized as a desirable ornamental and kitchen garden plant by the early eighteenth century, and seed was sent by John Bartram to England in 1744. It was reported that by 1760 there was "plenty in covent garden market" in London. Early American settlers, especially the Shakers in upstate New York, made a tea from the leaves, hence the name Oswego tea (which is now Earl Grey). The plant's citrusy flowers, which are very attractive to bees and hummingbirds, can be used as a garnish or a spice. Bernard McMahon listed "Crimson Monarda" in his 1804 broadside, and bee balm was cited as a garden-worthy plant by many nineteenth-century American garden writers, including A. J. Downing, Peter Henderson, Joseph Breck, and Robert Buist. Deer tend to avoid this plant's fragrant foliage.

HARDINESS ZONES 4 TO 9

1790: WF, "Bergamot Balm"
1802, 1806: BMB and BM, "Crimson Monarda"
1810: WB, "Monarda Scarlet lion's tail"

MONARDA FISTULOSA L.

MINT FAMILY

Wild Bergamot

Philadelphia nurseryman Bernard McMahon listed this robust, North American mint as "Purple Monarda" in *The American Gardener's Calendar* (1806). While not as showy as its crimson-flowered cousin, *Monarda didyma,* this species is less susceptible to powdery mildew, which often blights late-season perennials. Settlers noted wild bergamot quite early, and plants were sent to Europe by 1656. Native Americans used the roots to make a decoction for stomach pain. The leaves of bergamot add a distinct flavor to foods and drinks, such as Earl Grey tea.

HARDINESS ZONES 3 TO 9

1783: BGB, "Monarda didima"
1790: WF, "Bergamot"
1800: HM, "Wild Bergamot"
1804: BM, "*M. fistulosa* Purple Bee Balm"
1810: WB, "Monarda Scarlet lion's tail . . . White ditto . . . Purple ditto"

MUSCARI COMOSUM (L.) MILL.

ASPARAGUS FAMILY

Syn. Hyacinthus comosus L.; Leopoldia comosa (L.) Parl.

◊ Tassel Hyacinth

Muscari comosum, commonly called tassel hyacinth, is native to the Mediterranean region (southern Europe, Asia Minor, and northern Africa). Species plants grow eight to twelve inches tall and produce large conical racemes in early spring of urn-shaped, grape-like, drooping, olive brown/yellow fertile flowers that are topped by unusual tassel-like plumes of rounded, violet-purple, sterile flowers. The specific epithet means "with a tuft"—a tuft of sterile flowers in this case.

HARDINESS ZONES 4 TO 8

1806: BM, "*Hyacinthus comosus* Two-coloured Hyacinth"

MUSCARI COMOSUM 'PLUMOSUM' L.

ASPARAGUS FAMILY

◊ "Feathered Hyacinth"

TJ 1767, 1791

Feathered hyacinth, which is native to the Mediterranean region, has been in cultivation since 1612. Jefferson noted it blooming on April 25, 1767, at his boyhood home, Shadwell. His son-in-law Thomas Mann Randolph Jr. mentioned its blooming time in a letter to Jefferson in 1791. Philadelphia nurseryman Bernard McMahon forwarded bulbs to Jefferson in 1812 for planting along the flower borders at Monticello. Today the tassel hyacinth (*Muscari comosum*), the species form, has spread throughout the gardens and south orchard at Monticello. This hardy, late spring flowering bulb bears feathery plumes of mineral-violet flowers resembling puffs of cotton candy.

HARDINESS ZONES 4 TO 8

1793: JS, "Feathered Hyacinths"
1800: HM, "Feathered Hyacinths"
1806: BM, "*Hyacinthus monstrosus* Monstrous or Feathered Hyacinth"

NARCISSUS SPP.

AMARYLLIS FAMILY

Jefferson was never very specific about the types of daffodils he grew, but the second entry on the first page of his Garden Book, dated April 6, 1766, read, "Narcissus and Puckoon open." The following year, on March 23, 1767, he noted "Purple Hyacinth & Narcissus bloom." The early date of this entry suggests one of the early species, such as *Narcissus pseudonarcissus* or Lent lily. In 1782 he also charted the flowering of narcissus species over a longer period: from mid-March through mid-May. In 1812 he directed his daughter Martha to have the enslaved gardener Wormley Hughes bring "some of the hardy bulbous roots" divided from Monticello to his retreat home at Poplar Forest, including "daffodils, jonquils, Narcissuses, flags & lillies of different kinds, refuse hyacinths E[t]c."

The following historic varieties are possibilities for narcissus, jonquils, and daffodils grown by Jefferson.

Narcissus bulbocodium, Hoop-petticoat Daffodil: A diminutive daffodil species native to the Mediterranean, with grass-like leaves and trumpet-shaped flowers.

Narcissus jonquilla, Jonquil: Cultivated since the 1700s, it is native to Spain and Portugal and has naturalized throughout Europe and the southeastern United States.

Narcissus × medioluteus, Twin Sisters Daffodil: A fragrant, late-blooming variety with white petals and a short, citron-yellow cup. Flowers are held in pairs on each stem. Also known as cemetery ladies, loving couples, April beauty, and primrose peerless. According to John Gerard's 1597 herbal, this narcissus was generally widespread in the English countryside.

Narcissus obvallaris, Tenby Daffodil: This small yellow daffodil was introduced to cultivation by 1613 and is now naturalized in parts of Wales. It is known as a vigorous grower and was being used in American gardens by the end of the eighteenth century.

Narcissus × *odorus* 'Plenus', Double Campernelle: A sixteenth-century European variety and an early introduction to America. Thought to be a natural hybrid between jonquil (*N. jonquilla*) and the Lent lily (*N. pseudonarcissus*).

Narcissus poeticus, Pheasant's Eye Daffodil: Grows wild in mountain meadows from France into Greece. It has grown in Britain since Roman times and in America since the 1600s.

Narcissus pseudonarcissus, Lent Lily: Species native to western Europe from Spain to Portugal, east to Germany, and north to England and Wales. Often found at old homesites in the United States, this species was documented as early as 1753 in the Upland Gardens of Bethabara, a Moravian village in North Carolina.

HARDINESS ZONES 3 TO 9

NICOTIANA ALATA LINK & OTTO

NIGHTSHADE FAMILY

Flowering Tobacco, Jasmine Tobacco

Flowering tobacco, also referred to as night-scented tobacco, is a self-sowing, summer- and fall-blooming annual or perennial that bears fragrant white flowers that open only in the evening or during the cooler parts of the day. The aromatic flowers attract hummingbirds as well as moths that pollinate at night. A native of Brazil and Argentina, flowering tobacco was introduced into garden cultivation in England in 1829.

HARDINESS ZONES 10 TO 11

NIGELLA DAMASCENA L.

BUTTERCUP FAMILY

Love-in-a-Mist

Love-in-a-mist has been cultivated in gardens since the late sixteenth century. This self-seeding, cool-season annual produces handsome blue, white, or pink flowers amidst the delicate, lacy foliage. The unusual balloon-shaped, striped seed capsules add interest to the garden and dried arrangements. Thomas Jefferson sowed a related species, nutmeg flower (*Nigella sativa*), in an oval flower bed at Monticello on April 18, 1810.

1760: JT, "nigella"
1800: HM, "Love in a Mist, 2 sorts"
1802, 1806: BMB and BM, "Love in a Mist"
1810: WB, "Nigella, blue-flowered"

NIGELLA SATIVA L.

BUTTERCUP FAMILY

◊ "Nutmeg Plant," Nigella, Black Caraway, Black Cumin

TJ 1810

Seeds of "Nutmeg Plant" were planted in a Monticello oval bed in 1810. Also called black cumin and fennel flower, this hardy annual has been grown for centuries for the aromatic seed, which has many culinary and medicinal uses. Nutmeg plant bears feathery, finely cut leaves and delicate white to pale blue flowers.

HARDINESS ZONES 5 TO 10

1790: WF, "Nutmeg (Indian)"
1826: O&L, "Coriander"

PAEONIA LACTIFLORA PALL.

PEONY FAMILY

Syn. Paeonia albiflora Pall.
Chinese peony, herbaceous peony

This herbaceous perennial flowering plant is native to central and eastern Asia, from Tibet to eastern Siberia. When first introduced to Europe in the mid-eighteenth century it was known as the white peony, but it has been grown as an ornamental in China since the seventh century. Several mid-nineteenth century horticultural varieties have been on display in the Monticello gardens and were likely planted soon after the garden restoration.

'Duchesse de Nemours': The extremely fragrant and unusual 'Duchesse de Nemours' was introduced by 1856, although some believe it was earlier. Flowers bear large, cupped, white guard petals and light canary-yellow center petals, which are pale green at the base.

Felix Crousse' bears fragrant, double, brilliant ruby-red flowers with a silky luster in late spring. This variety was introduced in 1881.

'Festiva Maxima': This classic peony bears large, fragrant, double white flowers with prominent crimson flakes on a few central petals. It was introduced in 1831.

HARDINESS ZONES 3 TO 8

1806: BM, "*Paeonia albiflora* White-flowered Peony"

PAEONIA OFFICINALIS L.

PEONY FAMILY

◊ "Piony," Peony

TJ 1771, 1782

The ancient common or European peony, *Paeonia officinalis,* has been cultivated for centuries and has been found in the gardens of France and Britain, where it was grown in the medicinal gardens of monasteries since the sixteenth century. The genus name derives from the Greek name for Paeon, the physician of the gods and reputed discoverer of the medicinal properties of plants in this genus. Philadelphia nurseryman John Bartram sent several peonies to the botanical garden of Elizabeth and Thomas Lamboll of Charleston, South Carolina, in 1761, and Thomas Jefferson was most likely referring to the European peony when he noted "Piony" in a list of hardy perennials as early as 1771. This species was also included in the "Calendar of the bloom of flowers in 1782." Compared to the Asian sorts, European peony is a smaller perennial with soft, medium green foliage, and it comes into bloom earlier in the spring.

The variety 'Rosea Plena' has been in cultivation since at least 1613. 'Rubra Plena' has been documented since at least 1581 and is considered the first peony variety in American gardens, specifically in New England and the Middle Atlantic states.

HARDINESS ZONES 3 TO 8

1806: BM, "Common Peony" (listed as a tuberous rooted flowering plant)
1810: WB, "Paeonea Double red piony"

PAPAVER RHOEAS L.

POPPY FAMILY

◊ "Dwarf Poppy," "Lesser Poppy," Corn Poppy, Common Poppy
TJ 1767, 1807

Seed of "Papaver Rhoeas flor. Plen. Double poppy" was planted in an oval flower bed at Monticello in 1807. This was a double form of the common European field poppy, which was later immortalized in Flanders during World War I. This also is likely the "dwarf" or "lesser" poppy Jefferson observed blooming at Shadwell in 1767 and perhaps the "poppy" he found suitable for naturalizing in the shrubbery in 1771.

HARDINESS ZONES 3 TO 10

1790: WF, "Poppy"
1800: HM, "Poppys, 2 Sorts"
1806: BM, "Double Dwarf, Corn Poppy"
1810: WB, "Poppy"

PAPAVER SOMNIFERUM L.

POPPY FAMILY

◊ "White Poppy," "larger Poppy," Breadseed Poppy, Carnation Poppy
TJ 1812

Seed of "white poppy" was planted along the winding walk flower border in April 1812. This was one of the numerous hardy cool-season annuals to grace the flower gardens in late May and early June, before the heat of high summer. It is native to southeastern Europe and western Asia and had been cultivated as an ornamental in America prior to 1750. Flower colors range from white to deep rose and scarlet red.

Hardiness zones 3 to 8

1736: WBII, "Poppy"
1760: JT, "carnation poppy"

1800: HM, "Poppys, 2 Sorts"
1806: BM, "Double Carnation Poppy," "White Poppy"
1810: WB, "Poppy"

PELARGONIUM INQUINANS (L.) L'HÉR.

GERANIUM FAMILY
◊ Scarlet Geranium
TJ 1803, 1807

Imported from South Africa into Britain by the early 1700s, this species geranium was an exciting novelty that became one of the parents of our modern bedding geraniums. It is thought to be the species grown by Jefferson in the President's House. Prior to his retirement, Margaret Bayard Smith, a Washington socialite, asked for a geranium he was growing, and Jefferson replied: "It is in very bad condition, having been neglected latterly, as not intended to be removed . . . if plants have sensibility, as the analogy of their organisation with ours seems to indicate, it cannot but be proudly sensible of her fostering attentions." It bears velvety green foliage studded with clusters of bright scarlet flowers throughout the year.

HARDINESS ZONES 10 TO 11

1790: WF, "Geranium"
1793: MC, "Gerenium"
1810: WB, "Scarlet flowered Geranium"

PENTAPETES PHOENICEA L.

MALLOW FAMILY
◊ "Scarlet Mallow," Noon Flower
TJ 1811

On March 22, 1811, Jefferson wrote: "Pentapetes Phoenicia. Scarlet Mallow. Outer flower border. S. W. quarter." The seed for this planting along Monticello's winding flower walk undoubtedly came from Bernard McMahon, who included this obscure flower in the appendix of his *Calendar* (1806) as "Scarlet-flowered Pentapetes," but it is curiously absent from other period sources. It was introduced to the West before 1700, and an unusual hand-colored engraving by Jakob Christoph Keller appeared in Christoph Jakob Trew's *Plantae Rariores* (1763). Liberty Hyde Bailey's *The Standard Cyclopedia of Horticulture* (1935) briefly described it as a "tender annual, widely distributed in tropical Asia," and added that it was "rare in gardens."[40] The modern edition of *Hortus Third* (1976) omits *Pentapetes* completely. Despite the dearth of information, the scarlet mallow made its way back to Monticello thanks to a horticultural friend from Texas, who saw the flower on one of his plant-hunting excursions. He recognized it as a little-known Jefferson species and sent us seeds, in true "pass-along" fashion. Its genus name, from the

Greek meaning "having five leaves," refers to the five-petalled arrangement of its attractive red flowers, which open at noon and close the following morning, hence the name noon flower. The name *phoenicea* means scarlet. Once the season warms, its growth competes easily with the magnificent prince's feather, but its habit is more solidly pyramidal and erect. For a true annual, it is amazingly woody, with a strong, olive-brown central stem contrasting nicely with the long, deeply lobed leaves.

1806: BM, "Scarlet-flowered Pentapetes"
1810: WB, "Pentapetes, Scarlet-flowering"

PHLOX DIVARICATA L.

PHLOX FAMILY

Wild Blue Phlox

This North American species was introduced to British and European gardens as *Phlox canadensis* in 1746. Bernard McMahon listed it as the "early flowering phlox" in his 1806 *Calendar.* In *The American Flower Garden Directory* (1839), nurseryman, florist, and author Robert Buist considered the American genus phlox to be one of the most handsome in cultivation. Buist included the wild sweet William among the species he considered the finest. The flowers are attractive to butterflies.

HARDINESS ZONES 3 TO 8
1793: JS, "wild sweet William"
1806: BM, "early flowering phlox"

PHLOX PANICULATA L. (1753) OR PHLOX SUBULATA

POLEMONIUM FAMILY

◊ "Sawpit Phlox," Garden Phlox
TJ, ca. 1806-9

The identification of the "sawpit phlox" on an undated list of flowers in Jefferson's hand is uncertain. It may be one of the native North American phlox species that were developed into common garden varieties during the nineteenth and twentieth centuries. Curtis's *Botanical Magazine,* the premier British magazine for early botanical illustrations, presented numerous phlox illustrations, such as the "Hairy Phlox, Lychnidae."[41] Bernard McMahon included fourteen species of phlox, or "Lychnadea," in *The American Gardener's Calendar* (1806). Another candidate could be *Silene caroliniana,* a member of the dianthus family with rose-pink flowers that is commonly known as Carolina campion or sticky catchfly. This species is a rare occurrence in areas of the Monticello landscape.

HARDINESS ZONES 3 TO 9
1806: BM, "*Phlox subulata* Awl-shaped Phlox"

PHYSALIS ALKEKENGI L.

NIGHTSHADE FAMILY

Syn. Alkekengi officinarum Moench
◊ "European Winter Cherry," Chinese Lantern, Bladder Cherry
TJ 1807

This hardy species is native from southern Europe to northern Asia and Japan and was documented in European gardens as early as 1548. It is a member of the nightshade family, which includes the tomato, and is also known as Japanese lantern, bladder cherry, strawberry tomato, and winter cherry. In 1807, Thomas Jefferson listed in his Garden Book: "Physalis Alkekengi—European winter cherry," and he devoted an entire oval flower bed to this curious species. Jefferson's source may have been Bernard McMahon, who included "Physalis Alkekengi-European Winter-Cherry" in his 1806 *Calendar.* The fruits were once regarded as edible and of some medicinal value. The showy, bright orange-red ornamental seeds, which resemble paper lanterns, appear in late summer and are popular in dried flower arrangements.

HARDINESS ZONES 3 TO 9

1739–40: JC/PC, "Ground Cherry"
1802, 1806: BMB and BM, "Alkekengi-European Winter-Cherry"
1826: O&L, "Alkekendi or kite flower"

PODOPHYLLUM PELTATUM L.

BARBERRY FAMILY
◊ "May Apple," Mayapple
TJ, ca. 1806-9

This North American spring-flowering perennial carpets large areas of the Monticello woodlands with broad, dark green leaves that resemble parasols. The mayapple was noted on an undated list of cultivated flowers and was another of Jefferson's collection of native botanical species. Margaret Bayard Smith described Jefferson's plans for the grounds of the President's House in *The First Forty Years of Washington Society* (1906): "It was Mr. Jefferson's design to have planted them exclusively with Trees, shrubs and flowers indigenous to our native soil. He had a long list made out in which they were arranged according to their forms and colours and the seasons in which they flourished."[42] The fruits, which form in May, also give it the common names hog apple and wild lemon. Mayapples are associated with rich forests from western Quebec south to Florida and Texas and occur abundantly throughout the forests of Monticello. Its fruit is food for wildlife (but the leaves, roots, and unripe fruit are poisonous to humans).

HARDINESS ZONES 3 TO 8

1806: BM, "*Podophyllum peltatum* May Apple"

POLIANTHES TUBEROSA L.

◊ See Agave amica (Medik.) Thiede & Govaerts

POLYGONUM ORIENTALE L.

KNOTWEED FAMILY
Syn. Persicaria orientalis (L.) Spach
Tall Persicary, Prince's Feather

The earliest date documenting this Asian polygonum in America is 1736–37. That was the year Peter Collinson sent seeds to the Quaker botanist John Bartram of Philadelphia and to Williamsburg's John Custis. In a letter to Bartram, Collinson wrote, "Inclosed, is some seed of a noble annual,—grows six or seven feet high, and makes a beautiful show with its long bunches of red flowers. . . . It is called the great oriental Persicaria." In 1792, William Curtis's *Botanical Magazine* contained one of the first color illustrations and described the tall persicary: "The present well-known native of the East . . . is the principal one cultivated in our gardens for ornament, and is distinguished not less for its superior stature than the brilliancy of its flowers; it will frequently grow to the height of eight or ten feet, and become a formidable rival to the gigantic sun-flower. . . . [It] produces [an] abundance of seed, which, falling on the borders, generally comes up spontaneously . . . but it is most commonly sown in the spring with other annuals. . . . This plant requires very little care, and will bear the smoke of London better than many others."[43]

Hardiness zones 7 to 10

1736–37: PC to JC, "Oriental Persicary"
1802, 1806: BMB and BM, "Persicaria"

PRIMULA AURICULA L.

PRIMROSE FAMILY

◊ Auricula
TJ 1767, 1786, 1807, 1809, 1811, 1812, 1813

Bernard McMahon sent "6 pots of Auriculas, different kinds" to Monticello in 1812. The species auricula, also known as "bear's ear," is an alpine flower that was known by the Romans. The garden auricula was much improved over its wild Swiss ancestor and much admired by McMahon, who included detailed descriptions of the character and culture of what was considered a choice pot plant in his *Calendar* (1806). McMahon also gave directions for displaying the plants on greenhouse shelves, the proper compost including "One twenty-fourth, ashes of burned vegetables," and devoted an entire page to the "Properties of a fine Variegated Auricula."[44] The auricula primrose is a hardy, spring-flowering perennial with umbels of large, flat, richly colored flowers ranging from maroon-carmine, coral pink, and deep orange to deep maroon with primrose yellow centers.

HARDINESS ZONES 3 TO 8

1793: MC, "Auricula"
1799, 1800: GF, "Auricula"
1800: HM, "Double Primula"
1802, 1806: BMB and BM, "Garden Auricula"

PRIMULA × *POLYANTHA* L.

PRIMROSE FAMILY

◊ Polyanthus
TJ 1806, 1812

In 1812 Bernard McMahon sent "a beautiful polyanthus" to Monticello. The polyanthus was another improved early nineteenth-century flower and was the result of the cross between the yellow English primrose (*Primula vulgaris*) and a red form of the English cowslip (*P. veris*). McMahon's directions for the culture of the polyanthus were as detailed as for the auricula, and there was much interest in displaying the most fanciful colored flowers in pots.

HARDINESS ZONES 3 TO 8

1800: HM, "Double Polyanthus Primrose"
1810: WB, "Polyanthus, in varieties, Double Polyanthus or hose-in-hose"

PRIMULA VULGARIS HUDS.

PRIMROSE FAMILY

◊ Common Primrose

TJ 1771

When Jefferson listed the primrose among the "hardy perennial flowers" suitable for naturalizing in 1771, he was likely referring to this fragrant, pale yellow-flowering native of the woodlands of Britain and southern Europe to western Asia. The flowers of this spring-blooming perennial are formed on short slender stems from the center of the basal rosette of semi-evergreen leaves.

HARDINESS ZONES 3 TO 8

1790: WF, "primrose"
1800: HM, "Double Cowslip Primrose"
1806: BM, "Common European Primrose"
1810: WB, "Double purple primrose"

PUNICA GRANATUM L.

LYTHRUM FAMILY

◊ Pomegranate

TJ 1769

Pomegranates are an ancient fruit thought to have originated in Afghanistan and Iran and introduced to America by the Spanish in the late sixteenth century. Jefferson's early plans for a fruitery on the south slope of Monticello included pomegranates, which were planted 12½ feet apart in a row "in the hollow" on March 14, 1769. Because pomegranates are marginally hardy, this was likely a failed experiment. An ornamental, double-flowering, non-fruiting pomegranate (*Punica granatum* 'Flore Pleno') is on display in an East Front oval flower bed.

HARDINESS ZONES 8 TO 10

1806: BM, "common pomegranate" (a **"Greenhouse Tree and Shrub"**)

PULMONARIA OFFICINALIS L.

BORAGE FAMILY

Common Lungwort

Lungwort is an herbaceous perennial native to Britain and Europe and has been in cultivation since the fifteenth century. It was used as a potherb and was once thought to be good for the lungs because the spotting on the foliage gives the leaf the appearance of a human lung. (This notion was founded on the principle of the "doctrine of signatures.") Lungwort formerly found a place in almost every garden, and it was held in great esteem for its reputed medicinal qualities in diseases of the lungs. It flowers in early spring and grows well in partial shade.

HARDINESS ZONES 3 TO 9

1735: PC/ JC, "Jerusalem Cowslip"

RANUNCULUS ASIATICUS FLORA PLENA L.

BUTTERCUP FAMILY

◊ Persian Buttercup

TJ 1807

Like the other bulbs planted in the 1807 oval bed scheme, the ranunculuses were at least immediately successful. By 1812, however, Jefferson ordered more from Bernard McMahon, which suggests that these tender bulbs were not lifted and properly stored during the winter months.

HARDINESS ZONES 8 TO 11

1741: JC/PC, "ranunculus"
1786: PC&Co., "double ranunculus, 400 sorts"
1792: MC, "Fine mixed ranunculus"
1793: JS, "12 ranunculus"
1799: GF, "Ranunculus"
1800: HM, "Ranunculus-double"
1802, 1806: BMB and BM, "Double Persian," "many varieties" and "Double Bulbous Crowfoot"
1810: WB, "Persian ranunculus, in varieties"

RESEDA ODORATA L.

MIGNONETTE FAMILY

◊ Garden Mignonette

TJ 1803, 1811

Mignonette was introduced to ornamental gardens in Europe about 1725, and because of its sweet fragrance, its popularity both as a garden plant and as a cut flower grew steadily on both sides of the Atlantic through the nineteenth century. In 1803 Jefferson's granddaughter Anne Cary Randolph wrote to her grandfather that "we were so unfortunate as to lose the Mignonett entirely although Mama divided it between Mrs. Lewis Aunt Jane & herself but none of it seeded." Jefferson recorded sowing seeds at Monticello on March 22, 1811. The tiny, pale green and white flowers emit a fresh, fruity scent in summer and are attractive to bees and butterflies.

HARDINESS ZONES 5 TO 11

1790: WF, "Mignonette"
1793: JS, "Mignonette"
1799, 1800: GF, "Mignonette"
1800: HF, "Mignonette, 1 oz."
1802, 1806: BMB and BM, "Mignonette"

ROBINIA HISPIDA L.

BEAN FAMILY

◊ "Red Locust," Prickly Locust, Moss Locust, Rose Acacia

TJ 1807, 1816, 1817

Jefferson's planting schemes for shrubbery clumps at Monticello in 1807 and at Poplar Forest in 1816 included this deciduous shrub, native to the southeastern United States. Commonly called bristly or moss locust, the shrub grows eight feet wide and ten feet high, bearing showy pendulous clusters of pink or purplish pealike flowers in early summer on arching, bristly (hispid) stems. The Cherokee were known to have used the root medicinally for toothaches. In 1807 Jefferson purchased *Robinia* from the Thomas Main Nursery in Georgetown and sent plants to Poplar Forest for the oval planting beds on the north of the house.

HARDINESS ZONES 6 TO 10

1783: BGB, "*Robinia villosa,* Peach Blossom Acacia"
1790: William Prince Nursery, Long Island, NY, "dwarf acacia with red flowers"
1802, 1806: BMB and BM, "Rose Acacia"

ROSA / ROSES

See appendix B.

RUDBECKIA HIRTA L.

ASTER FAMILY
Black-eyed Susan

This showy, long-blooming wildflower is native to a range of soil types in meadows, open woods, and thickets from New York south to Florida and west to Missouri. It was introduced to European gardens as early as 1714. This self-seeding, biennial species is resistant to deer and has long been recognized as a worthy garden plant. The flowers are good for cutting and attract a range of butterflies, native bees, and other pollinators; the seeds are later enjoyed by songbirds.

HARDINESS ZONES 3 TO 9

1806: BM, "*Rudbeckia hirta* Rough Rudbeckia"

SALVIA COCCINEA BUC'HOZ EX ETL.

MINT FAMILY
Texas Sage, Scarlet Sage

Texas or scarlet sage is native across the southern United States, from Florida to Texas. It has been grown as a self-seeding ornamental annual in North American gardens since the mid- nineteenth century. The spreading plants reach two to three feet and, from midsummer until the first frost in autumn, they produce slender spikes of scarlet flowers that are highly attractive to hummingbirds.

HARDINESS ZONES 8 TO 10

SALVIA VIRIDIS L.

MINT FAMILY
Syn. Salvia horminum
Horminum Sage, Annual Clary Sage

Horminum sage is a hardy annual native to the Mediterranean region. Grown in Britain as an ornamental in the sixteenth century, horminum sage was cultivated in American gardens as early as 1761, when it appeared on a plant list for a Moravian farm in North Carolina. Compact plants form spikes of colorful bracts in hues of pink, blue, and purple, which make long-lasting cut flowers.

HARDINESS ZONES 5 TO 9

1759: MGB, "Horminum"
1810: WB, "Horminum"

SANGUINARIA CANADENSIS L.

POPPY FAMILY

◊ "Puckoon," Bloodroot

TJ 1766

This North American ephemeral wildflower grows along the northern slopes and river bottoms of Monticello. Jefferson observed it blooming on April 6, 1766, calling it "Puckoon," a name used by Indigenous Americans. He watched its spring progression along with narcissus, Virginia bluebells, and purple flag iris. By April 13, its flowers had fallen. Bloodroot was introduced to Europe by 1680, and early American botanist John Bartram collected specimens and sent them to his European patrons. Although the roots can be poisonous, they were prescribed as a headache remedy. The sap from the roots produced a red dye.

HARDINESS ZONES 3 TO 8

1810: WB, "Canadian puccoo"

SAPONARIA OFFICINALIS L.

DIANTHUS FAMILY

◊ Common Soapwort

TJ, ca. 1806–9

This robust perennial was listed on an undated manuscript of cultivated flowers. Philip Miller said it was "a plant of no great Beauty; and being a very great Runner in Gardens, has been almost excluded from all curious Gardens; but as it is a Plant which requires very little Culture, it may be admitted to have a Place in some abject Part of the Garden."[45] Bernard McMahon listed both the single and double flowering forms. The soapwort, like the daylily, perennial pea, and other aggressive early introductions into American flower gardens, is a common escape from cultivation today.

HARDINESS ZONES 3 TO 8

1800: HM
1802, 1806: BMB and BM, "Field Burnet" and *S. officinalis plena* "Double Soapwort"
1810: WB, "Double soap-wart"

SCABIOSA ATROPURPUREA L.

HONEYSUCKLE FAMILY

◊ "Mourning Bride," Pincushion Flower

TJ 1811

When Thomas Jefferson requested roots of the "Mourning bride" from his friend and neighbor Isaac Coles in 1811, he may have been referring to the pincushion flower. The plant is also known as scabiosa, because of its skin-healing medicinal qualities, and mourning bride, because of its association with grieving widows in eighteenth-century England. The dark purple "Sweet Scabious" was documented as a hardy annual in Europe as early as 1629 and was sold by Bernard McMahon in 1804.

HARDINESS ZONES 3 TO 11

1793: JS, "Sweet Scabios"
1802, 1806: BMB and BM, "Purple Sweet Scabious"
1810: HM, "Pincushion Flower, 2 sorts"
1810: WB, "Sweet scabius"
1826: O&L, "Purple Scabius"

SCILLA SIBERICA HAW.

ASPARAGUS FAMILY

Siberian Squill

This hardy, early spring–flowering bulb is native to southern Russia, the Caucasus, and Turkey and has naturalized throughout central Europe. It has been known in cultivation since 1796 and became popular in rockeries during the late nineteenth century. Tiny, metallic-blue flowers with violet anthers appear on four-to-six-inch stems. Siberian squill is naturalized in an East Front oval flower bed at Monticello.

HARDINESS ZONES 4 TO 8

SILENE ARMERIA L. OR SILENE CAROLINIANA WALTER

DIANTHUS FAMILY

Syn. Atocion armeria (L.) Raf.
◊ Sweet William Catchfly, Lobel's Catchfly
TJ 1791

Jefferson's son-in-law Thomas Mann Randolph wrote to Jefferson from Monticello on April 30, 1791, with a detailed account of the blooming time for plants including "Silene" on April 4. Sweet William catchfly, *Silene armeria,* is a showy, self-seeding annual flower native to Europe with blue-green leaves and a long succession of purplish-pink flowers from late spring into summer. Sometimes called Lobel's catchfly or none-so-pretty, it was established in American gardens by the 1820s. The 1804 broadside of Philadelphia nurseryman Bernard McMahon offered seed for both red and white forms. The early April flowering date, however, suggests the "silene" that Thomas Mann Randolph reported could have been a native species, *S. caroliniana* Walter, commonly called Carolina campion, sticky catchfly, and wild pink.

HARDINESS ZONES 5 TO 8

1760: JT, "catch fly"
1804, 1806: BMB and BM, "Lobel's Catchfly"
1806: BM, "*Silene virginica* Virginian Catchfly"

SISYRINCHIUM ANGUSTIFOLIUM MILL.

IRIS FAMILY

◊ "[A] little blue flower from woods Bermudian," Blue-eyed Grass
TJ, ca. 1806-9

Jefferson included "a little blue flower from woods Bermudian" on an undated list of cultivated flowers. This delicate, spring-flowering perennial bears bright blue-violet flowers with a yellow eye on stalks above the stiff, upright, sword-shaped leaves. This member of the iris family is found in the Monticello woodlands on the north slope of the mountain.

HARDINESS ZONES 4 TO 9

1793: JS, "Bermudian (see Sizranchium) the blue flower with grasslooking stalks"
1806: BM, three species listed, including the "Bermudian Sisyrinchium"

SOLANUM PSEUDOCAPSICUM L.

NIGHTSHADE FAMILY
◊ Jerusalem Cherry
TJ 1808

On April 21, 1808, Ellen Wayles Randolph wrote to her grandfather from Edgehill: "I have got the seed of the Jerusalem Cherry which I am told is very pretty." This shrubby plant is native to Bolivia, Brazil, and other parts of South America. It was introduced to Europe as a greenhouse evergreen in the late sixteenth century. Presently this tender plant is generally regarded as a cheery houseplant with its showy red berries, which are inedible and can be toxic.

HARDINESS ZONES 8 TO 10

1790: WF
1806: BM, "Shrubby winter Cherry"

SOLIDAGO GLOMERATA MICHX.

ASTER FAMILY
◊ Clustered Goldenrod "of Bartram"
TJ 1805

In a letter from 1805, the botanist Benjamin Smith Barton identified several goldenrod and aster species that Jefferson had sent to him in Philadelphia, including the "Solidago glomerata of Bartram." Jefferson had received the specimens from William Dunbar, a Scottish-born American scientist and explorer who helped Jefferson plan some of the first expeditions into the newly purchased Louisiana Territory. The specimens had been collected along the Washita River, a tributary of the Red River in Oklahoma.

HARDINESS ZONES 5 TO 8

SOLIDAGO ODORA AITON

ASTER FAMILY
Syn. Solidago suaveolens
◊ Sweet-scented or Anise-scented Goldenrod "of NJ"
TJ 1805

Native from New Hampshire to Florida and west to Texas, this showy, fragrant-leaved perennial goldenrod is well-behaved and does not spread aggressively like others of its genus. It was included as *Solidago anisatum* in a list of plants "sent to Europe for Mr. Pierepont by John and Wm. Bartram, Philadelphia, October 1784." In 1805, Thomas Jefferson asked botanist and physician Benjamin Smith Barton to identify several plants sent to him from an expedition up the Washita River in Texas and Oklahoma; Barton identified one of the plants as "Solidago suaveolens: The Sweet-scented or Anise-seed, golden rod of New Jersey." A deer-resistant plant, the flowers attract butterflies, bees, and many other beneficial insects.

HARDINESS ZONES 4 TO 10

SPREKELIA FORMOSISSIMA (L.) HERB.

◊ "AMARYLLIS FORMOSISSIMA," JACOBEAN LILY
TJ 1807

Bernard McMahon sent six bulbs of the "Amaryllis formosissima" to Monticello in 1807. The flower of this tender bulb can be compared to a stunning scarlet insect—and even resembles the flower of the bird-of-paradise. It was described by McMahon as "very admirable," "of extraordinary beauty," and "making a most beautiful and grand appearance."[46]

In a letter dated April 2, 1807, accompanying the bulbs McMahon sent from Philadelphia, he wrote, "In the small box I send you 24 roots Double Tuberoses and 6 roots of the Amarylis formosissima; for the management of these, see pages 349 & 350 of my work on Gardening [i.e., *The American Gardener's Calendar* (1806)]."[47]

HARDINESS ZONES 8 TO 11

1790: WF, "Jacobin Lilley"
1800: HM, "Sprekelia f."
1806: BM, "*Amaryllis formosissima* Jacobea Lily"

STERNBERGIA LUTEA (L.) KER GAWL. EX SPRENG.

AMARYLLIS FAMILY
Yellow Autumn Daffodil, Winter Daffodil

This native of southeastern Europe and the Middle East has been known by a variety of names since it first came into cultivation in the late sixteenth century, including autumn daffodil, winter daffodil, and yellow amaryllis. The bulb was among the plants that Williamsburg's John Custis received from Peter Collinson, the wealthy English Quaker woolen merchant and patron of early American naturalists, including John Clayton and John Bartram.

HARDINESS ZONES 7 TO 9

1739–40: PC to JC, "Autumn Narciss with a yellow Crocus Like flower"
1793: JS, "Yellow Autumnal Amaryllis Daffodils"

SULLA CORONARIA (L.) MEDIK.

BEAN FAMILY
Syn. Hedysarum coronarium L.
◊ "Sulla," "Spanish St. Foin," French Honeysuckle
TJ 1786

On May 6, 1786, Jefferson wrote to William Drayton, chair of the South Carolina Society for Promoting Agriculture, accepting membership in that society. He sent Drayton seeds of a southern European grass known as "Sulla," or "Spanish St. foin," saying it was the *Hedysarum coronarium* of Linnaeus. This member of the bean family has clusters of showy, deep rose–colored flowers like wild vetch. In his 1806 *Calendar* Bernard McMahon included "Hedysarums" among the "many beautiful ornamental plants . . . which would grace and embellish the Flower-garden and Pleasure-grounds, if introduced thereinto."[48]

HARDINESS ZONES 8 TO 10

1806: BM, "*Hedysarum coronarium* French Honeysuckle"

SYMPHORICARPOS ALBUS

HONEYSUCKLE FAMILY

◊ Snowberry bush

TJ 1806, 1812

On August 13, 1805, Meriweather Lewis wrote in his journal after crossing the Lemhi Pass in Idaho that he had seen a species of honeysuckle bearing "a globular berry as large as a garden pea and as white as wax."[49] Thomas Jefferson sent seeds of the snowberry that were brought back from the Lewis & Clark Expedition to his nurseryman friend Bernard McMahon. In 1812, McMahon sent Jefferson young plants, saying, "This is a beautiful shrub brought by C. Lewis from the River Columbia, the flower is small but neat, the berries hang in large clusters are of a snow white colour and continue on the shrubs, retaining their beauty, all the winter; especially if kept in a Green House. . . . I have given it the trivial english name of Snowberry-bush."[50]

This shrub became a popular garden novelty in England after seed was first exported in 1817. The tiny pink blossoms form in late spring and are followed by the large white berries that are especially striking after the leaves drop.

HARDINESS ZONES 3 TO 7

1805: L&C, a species of honeysuckle

SWERTIA CAROLINIENSIS (WALTER) KUNTZE

GENTIAN FAMILY

◊ Syn. Frasera caroliniensis

"American Columbo," Yellow Gentian

TJ 1810

On April 18, 1810, Jefferson recorded in his Garden Book, "S. oval bed on S.W. side. American Columbo." Peter Collinson, an early English botanist and sponsor of plant explorer John Bartram, described this rare herbaceous perennial as the "pyramid of Eden" because of its stately two-foot panicle of purple-spotted light green to white flowers. Found in calcareous grasslands and savannas over much of east-central North America, this uncommon species, also known as yellow gentian, is a monocarpic perennial, meaning it flowers once after multiple seasons and then dies.

HARDINESS ZONES 4 TO 8

TAGETES ERECTA L.

ASTER FAMILY

◊ African Marigold ("two kinds of Marigolds")

TJ 1808, 1810

Anne Cary Randolph wrote to her grandfather from Edgehill on January 22, 1808, that "we have plenty of the two kinds of Marigolds that you gave us." She likely was referring to the French and African marigold species, which had been introduced by the Spanish to Europe and northern Africa from South America in the late 1500s. Seeds of the African marigold were planted along the winding walk flower border on April 8, 1810. While double garden forms were common by 1800, the species, or wild form, of African marigold features rare single-petaled yellow flowers, which are illustrated in the *The Herball or Generall Historie of Plants* (1597) by the English herbalist John Gerard.

HARDINESS ZONES 10 TO 11

1760: JT, "Africans"
1799, 1800: GF
1802, 1806: BMB and BM, "Double Lemon African Marigold," "Double Orange African Marigold," "Double Orange Quilled Marigold"
1806: BM, "*Tagetes erecta,* v. fl. pleno Double African Marigold," "*T. erecta* v. *fistulosa* Quilled African Marigold"

TAGETES PATULA L.

◊ FRENCH MARIGOLD

TJ 1808

Both French and African marigolds originated in South America and were introduced in England and Europe by the Spanish after a circuitous route through north Africa and the coast of France. Anne Cary Randolph wrote to her grandfather on January 22, 1808, that she had saved seed of various annuals, including "the two kinds of Marigolds that you gave us." This suggests that both species of *Tagetes,* the French and African marigolds, were being grown at Monticello. A distinctive red-and-yellow-striped form of the French marigold was illustrated in Curtis's *Botanical Magazine* in 1791 and listed as "Striped French Marigold" by Jean Skipwith at Prestwould plantation in 1793.

HARDINESS ZONES 10 TO 11

1793: JS, "Striped French Marigold"
1799: GF, "French Marigold"
1800: HM, "French Marigold, 4 Sorts"
1802: BMB, "Double French Marigold," "Sweet Scented Marigold"
1806: BM, "*Tagetes patula,* v. fl. pleno Double French Marigold"

TRADESCANTIA VIRGINIANA L.

COMMELINA FAMILY

Virginia Spiderwort

This lushly growing native species with deep to pale blue iris-like flowers was introduced to European gardens by 1629 and named for the famous British plant explorer John Tradescant. One of the earliest mentions in America was made in 1793 by Jean Skipwith of Prestwould plantation. In 1897 Thomas Meehan of Philadelphia described many beautiful color forms, including reddish violet, pale to deep rose, vermilion, carmine, light purple, and white.

HARDINESS ZONES 3 TO 9

1793: JS, "Virginia Spiderwort"
1806: BM, "Virginian Spiderwort"

TRITONIA CROCATA (L.) KER GAWL.

IRIS FAMILY

Syn. Tritonia hyalina L.f.
◊ Flame Freesia

TJ 1812

This South African bulb with bright yellow to orange flowers was sent by Bernard McMahon to Jefferson in 1812. Many plant explorers were engaged to collect South African plants for Kew Gardens in London during the late eighteenth century, and it seems likely that McMahon was the chief American curator for this collection.

HARDINESS ZONES 9 TO 11

1806: BM, six species of Tritonia (under "Greenhouse Bulbous Rooted Plants, &c")

TROLLIUS EUROPAEUS L. OR *TROLLIUS ASIATICUS* L.

BUTTERCUP FAMILY

◊ "Anemone," Globe Flower

TJ 1771

Jefferson included "Trollius=anemone" among the "hardy perennial flowers" suitable for the "Open Ground on the West" in 1771. It is uncertain if he was referring to the European or Asian globeflower, however. Both species are clump-forming members of the buttercup family bearing bright yellow, globe-shaped flowers in spring and are native to damp meadows, moist open woodlands, stream banks, and wet pastures in northern parts of Europe and Asia. The European species is now protected in the wild.

HARDINESS ZONES 3 TO 6

1806: BM, "*Trollium asiaticus* Asiatic Globe-flower"

TROPAEOLUM MAJUS L.

NASTURTIUM FAMILY

◊ "Nasturcium," Nasturtium, Indian Cress

TJ 1774

Jefferson recorded planting "Nasturcium," "Cresses," "Celery," and "Radichio" on March 26, 1774, "in the meadow" (the location of which has not been determined). This is in keeping with the popular use of nasturtium as an edible plant, either by pickling its seeds and flower buds (much like capers) or by using its leaves in salads. Later, however, Jefferson listed "Nasturtium" with other ornamental plants in a "Calendar of the bloom of flowers in 1782" and showed it blooming from July until the end of September. Bernard McMahon sold nasturtium in his 1803 seed list as an "esculent" plant.

HARDINESS ZONES 10 TO 11

1759: MGB, "Nasturtium 'Kaper'"
1790: WF, "Nasturtium"
1793: MC, "Large Nerstertion"
1802, 1806: BMB and BM, "Large Nasturtium"
1810: WB, "Nasturtium large and dwarf"
1825: S&M, "Nasturtium"
1826: O&L, "Nasturtium (fine pickle)"

TULIPA CLUSIANA L.

LILY FAMILY

Lady Tulip

Charles de l'Ecluse (also known as Carolus Clusius), a botany professor at Leiden, was largely responsible for the introduction of tulips from Turkey to Europe beginning around 1570. Lady tulip was later named for him in order to honor his contributions to botany and horticulture. This bulb, a native of Asia Minor, bears small flowers with ivory white petals striped deep pink. It grew in English gardens by 1636 and made its way to the New World shortly thereafter. The story persists that when the Garden Club of Virginia restored the Monticello flower gardens in 1941, lady tulips were brought from Edgehill, a nearby estate and former home of Jefferson's daughter Martha Jefferson Randolph. These bulbs were planted at

Monticello, where they have naturalized and still flower in mid-April.

HARDINESS ZONES 4 TO 10

TULIPA GESNERIANA L.

LILY FAMILY

Garden Tulip

TJ 1782, 1786, 1806, 1807, 1808, 1809, 1811, 1812, 1816

Bernard McMahon regularly sent the "best Tulips of Various kinds," including classic florists' types known as Bizarre, Bybloemen, Rose, Baguet Rigauts, and Primo Baguets. In 1812 McMahon sent "2 Roots Parrot Tulips . . . red, green and yellow mixed," and he instructed that they be "planted as directed in page 528 of my book."[51] The bulbs at Monticello were dug following flowering, stored, and then divided and replanted in the fall. In 1816 Jefferson asked his daughter Martha Randolph to have Wormley Hughes dig and transport "some of the hardy bulbous roots of flowers," including tulips, for planting in the gardens at Poplar Forest. Peter Crouwells & Co. of Philadelphia advertised hundreds of "rare bulbous flowers," including six hundred sorts of hyacinths, twenty-six jonquils, forty double narcissus, four hundred sorts of tulips, four hundred double ranunculus, and six hundred double anemones.

HARDINESS ZONES 3 TO 8

1730s: PC to JC, "double tulips" and "early tulips"
1786: PC&Co, "tulips, 400 sorts"
1790: WF, "tulips"
1792: MC, "mixed tulips"
1793: JS, "6 tulips"
1800: GF, "double tulips"
1800: HM, "best mixed tulips"
1802, 1806: BMB and BM, tulips
1810: WB, "fine striped tulips, in varieties," "early blowing tulips, in varieties," "double tulips, in varieties," "Parrot tulips, in varieties"

TULIPA SYLVESTRIS L.

LILY FAMILY

Florentine Tulip, Woodland Tulip

This diminutive species is a European native introduced very early into American gardens. Although Jefferson did not mention it in his Garden Book, it is now naturalized through the lawns and flower beds at Monticello. It blooms with the Virginia bluebells in mid-April. Florentine tulips bear clear yellow flowers with pointed petals. They have a distinctly sweet fragrance and multiply freely once planted, two qualities lost with the development of modern tulip cultivars.

HARDINESS ZONES 3 TO 8

1806: BM, "Italian Yellow Tulip"

VERBESINA ENCILIOIDES (CAV.) BENTH. & HOOK F. EX A. GRAY

ASTER FAMILY

◊ "Ximensesia Encelioides," Golden Crownbeard

TJ 1811

André Thoüin of the Jardin des Plantes sent seeds of this Mexican annual to Monticello, where it was planted in an oval bed in 1811. Thoüin described it as a "belle grande plante annuelle d'ornement." Although most of the seeds sent from Paris were relayed by Jefferson to American botanical gardens and plantsmen such as Philadelphians Bernard McMahon and William Hamilton of The Woodlands, one laments that so few of these species were documented as actually planted at Monticello. Golden crownbeard is a perennial generally grown as an annual.

HARDINESS ZONES 5 TO 10

VIBURNUM OPULUS 'ROSEUM' L.

VIBURNUM (ADOXA) FAMILY

◊ "Gelder Rose," Snowball Bush

TJ 1794, 1807, 1812

This sterile garden form was known in Europe by 1554 and has been a favorite ever since. The flowers, described in 1770 as "balls of snow, lodged in a pleasing manner all over its head," have inspired other common names such as Whitsun-boss, love-roses, and pincushion-tree. In 1794, Thomas Jefferson included "gelder rose" in his "Objects for the garden this year." On April 16, 1807, Thomas Jefferson planted *Viburnum opulus* 'Roseum' on the "N.W. brow of the slope" of Monticello Mountain. That same day he also planted the species guelder rose or cranberry viburnum (*Viburnum opulus*). Jefferson's "Planting Memorandum for Poplar Forest, 1812" included "Gelder roses" for the banks of the sunken lawn to the south of the house.

HARDINESS ZONES 3 TO 8

1806: BM, "European Guelder Rose, or Snow-ball"
1810: WB, "Gelder-rose"

VIGNA CARACALLA (L.) VERDC.

BEAN FAMILY

Syn. Cochliasanthus caracalla (L.) Trew

◊ Caracalla Bean, Snail Flower, Corkscrew Flower

TJ 1792

The caracalla bean has a long and colorful history in ornamental gardens. On April 1, 1792, Jefferson wrote to Benjamin Hawkins that "the most beautiful bean in the world is the Caracalla bean which, though in England an green-house plant, will grow in the open air in Virginia and Carolina." Also known as snail flower or corkscrew flower, caracalla bean is a tender perennial with highly fragrant, striking purplish-blue and white flowers. Whether Jefferson ever received seeds or plants of this vine is not known. In the 1768 edition of *The Gardeners Dictionary,* Philip Miller described it as "a kidney-bean with twining stalk." Miller expanded on its introduction, stating that it "grows naturally in the Brazils, from whence the seeds were brought to Europe. . . . It is very common in Portugal, where the inhabitants plant it to cover arbours and seats in gardens, for which it is greatly esteemed . . . for its beautiful sweet smelling flowers."[52] Bernard McMahon listed *Phaseolus caracalla* as "twisted-flowered kidney-bean" under the category "Hot-House Herbaceous Perennial Plants" in *The American Gardener's Calendar* (1806). By 1839, Robert Buist described it in *The American Flower Garden Directory* as "a very curious blooming plant, with flowers of a greenish yellow, all spirally twisted, in great profusion when the plant is well grown."[53] Throughout the nineteenth century the flowers were valued by florists for their delicious fragrance and resemblance to orchids. Yet by the early twentieth century, Liberty Hyde Bailey indicated its loss in popularity: "It is an old-fashioned glasshouse plant in cold climates but is now rarely seen."[54]

HARDINESS ZONES 9 TO 11

1806: BM, "Phaseolus caracalla, twisted flowered kidney-bean"

VIOLA TRICOLOR L.

VIOLET FAMILY

◊ "Tricolor," Johnny-jump-up, Heart's-ease, Wild Pansy

TJ 1767

Viola tricolor flourished in American gardens well before 1700, and Thomas Jefferson recorded sowing seeds of "Tricolor" at Shadwell, his boyhood home, on April 1, 1767. Native over large areas of Europe and western Asia, this ancestor of our modern pansy is also known as wild pansy, panse, and heartsease. The name "pansy" is believed to derive from the French word "pensée," an analogy used by Ophelia in Shakespeare's *Hamlet:* "and there is pansies, that's for thoughts." Darker forms, including types with nearly black petals such as 'Black Violet', were selected by the early nineteenth century.

HARDINESS ZONES 4 TO 9

1799, 1800: GF, "Heart's Ease"
1800: HM, "*Viola Tricolor*"
1802, 1806: BMB and BM, "Heart's Ease, Three-coloured Violet"
1826: O&L, "Hearts Ease"

VINCA MINOR L.

DOGBANE FAMILY

◊ Periwinkle

TJ 1771, 1794

Jefferson listed "Periwinkle" among "hardy perennial flowers" for planting in a note dated September 30, 1771, and again as "Perywinkle" in 1794 among a list of "Objects for the garden this year." A native of Europe and western Asia, periwinkle is a hardy trailing plant ideally suited for ground cover in shady areas. Its small, five-petaled flowers are typically shaded purple or blue, but they sometimes show in white.

HARDINESS ZONES 4 TO 9

1810: WB, "Periwinkle"
1806: BM, "Small Periwinkle"

WATSONIA MERIANA (L.) MILL.

IRIS FAMILY

◊ Bulbil Bugle-Lily, Wild Watsonia

TJ 1812

On October 24, 1812, Bernard McMahon sent "6 roots" of this perennial greenhouse bulb from the Cape of Good Hope, adding, "and consequently, with you, belonging to the Green-House department."[55] This ornamental South African bulb has sword-shaped leaves and bears delicate, soft apricot–colored flowers on tall spikes that resemble a bugle. In more temperate climates, including coastal regions of California and Australia, it is considered an invasive species where it has escaped cultivation.

HARDINESS ZONES 8 TO 10

1793: JS, "Mariana. Bulbous, kidney-shaped root, red flower. Well fr. Seed"

WISTERIA FRUTESCENS (L.) POIR.

BEAN FAMILY

Syn. *Clycine frutescens*, *Kraunhia frutescens*, *Kraunhia macrostachya*

◊ "Carolina kidney bean tree with purple flowers," American Wisteria

TJ 1791

The native or American wisteria is a twining, deciduous, woody vine that grows to forty feet or more. It is native primarily to moist thickets, swampy woods, pond peripheries, and stream borders from Virginia to Illinois south to Florida and Texas. In Missouri, *Wisteria frutescens* var. *macrostachya* is found in the far southeastern bootheel area. Fragrant, pea-like, lilac-purple flowers in drooping racemes to six inches long bloom in April and May, after the leaves emerge but before they fully develop. Limited additional summer bloom may occur. Flowers give way to narrow, flattened, smooth seedpods (to five inches long) that ripen in summer. Pods typically split open in fall. Compound, odd-pinnate leaves (each leaf typically with nine to fifteen lance-shaped leaflets) are deep green. American wisteria is not as aggressive a spreader as Chinese wisteria (*W. sinensis*). The genus name honors Caspar Wistar (1761–1818), professor of anatomy at the University of Pennsylvania.

HARDINESS ZONES 5 TO 9

1793: JS, "Carolina Kidney-bean (see Glycine) Winged leaves & blue flowers growing in whorls-2nd sort. Got the seed from G. Skipwith"

YUCCA FILAMENTOSA L.

ASPARAGUS FAMILY

◊ "Beargrass," Yucca, Adam's Needle

TJ 1794

Native to the southeastern United States, *Yucca filamentosa* was introduced to gardens by 1675, and it was then known as silk grass or bear grass. Thomas Jefferson included "Beargrass" in a list of "Objects for the garden" at Monticello in 1794. Fiber obtained from the leaves is one of the strongest native to the United States and was used for basket weaving, binding, fishing nets, clothing, and more. At Monticello, rope made from this species was used in the vineyards for staking and tying up grapevines. The ornamental qualities and exotic appearance of this striking native plant, which bears tall spikes of showy, creamy white, bell-shaped flowers in early summer, were much admired in the late nineteenth and early twentieth centuries.

HARDINESS ZONES 4 TO 10

1735: JC to PC, "silk Grass"
1793: JS, "Bear Grass, Silk Grass"

ZEPHYRANTHES ATAMASCA (L.) HERB.

ACANTHUS FAMILY

◊ "Amaryllis Atamasco L.," Rain Lily, Atamasco Lily

TJ 1812

This native to the southeastern United States grows in swampy forests and coastal prairies, where it prefers acid, boggy soils. "Atamasco" is the Native American name for this species, meaning either "under grass-like leaves" or "stained with red." Bulbs were forwarded by Bernard McMahon to Jefferson at Monticello in 1812. Its large, lily-like white flowers gradually fade to pink in spring.

HARDINESS ZONES 7 TO 10

1793: JS, "Atamasco Lily (see Amaryllis 2nd sort)"

ZINNIA ELEGANS AND *ZINNIA PERUVIANA* (L.) L.

ASTER FAMILY

Syn. *Z. pauciflora* (for *Z. peruviana* [L.] L.)
Zinnia, Peruvian Zinnia

Although zinnias did not become popular garden plants until late in the nineteenth century, *Zinnia peruviana* was grown in eighteenth-century gardens and was sold by Philadelphia nurseryman Bernard McMahon in 1804. This South American annual grows to three or four feet and produces mixed yellow and orange pastel flowers throughout the summer. Its small but attractive flowers are very different from the improved hybrids now so popular.

HARDINESS ZONES 9 TO 11

1800: HM
1802, 1806: BMB and BM, "*Zinnia multiflora* Red Zinnia" "*Zinnia pauciflora* Yellow Zinnia"
1810: WB, "Red flowered, Yellow flowered"

APPENDIX B

JEFFERSON'S ROSES BY DATE OF DOCUMENTATION

ROSA GALLICA OFFICINALIS L.

APOTHECARY'S ROSE
1767, 1782, 1806, 1811–12

The apothecary's rose is a venerable garden plant with a long history, having originated before the time of the ancient Romans. The early herbalists listed it as a source of flavorings and medicines, such as rosewater, preserves, and potpourri. It was considered a common and useful plant in American gardens as early as the seventeenth century. The apothecary's rose may be the variety Thomas Jefferson called " crimson dwarf rose," in bloom at Monticello in 1782, and the rose that was later planted at his retreat home, Poplar Forest, in Bedford County, Virginia. The shrub bears large, semidouble, deep rose–colored flowers with a prominent central cluster of golden stamens. It is also known as red rose of Lancaster, rose of Provins, and double French rose. The apothecary's rose was likely the rose planted at Poplar Forest in 1811, 1812, and 1816 on the banks of the sunken lawn and possibly in the kitchen garden and oval flower beds.

ROSA RUBIGINOSA L.

SYN. *ROSA EGLANTERIA*
Sweetbriar
1771

This large European shrub is distinguished by its apple-perfumed foliage and densely prickled stems. Its small, single, blush-pink, highly fragrant flowers bloom once in spring, followed by long-lasting hips. Young growth exudes the strongest fragrance, so it is best to clip this shrub every year to encourage new growth. In 1771 Jefferson noted "sweet briar" in a list of shrubs "not exceeding" ten feet for the shrubbery at Monticello. It is possible that this is the climbing rose identified by Jane Cary

Smith, who remembered a flower bed "under each low French window" below Monticello's dining room with trellises "covered with yellow Jessamine & climbing roses, a nest of sweets."[1]

ROSA x CENTIFOLIA CV.

'POMPON DE BOURGOGNE' ROSE

1782

This miniature rose was introduced into cultivation before 1664 and was also identified as the Burgundian rose (*Rosa burgundica*). This is possibly the dwarf rose noted in "a Calendar of the bloom of flowers in 1782." Bernard McMahon listed Burgundy rose as a variety of *R. centifolia* in *The American Gardener's Calendar* (1806). It is a once-blooming rose with fragrant, rosy claret to purple flowers. It grows two feet high and spreads.

ROSA x CENTIFOLIA 'MAJOR' L.

LARGE PROVENCE ROSE, CABBAGE ROSE

1791 Prince Nursery

This rose, which dates to the late eighteenth century, is a large, sprawling shrub growing to six feet tall. The clear, deep pink flowers are typically fully double, of a distinct globose shape, and with a clearly defined button eye in the center.

ROSA x CENTIFOLIA MUSCOSA

MOSS ROSE, MOSS PROVENCE

1791 Prince Nursery

The moss roses were among the most sought-after roses in the late eighteenth century. The first moss rose was reported in 1728, although Peter Beales dates it to the seventeenth century. Mossy mutations on roses occurred at least three hundred years ago. The soft mossing on the flower buds has a distinct scent of pine, and they were very popular during the Victorian era.

ROSA CINNAMOMEA L.

SYN. ROSA MAJALIS HERRM.

Cinnamon Rose

1791 Prince Nursery

This rose is named for the color of its reddish-brown stems. Jefferson also called it the "May

Rose." It has small, fragrant, pale pink blossoms and prickly, cinnamon-red to mauve-purple upright stems. It is native to northern and western Asia and was cultivated before the seventeenth century.

ROSA x DAMASCENA BIFERA MILL.

MONTHLY ROSE (LIKELY THE AUTUMN DAMASK ROSE, WHITE DAMASK)

1791 Prince Nursery

This extremely ancient rose originated in the Middle East and was cultivated in Europe by the sixteenth century. It is thought to be a cross between a gallica, such as the apothecary's rose, and the musk rose (*Rosa moschata*). Autumn damask was known in France as 'Quatre Saisons', referring to its habit of reblooming by the end of the season. The fragrant petals of this rose were used for making perfume and for their medicinal properties in the practice of apothecaries. A popular white form, 'Quatre Saisons Blanc Mousseux', was developed by the French breeder Laffay in 1837 and available in the United States by 1844.

ROSA FOETIDA HERRM.

SYN. *ROSA LUTEA* MILL.

Yellow Rose

1791 Prince Nursery

This species bears single flowers of rich golden yellow with prominent stamens. It features erect growth, chestnut-brown stems, and distinct, globose hips. This species is native to southern, western, and central Asia, where it was grown since the sixteenth century. This rose is important for being largely responsible for bringing yellow to modern roses. The flowers have a slightly unpleasant smell.

ROSA GALLICA VERSICOLOR

ROSA MUNDI

1791 Prince Nursery

This low-growing shrub bears a striking mixture of light crimson-and-white-striped blossoms in spring. Rosa Mundi is a sport of the apothecary's rose (*Rosa gallica officinalis*) and is probably the oldest and best known of the striped roses. It originated in Europe and southwest Asia and has a long history in gardens. Many legends surround this rose; the most romantic is that it was named for Fair Rosamund, mistress of Henry II. The name more likely references the universal appeal of this variety, hence the "rose of the world." Rosa Mundi was cultivated in America by the eighteenth century.

ROSA MOSCHATA HERRM. AND *ROSA MOSCHATA PLENA*

MUSK ROSE

1791 Prince Nursery

This late-blooming, ancient species was introduced during the reign of Henry VIII. It grows into a large shrub and produces large, intensely fragrant clusters of cream-colored buds that change to pure white when fully open. The shapely, pointed, and slightly drooping foliage is of a rich gray-green color. The true musk rose is a species of southern Europe and the Middle East that was thought to be extinct until the late twentieth century. The musk rose is the parent of many important rose varieties and is desirable for its dense habit and late bloom season.

ROSA PENDULINE L.

THORNLESS ROSE (POSSIBLY THE ALPINE ROSE)

1791 Prince Nursery

This European species was in cultivation by 1700. The large shrub rose produces arching, reddish-purple stems and dark green foliage. The single, deep pink flowers are followed by handsome, orange-red hips.

ROSA PIMPINELLIFOLIA L.

FORMERLY R. SPINOSISSIMA

Prim Rose

1791 Prince Nursery

This European native is highly variable in nature. It was cultivated in Britain and Europe by 1600 and was introduced into American gardens before the eighteenth century. This rose may correspond to one Thomas Jefferson ordered from the Prince Nursery by the name "Prim rose," a possible reference to the flower's resemblance to primulas. Prim may also refer to a marbled or striped form of scotch briar rose. Varieties bearing yellow flowers, namely, *R. pimpinellifolia altaica* and *lutea,* were introduced from Asia in the late 1700s.

ROSA CHINENSIS CV. 'PARSON'S PINK CHINA' OR 'OLD BLUSH'

ROSA CHINENSIS SEMPERFLORENS 'SLATER'S CRIMSON CHINA'

Pre-1809

Margaret Bayard Smith's account of Jefferson's presidential apartment stated, "In the window recesses, were stands for the flowers and plants which it was his delight to attend and among his roses and geraniums was suspended the cage of his favorite mockingbird."[2] Indoor roses at that time could have been varieties of the species *Rosa chinensis,* including 'Parson's Pink China' or 'Old Blush' or 'Slater's Crimson China', which were in America by 1798. These are ancestors of all modern repeat-blooming garden roses.

ROSA CAROLINA L. AND ROSA VIRGINIANA L.

WILD ROSES
1802, 1804, 1805

On December 9, 1802, Jefferson wrote to his overseer Robert Bailey asking that a half bushel each of seed of "wild roses of every kind" be sent to his friend Madame de Tessé in France. These two North American species are similar in habit, both bearing single, soft pink flowers in late spring followed by round hips. The Carolina rose bears straight prickles (thorns) while the Virginia rose prickles are curved.

ROSA LAEVIGATA MICHX.

CHEROKEE ROSE
1804

This Asian species is believed to have been brought to America by the mid-eighteenth century and naturalized so extensively that it was thought to be native. Others believe it moved across the Asian landmass when the continents were connected. French botanist and explorer André Michaux saw it in great abundance in the south by 1803. John Milledge, a Revolutionary patriot and Governor of Georgia, sent Cherokee rose seed to Jefferson, which the enslaved gardener Goliah planted in rows and labeled with sticks in the nursery at Monticello.

ROSA GALLICA CV.

'TUSCANY' OR 'DOUBLE VELVET'
1808

Margaret Bayard Smith sent Jefferson "black-rose" plants from James Hugh McCulloch, possibly a deep purple to mauve-red variety of a gallica rose called 'Tuscany' or 'Double Velvet', which had been in cultivation since 1596. McCulloch was a merchant and public official appointed by Jefferson as Collector of the Port of Baltimore, Maryland.

ROSA ALBA SEMI-PLENA OR *ROSA ALBA MAXIMA*

WHITE ROSE OF YORK OR DOUBLE WHITE ROSE

1816

Jefferson's Poplar Forest planting memoranda stated that large roses of different kinds were planted in the North Front oval flower bed. These could be the ancient white, or "alba," roses that have been cultivated in Europe since the sixteenth century. The 'White Rose of York' is likely the identity of the "Yorkist" rose that Abigail Adams brought to Quincy (then Braintree), Massachusetts, from England in 1788. This rose, now at Peace field, a National Park Service property, continues to thrive on its original root system.

ROSA MULTIFLORA 'CARNEA' OR *ROSA MOSCHATA PLENA* OR *ROSA PLATYPHYLLA* 'SEVEN SISTERS' (HYBRID MULTIFLORA)

"MULTIFLORA ROSE"

1819

In a letter written from Poplar Forest to Martha Jefferson Randolph, Thomas Jefferson's granddaughter Ellen Wayles Randolph wrote, "I rely on Virginia's [Randolph Trist] care of my pride of Barbadoes [*Caesalpinia pulcherrima*] and multiflora rose if my mocking birds & other multiflora should arrive, I recommend them most particularly to the whole family." Multiflora rose is referenced again in a letter to Dolley Madison of Montpelier, this time written from Monticello and dated January 17, 1820: "Mama [Martha Jefferson Randolph] begs that you will tell Mrs. Reuben Conway, that [. . .] the Multiflora Rose which she promised her has been stuck and is very flourishing." The identity of the rose is uncertain, but it could be a hybrid of the Asian *Rosa multiflora* species. The renowned floral artist Pierre-Joseph Redouté illustrated *R. multiflora* 'Carnea' and *R. multiflora platyphylla,* known as 'Seven Sisters' or 'Russell's Cottage Rose', in his *Les roses* (1817–24). 'Carnea' was sent to England from China in 1804 and distributed throughout Europe. It bears profuse clusters of small, fully double, shell-pink roses in spring. 'Seven Sisters' is a vigorous, climbing polyantha variety bearing heavy clusters of highly scented, deep crimson to violet-red flowers that fade to pink. It is also possible that the "multiflora" Ellen Randolph referenced was the double musk rose (*R. moschata plena*).

APPENDIX C

UNDATED LIST OF FLOWERS

Garden historians are continually searching for primary documentation that can clarify and add deeper insights into the history of a site and the vision of the individuals who imagined it. While Jefferson left an enormous body of written information, there remains much to be discovered. An undated list of flowers in Jefferson's hand is one such document. The best determination of the creation of this listing of forty genera dates it sometime between 1806 and 1809, around the time of his retirement from the presidency. Most of the flowers are ornamental varieties, with cultural details taken directly from Bernard McMahon's *The American Gardener's Calendar,* a publication Jefferson received in 1806.

In this list of flowers, we find notes such as "Canada Martagon July or Aug. take & replt.," which echoes McMahon's *Calendar* instructions for the month of July: "Take up the bulbs of such late flowers as were not sufficiently ripe, nor their leaves decayed last month; as Ornithogalums, bulbous Irises, Martagon, and other lilies; . . . this being the season in which their roots are not in action, is the most proper time for transplanting them, before they put forth new fibers, after which, it would be very improper to remove them."[1] Jefferson's list also notes the time for planting tulips, hyacinths, and crown imperial lilies in October and digging the tender tuberose in November and replanting in April, all as instructed by McMahon.

The native species, many of which are found in the forests around Monticello, further reveal Jefferson's interest in the natural world. The most curious flowers on his list include two diminutive, spring-flowering native iris and lily species: blue-eyed grass (*Sisyrinchium angustifolium*), which Jefferson described as "a little blue flower from woods Bermudian," and yellow star-grass (*Hypoxis hirsuta*), which he called "a little yellow [flower from woods] star of Bethlehem." The memorandum included common spring-flowering woodland ephemerals such as Virginia bluebells ("mountain cowslip," *Mertensia virginica*) and mayapple (*Podophyllum peltatum*), which blanket the forest floor in April and May, as well as the rare pink lady slipper orchid ("mockasun," *Cypripedium acaule*), which is found in the woodlands at nearby Tufton Farm. Summer-flowering species included the cardinal flower ("cardinel," *Lobelia cardinalis*), also found at Tufton, and the curious evergreen pipsissewa or spotted wintergreen, which he called "Dragon's tongue" (*Chimaphila maculata*). "Columbines" could refer to both European varieties as well as the eastern North American red columbine (*Aquilegia canadensis*), which Thomas Mann Randolph Jr., Jefferson's son-in-law, also referenced in a letter to Jefferson from 1791, when he accounted for the flowers observed at Monticello on April 30 along with the fringe trees (*Chionanthus virginicus*) and yellow lady slipper orchids (*Cypripedium calceolus*), which grow on the north slope of Monticello.

The intention for this list is not specified. Was he envisioning possible flowers for the gardens at Monticello, or was Jefferson simply taking inventory of the flowers from the gardens and forest there?

TRANSCRIPTION

Tulips. May all June. mid Octobr.
Hyacinths all June Oct
feathered do
Cr. Imper. June {Aug Oct
~~Polyanthus~~
Amaryllis June Aug
Auricula offsets at any time. Aug.
Tuberose Nov. Apr.

———

Polyanthus Sep. or Oct. take up & replant
lilly valley plant spring or fall
Canada Martagon July or Aug. take & replt.
lillies—sumr. or aut. take up & plant, ~~Oct.,~~ End,
flags. July to Sep. take up & replant
Mockasun
Daffodils—take up any time aftr. flowrg. replant Oct.
Jonquils same.
Sweetwm
a little blue flower from woods Bermudian
a little yellow do. star of Bethlehem
Columbines

Hollyhocks
bullrush
snowdrop
mountain cowslip
French mallow
French pink bleuette
May apple
larkspur
poppy
amarenths
Dragon's tongue
Peony. take up & transplt. in Aug.
marigold
Nasturtium
Balsam
crocus
Marvel of Peru
~~feathered hyacinth~~
~~Mockasun~~
~~Balsam~~
Cardinel
soapwort. saponaria
sawpit phlox
red centaury

BOTANICAL NAMES

Tulips: *Tulipa gesneriana* cvs.
Hyacinths: *Hyacinthus orientalis* cvs.
feathered [Hyacinth]: *Muscari comosum,* possibly 'Plumosum'
Cr. Imper.: *Fritillaria imperialis*
Amaryllis: *Amaryllis* sp.
Auricula: *Primula auricula*
Tuberose: *Agave amica* (formerly *Polianthes tuberosa*)
Polyanthus: *Primula × polyantha*
lilly valley: *Convallaria majalis*
Canada Martagon: *Lilium canadense*
lillies: *Lilium spectabilis, L. canadense,* etc.
flags.: *Iris germanica* cv., *I. pallida, I. cristata,* etc.
Mockasun: *Cypripedium acaule*

Daffodils: *Narcissus* sp.
Jonquils: *Narcissus jonquilla*
Sweet wm. Sweet William: *Dianthus barbatus*
a little blue flower from woods Bermudian: *Sisyrinchium angustifolium*
a little yellow do. star of Bethlehem: *Hypoxis hirsuta*
Columbines: *Aquilegia canadensis* or *A. vulgaris*
Hollyhocks: *Alcea rosea*
bullrush: *Scirpus* sp.
snowdrop: *Galanthus nivalis*
mountain cowslip: *Mertensia virginica*
French mallow: *Malva sylvestris*
French pink bleuette: *Centaurea cyanus*
May apple: *Podophyllum peltatum*
larkspur: *Consolida ajacis*
poppy: *Papaver* sp.
amarenths: *Amaranthus* sp.
Dragon's tongue: *Chimaphila maculata*
Peony: *Paeonia officinalis* cv.
marigold: *Tagetes* sp. or *Calendula officinalis*
Nasturtium: *Tropaeolum majalis*
Balsam: *Impatiens balsamina*
crocus: *Crocus* sp.
Marvel of Peru: *Mirabilis jalapa*
Cardinel: *Lobelia cardinalis*
soapwort. saponaria: *Saponaria officinalis*
sawpit phlox: *Phlox subulata*
red centaury: *Centaurium erythraea*

APPENDIX D

WOODY PLANTS

The following list of trees, shrubs, and vines documented and grown at Monticello is arranged alphabetically by botanical name. Quotation marks surround names used by Jefferson.

TREES

Abies alba, silver fir
Abies balsamea, "Balm of Gilead fir," balsam fir
Acer pseudoplatanus, sycamore maple
Acer rubrum, "scarlet flowering maple," red maple
Acer saccharum, sugar maple
Acer tataricum, Tatarian maple
Aesculus hippocastanum, European horse chestnut
Aesculus octandra, "yellow horse chestnut," "Aesculus virginica," yellow buckeye
Aesculus pavia, "scarlet horse chestnut," "buck's-eye," red buckeye
Albizia julibrissin, "Chinese silk tree," mimosa
Amelanchier canadensis, "service tree," shadblow
Arbutus unedo, strawberry tree
Artocarpus altilis, breadfruit tree
Broussonetia papyrifera, "Otaheite," "paper mulberry tree," paper mulberry
Carpinus caroliniana, "hornbeam," ironwood, muscle wood
Carya illinoinensis, "paccan," pecan
Carya laciniosa, shellbark hickory
Carya ovata, shagbark hickory
Carya sp., "Gloucester hickory"
Castanea dentata, "common chesnut," American chestnut

Castanea sativa, "French chesnut," "Marronier," European chestnut
Catalpa bignonioides, southern catalpa
Cedrus libani, cedar of Lebanon
Ceratonia siliqua, carob tree
Cercis canadensis, redbud
Chamaecyparis thyoides, Atlantic white cedar
Chionanthus virginicus, fringe tree
Citrus aurantifolia, lime
Citrus aurantium, sour orange
Cornus florida, dogwood
Cornus mas, "ciriege corniole," Cornelian cherry
Corylus americana, "Hazel," hazelnut
Crataegus laevigata, "thorn haws from Algiers," English hawthorn
Crataegus phaenopyrum, "Thorn haws," Washington hawthorn
Diospyros virginiana, persimmon
Euonymus europaeaus, European spindle tree
Fagus grandifolia, "beach," American beech
Fagus sylvatica 'Atropunicea', "purple beach," copper beech
Firmiana simplex, Chinese parasol tree
Fraxinus americana, white ash
Fraxinus excelsior, European ash
Ginkgo biloba, "China maidenhair tree," ginkgo
Gleditsia triacanthos, "Kentucky locust," honey locust
Gymnocladus dioicus, Kentucky coffee tree
Halesia carolina, "snow drop tree," silver bell
Ilex aquifolium, English holly
Ilex opaca, American holly
Ilex vomitoria, "Cassioberry," "cassine," yaupon holly
Juglans nigra, black walnut
Juglans regia, "French walnut," "Madeira walnut," English walnut
Juniperus virginiana, red cedar
Koelreuteria paniculata, eastern red cedar, *"Paullinia aurea,"* golden rain tree
Laburnum anagyroides, *"Cytissus Laburnum,"* golden chain tree
Larix decidua, "Italian larch," European larch
Liriodendron tulipifera, tulip poplar
Maclura pomifera, "bow wood," "Osage apple," Osage orange
Magnolia acuminata, "cucumber tree," cucumber magnolia
Magnolia grandiflora, southern magnolia
Magnolia tripetala, "umbrella," umbrella magnolia
Magnolia virginiana, "swamp laurel," *"Magnolia glauca,"* sweet bay magnolia
Malus coronaria, "wild crab," wild crab apple
Malus sylvestris, European crabapple

Melia azedarach, "pride of China," "beadtree," Chinaberry
Morus alba, white mulberry
Morus nigra, "English mulberry," black mulberry
Morus rubra, red mulberry
Myroxylon balsamum var. *pereirae*, balsam of Peru
Olea europaea, olive
Picea abies, "Norway fir," Norway spruce
Picea glauca, "large silver fir," white spruce
Picea mariana, "Newfoundland fir," black spruce
Pinus rigida, pitch pine
Pinus strobus, "Weymouth pine," white pine
Pinus sylvestris, Scotch pine
Platanus × *acerifolia*, London plane tree
Platanus occidentalis, "plane-tree," sycamore
Populus balsamifera, "Tacamahac," balsam poplar
Populus deltoides, "cotton tree," cottonwood
Populus × *gileadensis*, balm of Gilead
Populus nigra var. *italica*, Lombardy poplar
Populus tremula, European aspen
Populus tremuloides, aspen, quaking aspen
Prunus avium, sweet cherry
Prunus cerasus, "dwarf cherry," sour cherry
Prunus persica, "double flowered peach," peach
Prunus serotina, black cherry
Prunus virginiana, "choak cherry," wild cherry
Quercus alba, "alba oak," white oak
Quercus coccifera, "prickly kermes," kermes oak
Quercus ilicifolia, "ground oak," "dwarf oak," bear oak
Quercus phellos, willow oak
Quercus robur, English oak
Quercus suber, "cork tree," cork oak
Robinia pseudoacacia, "common locust," "locust," black locust
Robinia viscosa, "red locust," clammy locust
Salix alba var. *vitellina*, "golden willow," yellow weeping willow
Salix babylonica, weeping willow
Sassafras albidum, sassafras
Sorbus aucuparia, "mountain ash," European mountain ash
Taxus baccata, English yew
Taxus canadensis, "dwarf yew," American yew
Thuja occidentalis, arborvitae
Thuja orientalis, Chinese arborvitae
Tilia sp., "Linden"

Tilia americana, American linden or basswood
Tsuga canadensis, "hemlock spruce," Canadian hemlock
Ulmus americana, "Elm," American elm
Ulmus procera, English elm
Viburnum prunifolium, "haw," blackhaw viburnum
Virgilia capensis, pink blossom tree
Zanthoxylum americanum, prickly ash
Ziziphus jujuba, common jujube

SHRUBS

Acacia farnesiana, *"Acacia nilotica,"* sweet acacia
Alnus incana ssp. *rugosa*, speckled alder
Berberis vulgaris, European barberry, common barberry
Callicarpa americana, "Callicarpa," American beautyberry
Calycanthus floridus, "Bubby flower shrub," sweet shrub, Carolina allspice
Castanea pumila, *"Fagus pumila,"* American chinquapin
Ceanothus americanus, New Jersey tea
Clethra alnifolia, sweet pepper bush
Colutea arborescens, bladder senna
Cornus sanguinea, "Dogberry," swamp dogwood
Coronilla emerus (syn. *Hippocrepis emerus*), scorpion senna
Cotinus coggygria, "Venetian sumach," smokebush
Cytisus scoparius, Scotch broom
Daphne cneorum, rose daphne
Daphne mezereum, "Mezereon" daphne, February daphne
Euonymus americanus, "Euonymus sempervirens," "evergreen spindle-tree," strawberry bush, hearts-a-bustin'
Gardenia jasminoides, "Cape jasmine," gardenia
Hibiscus syriacus, "Althaea," rose of Sharon
Ilex verticillata, winterberry holly
Jasminum officinale, "Jasmine," "White jasmine," "Star jasmine," poet's jasmine
Kalmia latifolia, "Ivy," "Dwarf laurel," mountain laurel
Ligustrum vulgare, common privet
Nerium oleander, oleander
Philadelphus coronarius, mock orange
Prunus triloba, "Amygdalus flore pleno," "Double blossomed almond," flowering almond
Pyracantha coccinea, "Mespilus," "Prickly medlar" pyracantha
Pyrularia pubera, "Oil shrub," buffalo nut
Rhododendron maximum, "Rose-bay," rosebay rhododendron

Rhododendron periclymenoides, "Wild honeysuckle," pinxter azalea
Ribes aureum, "Lewis' yellow currant," golden currant
Ribes odoratum, "Lewis' sweet-scented currant," buffalo currant
Robinia hispida, "Prickly locust," moss locust
Sambucus canadensis, "Elder," elderberry
Spartium junceum, Spanish broom
Symphoricarpos albus, snowberry
Syringa persica, "Persian jasmine," Persian lilac
Syringa vulgaris, common lilac
Taxus canadensis, "Dwarf yew," American yew
Ulex europaeus, "Furze," gorse
Viburnum opulus 'Roseum', "Snowball," "Guelder rose," snowball bush
Viburnum trilobum, "Bush cranberry," American cranberry
Vitex agnus-castus, chaste tree

VINES

Bignonia capreolata, "Trumpet Flower," cross vine
Campsis radicans, "Trumpet flower," trumpet vine
Clematis virginiana, "Virgin's Bower," woodbine, native clematis
Gelsemium sempervirens, "Yellow jasmine," Carolina jessamine
Hedysarum coronarium, "Scarlet monthly honeysuckle," French honeysuckle
Lonicera alpigena, "Red berried honeysuckle," alpine honeysuckle
Lonicera sempervirens, "Trumpet honeysuckle," coral honeysuckle
Rhus toxicodendron, "Poison oak," poison ivy
Vinca minor, periwinkle
Wisteria frutescens, "Carolina kidney bean tree with purple flowers," American wisteria

NOTES

Quotations from Thomas Jefferson preserve his capitalization, punctuation, and spelling as given in the sources.

ABBREVIATIONS

FLTJ Thomas Jefferson, *The Family Letters of Thomas Jefferson,* ed. Edwin Morris Betts and James Adam Bear Jr., rev. ed. (University Press of Virginia, 1995)

JMB Thomas Jefferson, *Jefferson's Memorandum Books: Accounts, with Legal Records and Miscellany, 1767–1826,* ed. James A. Bear Jr. and Lucia C. Stanton, 2 vols. (Princeton University Press, 1997)

PTJ Thomas Jefferson, *The Papers of Thomas Jefferson, Digital Edition,* ed. James P. McClure and J. Jefferson Looney (University of Virginia Press, Rotunda, 2008–25)

PTJ:RS Thomas Jefferson, *Papers of Thomas Jefferson: Retirement Series,* ed. J. Jefferson Looney, 13 vols. to date (Princeton University Press, 2004–)

TJGB Thomas Jefferson, *Thomas Jefferson's Garden Book, 1766–1824,* ed. Edwin Morris Betts, intro. Peter Hatch (Thomas Jefferson Foundation at Monticello, 1999)

TJW Thomas Jefferson, *Thomas Jefferson: Writings,* ed. Merrill D. Peterson (Library of America, 1984)

1. JEFFERSON'S EARLIEST FLOWER GARDENS

1. Thomas Jefferson, Garden Book [manuscript], 1766–1824. The original bound volume of sixty-six pages is held at the Massachusetts Historical Society. The version edited by Edwin Morris Betts, *Thomas Jefferson's Garden Book, 1766–1824, with Relevant Extracts from His Other Writings,* was originally published by the American Philosophical Society in 1944. The reprint with an introduction by Peter Hatch (Thomas Jefferson Foundation at Monticello, 2012) was consulted for this work and is cited hereafter as *TJGB.*
2. Susan Kern, *The Jeffersons at Shadwell* (Yale University Press, 2010), chaps. 1–2.
3. Peter Martin, *The Pleasure Gardens of Virginia, from Jamestown to Jefferson* (University Press of Virginia, 1991), 131.
4. Peter Collinson to John Custis, December 15, 1735, and Custis to Collinson, July 29, 1736, as cited in Andrea Wulf, *The Brother Gardeners* (Knopf, 2009), 24, 67. For correspondence between Collinson and Custin, see E. G. Swem, *Brothers of the Spade* (American Antiquarian Society, 1949).
5. Wulf, *Brother Gardeners,* 67–68; Martin, *Pleasure Gardens,* 79.
6. *PTJ,* 20:464.
7. Thomas Jefferson to de Volney, April 9, 1797, in *PTJ,* 29:352–53.
8. Dumas Malone, *Jefferson the Virginian* (Little, Brown, 1948), 430.
9. Malone, *Jefferson the Virginian,* 39, 48.
10. Sarah N. Randolph, *The Domestic Life of Thomas Jefferson* (University Press of Virginia, 1978), 39. Translation: "Ah, Joanna, the fairest of girls, / Ah forever covered with green flowers, / May the land be light for you; / Far, far away!"
11. "Puckoon" comes from the Powhatan word *poughkone* or *pohcoons,* meaning "red paint" or "red dye." The red sap that oozes from the plant's roots was used for dyeing clothing and baskets and for face painting.
12. Banister was a clergyman and plant collector who was sent to Virginia by Bishop Compton. His *Catalogue of Virginia Plants,* the first known work of its kind, was published in 1688. Banister also took part in the establishment of the College of William and Mary.
13. "Come to table" was a term Jefferson used throughout his gardening career to mean "harvested for the kitchen."
14. Suckering rose possibilities could be *Rosa gallica, R. pimpinellifolia, R. cinnamomea,* or a native rose such as *R. virginiana* or *R. carolina.*
15. Denise Wiles Adams, *Restoring American Gardens* (Timber Press, 2004), 169.
16. *TJGB,* 8.
17. John Hill, *The gardener's new kalendar; divided according to the twelve months of the year—containing the whole practice of gardening* (London, 1758).
18. Raymond Taylor, *Plants of Colonial Days* (Colonial Williamsburg, 1959), 45.
19. David Stuart and James Sutherland, *Plants from the Past* (Viking, 1987), 117–18.
20. *TJGB,* 464. Anne Cary Randolph married Charles Lewis Bankhead on September 19, 1808.
21. *TJGB,* 6.
22. Monticello is 868 feet above sea level and about 530 feet above the Rivanna River, which flows at the base of the mountain.
23. Thomas Jefferson, "Memorandum Books, 1771," *Founders Online,* National Archives, https://founders.archives.gov/documents/Jefferson/02-01-02-0005.
24. Jefferson, "Memorandum Books, 1771."
25. William Shakespeare, *A Midsummer Night's*

Dream 2.1.256.

26. Philip Miller, *The Gardeners Dictionary* (London, 1748), s.v. "Clematis."
27. Batty Langley, *New Principles of Gardening: Or the Laying Out and Planting Parterres, Groves, Wildernesses, Labyrinths, Avenues, Parks, &c.* (Battesworth and Batley, 1727).
28. Miller, *Gardeners Dictionary* (1748), s.v. "Clematis."
29. "Hardy perennial flowers" were enumerated in Jefferson's Memorandum Book in 1771: "Snapdragon [*Antirrhinum majus*]—Daisy [*Bellis perennis*]—Larkspur [*Consolida ajacis*]—Gilliflower [*Matthiola incana*]—Sunflower. [*Helianthus annuus* or *H. divericatus*]—Lilly [*Lilium* sp.]—Mallow [*Malva* sp. or *Hibiscus* sp.]—Flower de luce [*Iris pseudacorus*]—Everlasting pea [*Lathyrus latifolius*]—Piony [*Paeonia officinalis*]—Poppy [*Papaver* sp.]—Pasque flower [*Anemone pulsatilla*]—Goldy-lock. Trollius. =Anemone [*Trollius europaeus*]—Lilly of the Valley [*Convallaria majalis*]—Primrose [*Primula vulgaris*]—Periwinkle [*Vinca minor*]—Violet. [*Viola sp.*]—Flag [*Iris* sp.]." See Jefferson, "Memorandum Books, 1771."
30. Joel Fry (curator, Bartram's Garden, Philadelphia), personal correspondence, September 2, 2021.
31. Randolph, *Domestic Life*, 43–44.
32. *TJGB*, 75, entry for March 7, 1778: "Planted 19 Bubby flower shrubs, Calycanthus, from the Green mountain, the only place in this country I have ever heard of them. They are said to be very common in So. Carolina."
33. "Thomas Jefferson to Antonio Giannini, with a List of Seeds Wanted, 5 February 1786," *Founders Online*, National Archives, https://founders.archives.gov/documents/Jefferson/01-09-02-0218. George Granger Sr. (1730–1799) was a foreman of labor in 1793 and an enslaved overseer in 1796. While Jefferson served in Paris from 1784 to 1789, Granger was "reserved to take care of my orchards, grasses &c."
34. Thomas Jefferson to James Monroe, May 20, 1782, in *PTJ*, 6:186.
35. Annette Gordon-Reed, *The Hemingses of Monticello: An American Family* (Norton, 2008), 143; Rev. Hamilton Wilcox Pierson, *Jefferson at Monticello: The Private Life of Thomas Jefferson*, ed. James A. Bear Jr. (University Press of Virginia, 1967), 99.

2. JEFFERSON'S EUROPEAN TOUR

1. Thomas Jefferson, "Autobiography," in *TJW*, 46.
2. Dumas Malone, *Jefferson the Virginian* (Little, Brown, 1948), 405.
3. Extant signatures from Robert and James show that they spelled their family name differently, with Robert using the double "m" and James a single "m."
4. G. S. Wilson, *Jefferson on Display: Attire, Etiquette, and the Art of Presentation* (University of Virginia Press, 2018), 28; *JMB*, 1:562.
5. Thomas Jefferson to Maria Cosway, July 1, 1787, in *PTJ*, 11:519–20; George Green Shackelford, *Thomas Jefferson's Travels in Europe, 1784–1789* (Johns Hopkins University Press, 1995), 65–74.
6. Thomas Jefferson to Richard Cary, August 12, 1786, in *PTJ*, 10:127–28.
7. Thomas Jefferson to Bernard McMahon, December 28, 1808, Papers of Thomas Jefferson, Library of Congress, Washington, DC.
8. Thomas Jefferson to Martha Jefferson Randolph, October 18, 1808, in *FLTJ*, 351–52.
9. Alice Coats, *Flowers and Their Histories*, 3rd ed. (Adam and Charles Black, 1968), 111–12.
10. Thomas Jefferson to Madame de Tessé, Washington, January 30, 1803, in *PTJ*, 39:416–417.

11. Thomas Jefferson to Madame de Tessé, Washington, October 31, 1803, in *PTJ,* 41:644–45.
12. Thomas Jefferson to Madame de Tessé, December 8, 1813, in *PTJ:RS,* 7:33–36.
13. Thomas Whately, *Observations on Modern Gardening,* 3rd ed. (London, 1771).
14. Benton Seeley, *Stowe: A Description of the Magnificent House and Gardens of the Right Honourable Richard Grenville Temple* (London, 1744).
15. Thomas Jefferson, "Notes of a Tour of English Gardens," in *PTJ,* 9:369–70.
16. Whately, *Observations,* 31.
17. Thomas Jefferson to Ellen Randolph, July 10, 1805, in *FLTJ,* 276.
18. Whately, *Observations,* 152.
19. According to the National Gallery of Art's History of Early American Landscape Design project, "In colonial and federal America, 'pleasure ground' typically denoted an ornamented landscape composed of lawn, trees, shrubs, flowers, intersecting walks, and decorative structures." It applied to both public and private landscapes and "was consistently associated with beauty, order, and the improvement of nature." It was typically located near the house. See National Gallery of Art, "Pleasure Ground / Pleasure Garden," History of Early American Landscape Design, https://heald.nga.gov/mediawiki/index.php/Pleasure_ground/Pleasure_garden.
20. Whately, *Observations,* 177.
21. Whately, *Observations,* 147–48.
22. Jefferson, "Notes of a Tour of English Gardens," 170–71.
23. Thomas Jefferson to John Page in *PTJ,* 9:445.
24. Thomas Jefferson, "Notes of a Tour into the Southern Parts of France, &c.," in *PTJ,* 11:415–64.
25. "Jefferson's Hints to Americans Travelling in Europe," in *PJT,* 13:270. *Utile dulci:* Latin, meaning the combination of the useful with the pleasurable.
26. Jefferson, "Notes of a Tour into the Southern Parts of France, &c.," 442.
27. This sterile, double-flowered garden form of European viburnum was known by 1554. The flowers, described in 1770 as "balls of snow, lodged in a pleasing manner all over its head," have inspired other common names, such as Whitsun-boss, love-roses, and pincushion-tree. On April 16, 1807, Jefferson directed the planting of *Viburnum opulus* 'Roseum' in shrub circles on the northeast and southeast corners of Monticello.
28. March 3–April 23, 1788, in *PTJ,* 13:8–36.
29. "Jefferson's Hints to Americans Travelling in Europe," 267.
30. "Jefferson's Hints to Americans Travelling in Europe," 269.
31. Thomas Jefferson in *JMB,* 1:743, 747.

3. A BOTANIZING NORTHERN TOUR AND VISIT TO THE WILLIAM PRINCE NURSERY

1. Thomas Jefferson to James Madison, February 14, 1790, in *PTJ,* 16:182.
2. *JMB,* 1:758, June 7, 1790: "gave Bob for expenses to Fredsbg. £8."
3. Thomas Jefferson to Martha Jefferson Randolph, March 24, 1791, and Martha Jefferson Randolph to Thomas Jefferson, March 22, 1791, in *PTJ,* 19:604, 599. Cypress vine (*Ipomoea quamoclit*) is a member of the morning glory family.
4. Thomas Mann Randolph to Thomas Jefferson, April 30, 1791, in *PTJ,* 20:327–30. The flowers were wild violets (*Viola* sp.), dandelion ("Leontodon taraxacum," identified as *Taraxacum officinale*), catchfly or *Silene* sp. (a member of the dianthus family), fringe

tree (*Chionanthus virginicus*), yellow lady slipper orchid (*Cypripedium calceolus*), native columbine (*Aquilegia canadensis*), and tassel hyacinth (*Muscari comosum*).

5. Thomas Jefferson to Maria Jefferson, May 8, 1791, in *PTJ,* 20: 380–381.
6. Jefferson left Philadelphia on May 17 and returned on June 19. For his full itinerary, see *JMB,* 2:818–25.
7. James Madison to Thomas Jefferson, May 12, 1791, in *The Papers of James Madison, Digital Edition,* ed. J. C. A. Stagg (University of Virginia Press, Rotunda, 2010), 14:23.
8. "Northern Journey of Jefferson and Madison: Editorial Note," in *PTJ,* 20:434–53.
9. Thomas Jefferson to William Drayton, May 1, 1791, in *PTJ,* 20:332–33.
10. Benjamin Rush to Thomas Jefferson, January 26, 1792, in *PTJ,* 23:77.
11. Hosack, a botanist, educator, and physician, tended to the fatal injuries of Alexander Hamilton after his duel with Aaron Burr in July 1804.
12. Thomas Jefferson to William Prince, July 6, 1791, in *PTJ,* 20:603–4. "Roses. Moss Provence. Yellow. Rosa mundi. Large Provence. The monthly. The white damask. The primrose. Musk rose. Cinnamon rose. Thornless rose. 3 of each, making in all 30."
13. *Rosa rubiginosa* is a large European shrub rose distinguished by its apple-scented foliage and densely prickled stems. Its small, single, blush-pink flowers bloom once in late spring, followed by long-lasting hips. Young growth exudes the strongest fragrance.
14. This is a once-blooming rose with fragrant, rosy claret to purple flowers. It grows two feet high and spreads.
15. William Prince to Thomas Jefferson, November 8, 1791, in *PTJ,* 22:268–69.
16. A legendary "Yorkist Rose," which Abigail Adams brought from England in 1788, still survives at the Adams National Historic Park in Quincy, Massachusetts.
17. Pierre-Joseph Redouté, *Les roses* (Paris, 1817).
18. Thomas Jefferson to Robert Bailey, December 9, 1802, in *PTJ,* 39:125–126. Bailey (d. 1804) was an itinerant European gardener hired by Jefferson to work at Monticello for three years between 1794 and 1796. He subsequently became a gardener and nurseryman in Washington, DC. In 1803 Jefferson described him as "an old Scotch gardener of the neighborhood." It is believed that Bailey trained the enslaved gardener Wormley Hughes.
19. Thomas Jefferson to John Milledge, November 22, 1803, in *PTJ,* 42:29–30.
20. *TJGB,* 291.
21. Thomas Jefferson to Mary Jefferson Eppes, April 11, 1801, in *PTJ,* 33:570.
22. Margaret Bayard Smith, *The First Forty Years of Washington Society,* ed. Gaillard Hunt (C. Scribner's Sons, 1906), 385. Jefferson's favorite mockingbird was named Dick.
23. 'Old Blush', also known as 'Parson's Pink China' (*Rosa chinensis pallida*), introduced into the United Kingdom in 1789, is a possible candidate.
24. McCulloch was a friend of the Smiths and appointed by Jefferson as Collector of the Port of Baltimore. See *PTJ,* 10:407–8.
25. Mrs. Samuel Harrison Smith to Thomas Jefferson, March 26, 1808, Coolidge Collection of Thomas Jefferson Manuscripts, Massachusetts Historical Society, Boston; *TJGB,* 368. The "black rose" was most likely a deep red gallica rose. Although the name 'Tuscany' was not registered before 1819, this distinctive rose was illustrated in sixteenth-century herbals and botanical paintings.
26. Thomas Jefferson to Margaret Bayard Smith, March 27, 1808, *Founders Online,* National Archives, https://founders.archives.gov/

documents/Jefferson/99-01-02-7721. Thomas Main, a Scots gardener who settled at Georgetown near the Little Falls of the Potomac River circa 1804, was likely the first nurseryman in the district outside of Washington, DC. Jefferson spelled his name "Maine."

27. Jeremiah Augustus Goodman (ca. 1780–1857) was hired by Jefferson in 1809 as overseer at his Lego Farm and late in 1811 was transferred to Poplar Forest, where he remained until Jefferson dismissed him at the end of May 1815.

4. THE NATIVE FLORA OF VIRGINIA AND JEFFERSON'S CURIOUS MIND

1. Thomas Jefferson to Martha Jefferson Randolph, December 23, 1790, in *PTJ,* 18:350.
2. Thomas Jefferson to James Madison, June 9, 1793, in *PTJ,* 26:239–42. Jefferson wrote, "I have served my tour. . . . The motion of my blood no longer keeps time with the tumult of the world. It leads me to seek happiness in the lap and love of my family, in the society of my neighbors and my books, in the wholesome occupations of my farms and my affairs, in an interest or affection in every bud that opens, in every breath that blows around me, in an entire freedom of rest, of motion, of thought—owing account to myself alone of my hours and actions."
3. The American Philosophical Society, the oldest learned society in the United States, was founded by Benjamin Franklin in 1743 and modeled after the Royal Society of London for Improving Natural Knowledge.
4. James Madison to Thomas Jefferson, November 15, 1785, in *The Papers of James Madison, Digital Edition,* ed. J. C. A. Stagg (University of Virginia Press, Rotunda, 2010), 8:415–16.
5. Clayton, who also served as clerk of Gloucester County, collected and sent many North American plant specimens and manuscript descriptions to English naturalist Mark Catesby and to Gronovius, a Dutch botanist. John Bartram visited Clayton in 1738 and wrote that his was the finest garden in Virginia.
6. Ann Leighton, *American Gardens in the Eighteenth Century: "For Use or for Delight"* (University of Massachusetts Press, 1976), 423.
7. Michaux had arrived in Philadelphia in 1792. Jefferson originally considered him to lead an exploration of the western regions of America, an expedition later undertaken by Lewis and Clark.
8. Paul Russell Cutright, *Lewis and Clark: Pioneering Naturalists* (University of Illinois Press, 1969).
9. Thomas Jefferson to Bernard McMahon, January 6, 1807, Papers of Thomas Jefferson, Library of Congress, Washington, DC; transcription available in *TJGB,* 337.
10. Pursh, a German American botanist in Philadelphia, was Benjamin Smith Barton's part-time curator and collector. Pursh studied and described the plants collected on the Lewis and Clark Expedition and added this information to his manuscript *Flora Americae Septentrionalis,* published in 1814.
11. James Vick, *Vick's Floral Guide* (Rochester, NY, 1889), 11.
12. Thomas Jefferson to P. S. Dupont de Nemours, March 2, 1809, in *TJW,* 1203.
13. Thomas Jefferson to William Hamilton, July 31, 1806, in *TJW,* 1168.
14. Bernard McMahon to Thomas Jefferson, February 28, 1812; transcription available in *TJGB,* 481.
15. Bernard McMahon, *American Gardener's*

Calendar (1806; facsimile ed., Thomas Jefferson Memorial Foundation, 1997), 72.

16. Peter Kalm, *Travels into North America,* vol. 2 (London, 1771), 222.
17. Sandra Rebok, *Humboldt and Jefferson* (University of Virginia Press, 2014), chaps. 1 and 2.

5. THE ARDENT AMATEUR

1. L. H. Bailey, *The Standard Cyclopedia of Horticulture,* vol. 2 (Macmillan, 1935).
2. *Henderson's Handbook of Plants and General Horticulture* (P. Henderson, 1890), 355.
3. George Nicholson, *The Illustrated Dictionary of Gardening,* vol. 2 (L. U. Gill, 1885), 17.
4. Graeme Butler, "The Auricula: History and Cultivation," *Caledonian Gardener,* 2017, 42–49.
5. Bernard McMahon to Thomas Jefferson, February 25, 1807, Papers of Thomas Jefferson, Library of Congress, Washington, DC.
6. Bernard McMahon to Thomas Jefferson, February 28, 1812; transcription available in *TJGB,* 481.
7. Ian Thompson, *The Sun King's Garden: Louis XIV, André Le Nôtre and the Creation of the Gardens of Versailles,* (Bloomsbury Publishers, 2006), 163–65.
8. John Parkinson, *Paradisi in Sole Paradisus Terrestris* (London, 1629).
9. Miller, *Gardeners Dictionary* (1752), 614.
10. Bernard McMahon, *American Gardener's Calendar* (1806; facsimile ed., Thomas Jefferson Memorial Foundation, 1997), 155.
11. Montpelier, the lifelong home of James Madison, is thirty miles from Monticello in Orange County, Virginia.
12. Jane C. Slaughter, "Anne Mercer Slaughter: A Sketch," *Tyler's Quarterly Magazine,* July 1937, 30–44, Montpelier Research Database, MRD-S 115.
13. Jane Blair Cary Smith, "The Carysbrook Memoir," Special Collections, University of Virginia Library, Charlottesville, VA.
14. McMahon, *American Gardener's Calendar,* 78, 84.
15. McMahon, *American Gardener's Calendar,* 82.
16. M. Kent Brinkley, "The Green Spring Plantation Greenhouse/Orangery and the Probable Evolution of the Domestic Area Landscape: A Research Report," US Department of the Interior, National Park Service, 2004.
17. Brinkley, "Greenspring Plantation," viii.
18. *TJGB,* May 1778: "bought two Aegyptian Acacia (Mimosa Nilotica) from the Gardener at Greenspring. They are from seeds planted March 1777. Sept. 12 one of the Acacias 23 I. high the other 18 I. Oct. 12 their heights 28 ½ I. and 23. I."
19. Thomas Jefferson to Thomas Mann Randolph Jr., March 30, 1792, in *PTJ,* 23:355.
20. National Gallery of Art, "The Woodlands," History of Early American Landscape Design, https://heald.nga.gov/mediawiki/index.php/The_Woodlands.
21. Thomas Jefferson to William Hamilton, April 22, 1800, in *PTJ,* 31:533–35; Bernard McMahon to Thomas Jefferson, January 3, 1809, Papers of Thomas Jefferson, Library of Congress, Washington, DC.
22. The Mount Clare orangery was built by Charles Carroll around 1760.
23. George Washington to Margaret Carroll, September 16, 1789, in *Papers of George Washington, Presidential Series,* vol. 4, ed. Dorothy Twohig (University of Virginia Press, 1983), 43–47n.
24. Monticello: outbuildings (notes), ca. 1776–78, by Thomas Jefferson, N88, K57, Massachusetts Historical Society, Thomas Jefferson Papers: An Electronic Archive.
25. Thomas Jefferson to James Oldham, October

11, 1804, Coolidge Collection of Thomas Jefferson Manuscripts, Massachusetts Historical Society, Boston.

26. Anne Cary Randolph to Thomas Jefferson, November 9, 1807, in *FLTJ,* 31. Martha Jefferson Randolph and Thomas Mann Randolph's Edgehill was situated on land that was part of the Randolph family inheritance of 2,400 acres near Shadwell.
27. Anne Cary Randolph to Thomas Jefferson, January 22, 1808, in *FLTJ,* 323–24.
28. Margaret Bayard Smith to Thomas Jefferson, by March 6, 1809, addition to *PTJ,* 1:29.
29. Thomas Jefferson to Margaret Bayard Smith, March 6, 1809, in *PTJ:RS,* 1:20.
30. Margaret Bayard Smith, *The First Forty Years of Washington Society,* ed. Gaillard Hunt (C. Scribner's Sons, 1906), 71–72.
31. Thomas Jefferson to Martha Jefferson Randolph, November 23, 1807, in *FLTJ,* 315.
32. *TJGB,* 387 and 398n25.
33. Thomas Jefferson to Anne Cary Randolph Bankhead, December 29, 1809, in *TJFL,* 394.
34. Carl Linnaeus to C. Ryk Tulbagh, 1764, Linnean Society of London, Linnean Correspondence, translated synopsis, digital copy: ref. no. LC/9/177.
35. Curtis was an English botanist, apothecary, and publisher of *The Botanical Magazine or Flower-Garden Displayed,* the world's longest-running continuously published botanical journal, which began publication in 1787. It is widely recognized as *Curtis's Botanical Magazine.*
36. Carl Linnaeus, *Species Plantarum,* vol. 2 (1753), 293.
37. Bernard McMahon to Thomas Jefferson, October 24, 1812, in *PTJ:RS,* 5:412.
38. Thomas Jefferson to Bernard McMahon, April 8, 1811, in *PTJ:RS,* 3:544–45.
39. Thomas Jefferson to Martha Jefferson Randolph, November 10, 1816, in *PTJ:RS,* 10:517.
40. Cornelia J. Randolph to Ellen W. Randolph Coolidge, October 31, 1825, Ellen Wayles Randolph Coolidge Correspondence, 1810–1861, acc. no. 9090, 9090-c, 38–584, Special Collections, University of Virginia Library, Charlottesville, VA.
41. See the annotated list of Jefferson's roses in appendix B.
42. Mary Jefferson Randolph to Nicholas Trist, February 15, 1829, Nicholas P. Trist Papers, Library of Congress.
43. Mary J. Randolph to Ellen W. Randolph Coolidge, August 10, 1828, Ellen Wayles Randolph Coolidge Correspondence 1810–1861, acc. no. 9090, 9090-c, 38–584, Special Collections, University of Virginia Library, Charlottesville, VA. Transcription available at Jefferson Quotes & Family Letters, Thomas Jefferson Foundation Inc., https://tjrs.monticello.org/.

6. JEFFERSON'S RETIREMENT FLOWER GARDENS

1. Thomas Jefferson to Bernard McMahon, April 25, 1806, Papers of Thomas Jefferson, Library of Congress, Washington, DC.
2. Peter Hatch, introduction to Bernard McMahon, *The American Gardener's Calendar* (1806; facsimile ed., Thomas Jefferson Memorial Foundation, 1997).
3. Bernard McMahon to Thomas Jefferson, July 12, 1806, Papers of Thomas Jefferson, Library of Congress, Washington, DC.
4. Anna Pavord, *The Tulip: The Story of a Flower That Has Made Men Mad* (Macmillan, 1999).
5. Thomas Jefferson to Bernard McMahon, February 25, 1807, Papers of Thomas Jefferson, Library of Congress, Washington, DC.
6. Margaret Bayard Smith, *The First Forty Years of Washington Society,* ed. Gaillard Hunt (C.

Scribner's Sons, 1906), 394–95.

7. Thomas Jefferson to Anne Cary Randolph, June 7, 1807, in *FLTJ,* 307–8.
8. Anne Cary Randolph to Thomas Jefferson, November 9, 1807, in *FLTJ,* 314.
9. Thomas Jefferson to Anne Cary Randolph, February 16, 1808, in *FLTJ,* 328.
10. Anne Cary Randolph to Thomas Jefferson, April 15, 1808, in *FLTJ,* 342.
11. Thomas Jefferson to Bernard McMahon, July 6, 1808, Papers of Thomas Jefferson, Library of Congress, Washington, DC; transcription at *Founders Online,* National Archives, https://founders.archives.gov/documents/Jefferson/99-01-02-8274.
12. Anne Cary Randolph Bankhead to Thomas Jefferson, November 26, 1808, *Founders Online,* National Archives, https://founders.archives.gov/documents/Jefferson/99-01-02-9161; Jefferson to Anne Cary Randolph Bankhead, December 29, 1809, *Founders Online,* National Archives, https://founders.archives.gov/documents/Jefferson/03-02-02-0074. The "old French Gentleman," Andre Thoüin, regularly sent large packages of seeds from the Jardin des Plantes.
13. Ellen Wayles Randolph Coolidge to Thomas Jefferson, December 15, 1808, *Founders Online,* National Archives, https://founders.archives.gov/documents/Jefferson/99-01-02-9326.
14. Thomas Jefferson to Charles Willson Peale, February 6, 1809, Papers of Thomas Jefferson, Library of Congress, Washington, DC; transcription available at *Founders Online,* National Archives, https://founders.archives.gov/documents/Jefferson/99-01-02-9725.
15. *TJGB,* 387.
16. Bernard McMahon to Thomas Jefferson, February 28, 1812, in *PTJ:RS,* 5:523–24.
17. Thomas Jefferson to Bernard McMahon, October 11, 1812, in *PTJ:RS,* 5:382.
18. *TJGB,* 474.
19. Thomas Jefferson to Martha Jefferson Randolph, November 10, 1816, in *PTJ:RS,* 10:517; Martha Jefferson Thomas Randolph to Thomas Jefferson, November 20, 1816, in *PTJ:RS,* 10:536–37.
20. *TJGB,* 335.
21. Thomas Jefferson to Anne Cary Randolph Bankhead, May 26, 1811, in *PTJ:RS,* 3:633.
22. The "measuring line" used by Jefferson was likely the thirty-three-foot, two-pole metal "chain" that Jefferson used in his surveying. According to retired Garden Club of Virginia landscape architect Will Rieley, Jefferson's flower beds, like everything else on the grounds, were carefully planned and geometrically measured. Even the oval beds were almost certainly laid out as geometrically correct ovals or ellipses.
23. Henry S. Randall, *The Life of Thomas Jefferson* (Derby & Jackson, 1858), 3:346–47.
24. Barbara Wells Sarudy, *Gardens and Gardening in the Chesapeake, 1700–1805* (Johns Hopkins University Press, 1998).
25. Virginia Randolph Trist to Ellen Wayles Randolph Coolidge, March 28, 1827, Correspondence of Ellen Wayles Randolph Coolidge, 1810–1861, acc. no. 38–584, 9090, 9090-c, Special Collections, University of Virginia Library, Charlottesville, VA.
26. Thomas Jefferson to Benjamin Rush, August 17, 1811, in *PTJ:RS,* 4:87–88.
27. Thomas Jefferson to John Wayles Eppes, September 18, 1812, in *PTJ:RS,* 5:347–50.
28. Jack Gary, "Paper Mulberry Trees, Clumps, and Oval Beds: The First Phase of Landscape Restoration at Thomas Jefferson's Poplar Forest," *Magnolia* 25, no. 4 (2012): 1–7.
29. Jefferson admired paper mulberries, *Broussonetia papyrifera,* for the quality of shade they produced. Writing to his Poplar Forest neighbor Charles Clay in 1815, he noted they

were "valuable for their form, velvet leaf & for being fruitless. They are charming near a porch for densely shading it." See *TJGB,* 547.

30. C. Allan Brown, "Thomas Jefferson's Poplar Forest: The Mathematics of an Ideal Villa," *Journal of Garden History* 10, no. 2 (1990): 117–39.
31. *TJGB,* 494.
32. *TJGB,* 563.

7. THE FLOWER GARDEN RESTORED

1. Account by Samuel Whitcomb Jr., "An Interview with Thomas Jefferson," May 3, 1824 (transcript), acc. no. 2816, Special Collections, University of Virginia Library, Charlottesville, VA.
2. James A. Bear Jr., "The Last Few Days in the Life of Thomas Jefferson," *Magazine of Albemarle County History* 32 (1974): 77.
3. Cornelia Randolph to Ellen Randolph Coolidge, November 12, 1826. Transcription available at Jefferson Quotes & Family Letters, Thomas Jefferson Foundation Inc., tjrs.monticello.org/letter/1064.
4. Virginia Randolph Trist to Ellen Randolph Coolidge, March 28, 1827, Ellen Wayles Randolph Coolidge Correspondence, Special Collections, University of Virginia Library, Charlottesville, VA.
5. Marc Leepson, *Saving Monticello* (Free Press, 2001), 29–30, 32.
6. Leepson, *Saving Monticello,* 43, 68–70.
7. Leepson, *Saving Monticello,* 88–89.
8. Diary of Sarah Strickler, August 1, 1864, acc. no. 5633, Special Collections, University of Virginia Library, Charlottesville, VA.
9. Charles B. Coale, *The Life and Adventures of Wilburn Waters, the Famous Hunter and Trapper of White Top Mountain* (G. W. Gary, 1878), 237.
10. See Susanne Williams Massie and Frances Archer Christian, eds., *Homes and Gardens in Old Virginia* (J. W. Fergusson & Sons, 1930).
11. Peter Hatch, "Restoring the Monticello Landscape, 1923–1955," *Magnolia* 23, no. 1 (2009–10): 1, 3–8.
12. Fiske Kimball to Susan Massie, May 1938, Garden Club of Virginia archives, as cited by Hatch in "Restoring the Monticello Landscape," 5.
13. Hazlehurst Perkins to Fiske Kimball, November 28, 1938, Garden Club of Virginia archives, as cited by Hatch in "Restoring the Monticello Landscape," 5.
14. Morley J. Williams, "The Gardens at Monticello," *Landscape Architecture* 24, no. 2 (1934): 67.
15. Fiske Kimball, "The Gardens and Plantations at Monticello," *Landscape Architecture* 17, no. 3 (1927): 172.
16. Kimball, "Gardens and Plantations," 70.
17. Thomas Jefferson to William Hamilton, July 31, 1806, in *PTJ;* transcription at *Founders Online,* National Archives, https://founders.archives.gov/documents/Jefferson/99-01-02-4111.
18. Hatch, "Restoring the Monticello Landscape,"
19. Thomas E. Beaman Jr., "The Archaeology of Morley Jeffers Williams and the Restoration of Historic Landscapes at Stratford Hall, Mount Vernon, and Tryon Palace," *North Carolina Historical Review*79, no. 3 (2002): 352.
20. Dorothy Hunt Williams, *Historic Virginia Gardens: Preservations by the Garden Club of Virginia* (University Press of Virginia, 1975), 78.
21. Hazlehurst Perkins, quoted in *Follow the Green Arrow: The History of the Garden Club of Virginia, 1920–1970,* ed. Mrs. James Bland

Martin (Dietz Press, 1970), 85.

22. The setting stones came from Colonel L. L. Owen of Old Lynchburg Road, Charlottesville, VA.
23. Hatch, "Restoring the Monticello Landscape," 8.
24. Martin, *Follow the Green Arrow,* 74.
25. Martin, *Follow the Green Arrow,* 84–86.

EPILOGUE

1. Rudy J. Favretti and Joy Putnam Favretti, *Landscapes and Gardens for Historic Buildings: A Handbook for Reproducing and Creating Authentic Landscape Settings* (American Association for State and Local History, 1978).
2. C. Allan Brown, "Thomas Jefferson's Poplar Forest: The Mathematics of an Ideal Villa," *Journal of Garden History* 10, no. 2 (1990): 117.
3. According to Poplar Forest's consulting Landscape Architect Will Rieley, the fact that Jefferson's flower beds were carefully planned and geometrically measured revealed his consistently mathematical approach in laying out ovals and ellipses both at Monticello and Poplar Forest.
4. David C. Stuart and James Sutherland, *Plants from the Past* (Viking, 1987), 9.
5. On June 11, 1949, Hermond Norwood interviewed Fountain Hughes (ca. 1860–1957), a possible descendant of Wormley Hughes, for the Library of Congress. Freed from slavery after the American Civil War, Fountain Hughes eventually found his way to Baltimore, Maryland, where he worked for several decades for the Shirley family as a farmer and gardener.
6. "Getting Word African American Oral History Project" podcast, https://www.monticello.org/exhibits-events/livestreams-videos-and-podcasts/getting-word-mhpod/.
7. Thomas Jefferson to Étienne Lemaire, April 25, 1809, in *PTJ:RS,* 1:162.

APPENDIX A

1. Alice Morse Earle, *Old-Time Gardens Newly Set Forth* (Macmillan, 1901), 335.
2. Carl Linnaeus, *Species Plantarum,* vol. 2 (1753), 293.
3. Bernard McMahon, *The American Gardener's Calendar* (Philadelphia, 1806), 643.
4. Philip Miller, *The Gardeners Dictionary,* 8th ed. (London, 1768), s.v. "Antirrhinum."
5. Peter Henderson, *Henderson's Handbook of Plants and General Horticulture* (P. Henderson, 1890), 26.
6. John Parkinson, *Paradisi in Sole Paradisus Terrestris* (London, 1629), 269.
7. Philip Miller, *Figures of the Most Beautiful, Useful, and Uncommon Plants* (London, 1760), 1:34.
8. James L. Reveal and Joseph A. Mussulman, "Wild Ginger," Discover Lewis & Clark, https://lewis-clark.org/sciences/plants/wild-ginger/.
9. Robert Buist, *The American Flower Garden Directory* (Carey and Hart, 1839), 35.
10. *Curtis's Botanical Magazine,* 1807, plate 995, "Poinciana Pulcherrima. Barbadoes Flower-Fence."
11. Charles Lamb and Mary Lamb, *The Works of Charles and Mary Lamb,* vol. 2., ed. E. V. Lucas (2003), Project Gutenberg, https://www.gutenberg.org/cache/epub/10343/pg10343-images.html.
12. Scott Earle and James Reveal, *Lewis and Clark's Green World* (Farcountry Press, 2003), 151.

13. James Vick, *Vick's Floral Guide* (Rochester, NY, 1889), 11.
14. Philip Miller, *The Gardeners Dictionary* (London, 1735), s.v. "Clematis."
15. Joseph Breck, *The Flower-Garden; or Breck's Book of Flowers* (John P. Jewett, 1851), 119.
16. Bernard McMahon to Thomas Jefferson, September 24, 1812, *Founders Online,* National Archives, https://founders.archives.gov/documents/Jefferson/03-05-02-0303.
17. McMahon, *American Gardener's Calendar,* 440.
18. Thomas G. Fessenden, *The New American Gardener* (J. B. Russell, 1828), 126.
19. Breck, *Flower-Garden,* 119.
20. Bernard McMahon to Thomas Jefferson, September 16, 1812, *Founders Online,* National Archives, https://founders.archives.gov/documents/Jefferson/03-05-02-0290.
21. John Gerard, *The Herball or Generall Historie of Plantes* (London, 1597), 122.
22. Parkinson, *Paradisi in Sole Paradisus Terrestris,* 189.
23. Joan Parry Dutton, *Plants of Colonial Williamsburg* (The Colonial Williamsburg Foundation, 1979), 111.
24. Gerard, *Herball,* 827.
25. Breck, *Flower-Garden,* 125.
26. Bernard McMahon to Thomas Jefferson, November 24, 1812, *Founders Online,* National Archives, https://founders.archives.gov/documents/Jefferson/03-05-02-0397.
27. McMahon, *American Gardener's Calendar,* 154.
28. Elizabeth Lawrence, *Through the Garden Gate,* ed. Bill Neal (University of North Carolina Press, 1990), 155–56.
29. Bernard McMahon to Thomas Jefferson, September 23, 1812, *Founders Online,* National Archives, https://founders.archives.gov/documents/Jefferson/03-05-02-0302.
30. Buist, *American Flower Garden Directory,* 93.
31. Buist, *American Flower Garden Directory,* 185.
32. Miller, *Gardeners Dictionary* (1735), s.v. "Lathyrus."
33. "Thomas Jefferson to Antonio Giannini, with a List of Seeds Wanted, 5 February 1786," *Founders Online,* National Archives, https://founders.archives.gov/documents/Jefferson/01-09-02-0218.
34. Dutton, *Plants of Colonial Williamsburg,* 120.
35. Thomas Jefferson to William Fleming, November 28, 1809, *Founders Online,* National Archives, https://founders.archives.gov/documents/Jefferson/03-02-02-0017.
36. McMahon, *American Gardener's Calendar,* 461.
37. Bernard McMahon to Thomas Jefferson, March 27, 1807, *Founders Online,* National Archives, https://founders.archives.gov/documents/Jefferson/99-01-02-5367.
38. William Hanbury, *A Complete Body of Planting and Gardening* (London, 1771), 2:213.
39. McMahon, *American Gardener's Calendar,* 439.
40. L. H. Bailey, *The Standard Cyclopedia of Horticulture,* vol. 3 (Macmillan, 1935), 2538.
41. See Curtis's *Botanical Magazine,* 1810, plate 1307.
42. Margaret Bayard Smith, *The First Forty Years of Washington Society,* ed. Gaillard Hunt (C. Scribner's Sons, 1906), 1840–41.
43. See Curtis's *Botanical Magazine,* 1792, plate 213.
44. McMahon, *American Gardener's Calendar,* 338–39.
45. Miller, *Gardeners Dictionary* (1735), s.v. "Lychnis."
46. McMahon, *American Gardener's Calendar,* 350.

47. Bernard McMahon to Thomas Jefferson, April 2, 1807, *Founders Online,* National Archives, https://founders.archives.gov/documents/Jefferson/99-01-02-5404.
48. McMahon, *American Gardener's Calendar,* 461.
49. Earle and Reveal, *Lewis and Clark's Green World,* 74.
50. Bernard McMahon to Thomas Jefferson, February 28, 1812, in *PTJ:RS,* 5:523–24.
51. Bernard McMahon to Thomas Jefferson, July 12, 1806, Papers of Thomas Jefferson, Library of Congress, Washington, DC.
52. Miller, *Gardeners Dictionary* (1768), s.v. "Phaseolus."
53. Buist, *American Flower Garden Directory,* 285.
54. Bailey, *Standard Cyclopedia of Horticulture,* 1294.
55. Bernard McMahon to Thomas Jefferson, October 24, 1812, in *PTJ:RS,* 5:412.

APPENDIX B

1. Jane Blair Cary Smith, "The Carysbrook Memoir," Special Collections, University of Virginia Library, Charlottesville, VA.
2. Margaret Bayard Smith, *The First Forty Years of Washington Society,* ed. Gaillard Hunt (C. Scribner's Sons, 1906), 385.

APPENDIX C

1. Bernard McMahon, The American Garden's Calendar (1806; facsimile ed., Thomas Jefferson Memorial Foundation, 1997), 437.

BIBLIOGRAPHY

UNPUBLISHED PRIMARY SOURCES

HISTORICAL SOCIETY OF PENNSYLVANIA, PHILADELPHIA

Original Plans of the Monticello Gardens

MASSACHUSETTS HISTORICAL SOCIETY, BOSTON

Coolidge Collection of Thomas Jefferson Manuscripts
Original Plans of the Monticello Gardens

UNIVERSITY OF VIRGINIA LIBRARY, SPECIAL COLLECTIONS, CHARLOTTESVILLE

Edgehill-Randolph Collection, MSS 1397
Ellen Wayles Randolph Coolidge Correspondence, MSS 9090
Jane Blair Cary Smith, The Carys of Virginia, Accession No. 1378
Sarah Strickler, Diary, Accession No. 5633
Trist-Burke Family Papers, 1825–1936, MSS 6696
Samuel Whitcomb Jr., "An Interview with Thomas Jefferson, May 3, 1824," Accession No. 2816

PUBLISHED PRIMARY SOURCES

Jefferson, Thomas. *The Family Letters of Thomas Jefferson.* Rev. ed. Edited by Edwin Morris Betts and James Adam Bear Jr. University Press of Virginia, 1995.

———. *Jefferson's Memorandum Books: Accounts, with Legal Records and Miscellany, 1767–1826.* Edited by James A. Bear Jr. and Lucia C. Stanton. 2 vols. Princeton University Press, 1997.

———. *Notes on the State of Virginia.* Edited by William Peden. University of North Carolina Press, 1954.

———. *Papers of Thomas Jefferson.* Edited by Julian P. Boyd et al. 38 vols. to date.

Iris domestica

Princeton University Press, 1950–.
———. *The Papers of Thomas Jefferson, Digital Edition.* Edited by James P. McClure and J. Jefferson Looney. University of Virginia Press, Rotunda, 2008–25.
———. *Papers of Thomas Jefferson: Retirement Series.* 13 vols. to date. Edited by J. Jefferson Looney. Princeton University Press, 2004–.
———. *Thomas Jefferson: Writings.* Edited by Merrill D. Peterson. Library of America, 1984.
———. *Thomas Jefferson's Garden Book, 1766–1824.* Edited by Edwin Morris Betts. Introduction by Peter Hatch. Thomas Jefferson Foundation at Monticello, 1999.
Madison, James. *The Papers of James Madison, Digital Edition.* Edited by J. C. A. Stagg. University of Virginia, Rotunda, 2010.
———. *The Papers of James Madison, Secretary of State Series.* Edited by Robert J. Brugger et al. 9 vols. University of Virginia Press, 1986–.
Pierson, Rev. Hamilton Wilcox. *Jefferson at Monticello: The Private Life of Thomas Jefferson.* Edited by James A. Bear Jr. University Press of Virginia, 1967.
Smith, Margaret Bayard. *The First Forty Years of Washington Society.* Edited by Gaillard Hunt. C. Scribner's Sons, 1906.
Washington, George. *The Papers of George Washington, Presidential Series.* Edited by W. W. Abbot and Dorothy Twohig. 21 vols. University Press of Virginia, 1987–2020.
———. *The Writings of George Washington.* Edited by John C. Fitzpatrick. 39 vols. United States Printing Office, 1931–44.

SECONDARY SOURCES

Adams, Denise Wiles. *Restoring American Gardens.* Timber Press, 2004.
Bailey, L. H. *The Standard Cyclopedia of Horticulture.* 3 vols. Macmillan, 1935.
Beaman, Thomas E., Jr. "The Archaeology of Morley Jeffers Williams and the Restoration of Historic Landscapes at Stratford Hall, Mount Vernon, and Tryon Palace." *North Carolina Historical Review* 79, no. 3 (2002): 347–72.
Bear, James A., Jr. "The Last Few Days in the Life of Thomas Jefferson." *Magazine of Albemarle County History* 32 (1974): 63–79.
Brinkley, M. Kent. "The Green Spring Plantation Greenhouse/Orangery and the Probable Evolution of the Domestic Area Landscape: A Research Report." US Department of the Interior, National Park Service, 2004.
Brown, C. Allan. "Thomas Jefferson's Poplar Forest: The Mathematics of an Ideal Villa." *Journal of Garden History* 10, no. 2 (1990): 117–39.
Butler, Graeme. "The Auricula: History and Cultivation." *Caledonian Gardener,* 2017, 42–49.
Coale, Charles B. *The Life and Adventures of Wilburn Waters, the Famous Hunter and Trapper of White Top Mountain.* G. W. Gary, 1878.

Coats, Alice. *Flowers and Their Histories.* 3rd ed. Adam and Charles Black, 1968.
Curtis's Botanical Magazine. Royal Botanic Gardens, Kew, 1787–.
Cutright, Paul Russell. *Lewis and Clark: Pioneering Naturalists.* University of Illinois Press, 1969.
Favretti, Rudy J., and Joy Putnam Favretti. *Landscapes and Gardens for Historic Buildings: A Handbook for Reproducing and Creating Authentic Landscape Settings.* American Association for State and Local History, 1978.
Gary, Jack. "Paper Mulberry Trees, Clumps, and Oval Beds: The First Phase of Landscape Restoration at Thomas Jefferson's Poplar Forest." *Magnolia* 25, no. 4 (2012): 1, 3–7.
Gordon-Reed, Annette. *The Hemingses of Monticello: An American Family.* Norton, 2008.
Hatch, Peter. "Restoring the Monticello Landscape, 1923–1955." *Magnolia* 23, no. 1 (2009–10): 1, 3–8.
Hill, John. *The gardener's new kalendar; divided according to the twelve months of the year—containing the whole practice of gardening.* London, 1758.
Kern, Susan. *The Jeffersons at Shadwell.* Yale University Press, 2010.
Kimball, Fiske. "The Gardens and Plantations at Monticello." *Landscape Architecture Magazine* 17, no. 3 (1927): 172–81.
Langley, Batty. *New Principles of Gardening: Or the Laying Out and Planting Parterres, Groves, Wildernesses, Labyrinths, Avenues, Parks, &c.* Battesworth and Batley, 1727.
Leepson, Marc. *Saving Monticello.* Free Press, 2001.
Leighton, Ann. *American Gardens in the Eighteenth Century: "For Use or for Delight."* University of Massachusetts Press, 1976.
Malone, Dumas. *Jefferson the Virginian.* Little, Brown, 1948.
Martin, Mrs. James Bland, ed. *Follow the Green Arrow: The History of the Garden Club of Virginia, 1920–1970.* Dietz Press, 1970.
Martin, Peter. *The Pleasure Gardens of Virginia, from Jamestown to Jefferson.* University Press of Virginia, 1991.
Massie, Susanne Williams, and Frances Archer Christian, eds. *Homes and Gardens in Old Virginia.* J. W. Fergusson & Sons, 1930.
McMahon, Bernard. *The American Gardener's Calendar.* 1806. Facsimile edition. Thomas Jefferson Memorial Foundation, 1997.
Miller, Philip. *The Gardeners Dictionary.* London, 1768.
———. *The Gardeners Kalendar.* London, 1732.
Parkinson, John. *Paradisi in Sole Paradisus Terrestris.* London, 1629.
Pavord, Anna. *The Tulip: The Story of a Flower That Has Made Men Mad.* Macmillan, 1999.
Pursh, Frederick Traugott. *Flora Americae Septentrionalis; or, A Systematic Arrangement and Description of the Plants of North America.* White, Cochrane, 1814.
Randall, Henry S. *The Life of Thomas Jefferson.* 3 vols. Derby & Jackson, 1858.

Randolph, Sarah N. *The Domestic Life of Thomas Jefferson.* 1871. Reprint, University Press of Virginia, 1978.

Rebok, Sandra. *Humboldt and Jefferson.* University of Virginia Press, 2014.

Redouté, Pierre-Joseph. *Les roses.* Paris, 1817–24.

Sarudy, Barbara Wells. *Gardens and Gardening in the Chesapeake, 1700–1805.* Johns Hopkins University Press, 1998.

Seeley, Benton. *Stowe: A Description of the Magnificent House and Gardens of the Right Honourable Richard Grenville Temple.* London, 1744.

Shackelford, George Green. *Thomas Jefferson's Travels in Europe, 1784–1789.* Johns Hopkins University Press, 1995.

Slaughter, Jane C. "Anne Mercer Slaughter: A Sketch." *Tyler's Quarterly Magazine,* July 1937, 30–44.

Stuart, David, and James Sutherland. *Plants from the Past.* Viking, 1987.

Swem, E. G. *Brothers of the Spade: Correspondence of Peter Collinson, of London, and of John Custis, of Williamsburg, Virginia, 1734–1746.* American Antiquarian Society, 1949.

Taylor, Raymond. *Plants of Colonial Days.* Colonial Williamsburg, 1959.

Thompson, Ian. *The Sun King's Garden: Louis XIV, André Le Nôtre and the Creation of the Gardens of Versailles.* Bloomsbury Publishers, 2006.

Whately, Thomas. *Observations on Modern Gardening.* 3rd ed. London, 1771.

Williams, Dorothy Hunt. *Historic Virginia Gardens: Preservations by The Garden Club of Virginia.* University of Virginia Press, 1975.

Williams, Morley J. "The Gardens at Monticello." *Landscape Architecture* 24, no. 2 (1934): 65–71.

Wilson, G. S. *Jefferson on Display: Attire, Etiquette, and the Art of Presentation.* University of Virginia Press, 2018.

Wulf, Andrea. *The Brother Gardeners.* Knopf, 2009.

ILLUSTRATION CREDITS

American Philosophical Society Library, Philadelphia, PA, Violetta Delafield-Benjamin Smith Barton Collection: page 49

Historical Society of Pennsylvania, Ferdinand J. Dreer autograph collection, 137: page 75

By permission of the Corporation for Jefferson's Poplar Forest: page 85

Massachusetts Historical Society: pages 17, 77 (N147gg)

Minneapolis Institute of Art, Minnich Collection, Ethel Morrison Van Derlip Fund, P.18,334: page 59

National Gallery of Art, Washington, DC, Patrons' Permanent Fund, 1985.59.1: page 64

Watercolors by Debbie Donley: pages 124, 166 (right), 167 (right)

Painting by Pat Brodowski: pages 70 and 103

Paintings by Tim O'Kane: pages viii, 121 (bottom left), 129, 130 (top right), 137 (left), 150, 154 (left), 165, 172

INDEX

< *Tulipa Duc van Tol* "Red and Yellow"